SHIRLEY BASSEY

DIAMONDS ARE FOREVER

SHIRLEY BASSEY

DIAMONDS ARE FOREVER

A CELEBRATION OF MY 50 YEARS AS HER GREATEST FAN

MARY LONG

JOHN BLAKE

Published in Great Britain by
John Blake Publishing Limited
3 Bramber Court, 2 Bramber Road
London W14 9PB

www.johnblakepublishing.co.uk

www.facebook.com/johnblakebooks
twitter.com/jblakebooks

First published in hardback in 2017

ISBN: 978-1-78606-249-9

British Library Cataloguing-in-Publication Data:

A catalogue record for this book is available from the British Library.

Design by www.envydesign.co.uk

Printed in Great Britain by CPI Group (UK) Ltd

1 3 5 7 9 10 8 6 4 2

CONTENTS
(THE SET)

To Dame Shirley Bassey,
in celebration of her eightieth birthday
on 8 January 2017,
with gratitude and love.

ACKNOWLEDGEMENTS

Three years ago, aiming to fulfil a dream, I began writing the opening chapters to this book. The journey leading to the publication of *Diamonds Are Forever* has been a remarkable one. I owe thanks to several friends and family members for the continued support they have shown me. They know who they are.

Special thanks go to my friends for over fifty years, Joyce and Reon, who are also most devoted fans of Dame Shirley. We have shared so many happy memories together and I treasure our long friendship.

Whilst I had a clear idea from the beginning about what I wanted to write, my knowledge of publishing was limited, so I knew I would need help. Initial advice came from a gentleman at the Waterstones bookshop in Newport, Isle of Wight, to whom I am indebted. He recommended to me the *Writers' and Artists' Yearbook*, where I researched a list of literary agents. One shone out from the rest, Robert Smith Literary Agency. Within days of sending off my submission, to my delight came a reply from Robert. Then we spoke on the phone and it felt as though we had known each other for years. Robert, I thank you so much for believing in me and in *Diamonds Are Forever*, and for offering to be my literary agent. I certainly could not have chosen better, nor done it without you. My thanks, too, to Robert's ever friendly and helpful assistant, Gemma Quinn.

Through Robert, I gained a contract with John Blake Publishing. I am extremely grateful to my editor, Toby Buchan and his colleagues for their hard work and the commitment necessary to achieve publication to coincide with Dame Shirley Bassey's eightieth birthday.

Finally, my love and special thanks to Bernard, husband and photographer, for his photographic contribution to this work.

Thank you all for making my dream come true.

MARY LONG

November 2016

CHAPTER 1

WHERE DO I BEGIN?

I do not know when I first heard Shirley Veronica Bassey sing, but I remember vividly the day I first saw her in concert: it was Good Friday, 12 April 1963, and that was the day I became an ardent fan.

My mum and dad had been fans for several years prior to '63. I can remember my parents always listening with a special intensity whenever Shirley came on the radio, and particularly enjoying Miss Bassey on television. Living in the London suburb of Ilford in the early sixties, we didn't have a record player, let alone a radiogram, so those televised 'appearances' presented us with the rare opportunity to see Shirley and hear her incredible voice. So when, by chance, on a March evening I bought an evening paper and saw the advertisement announcing the 'fabulous Shirley Bassey' would be appearing in concert at the London Palladium, I couldn't believe my eyes. Would it be possible to go to this famous theatre and attend my first concert? What a place to start.

Fortunately, the April date fell close to my mum's birthday, so my dad didn't need much persuading when I suggested we take Mum as a birthday treat (I hasten to add it was a wonderful treat for us too). As I seem to remember, my dad, almost immediately, telephoned the London Palladium box office, from the nearby telephone box, and reserved three tickets for the Good Friday concert. In the sixties it was quite normal to reserve theatre tickets that were then paid for on collection from the theatre box office at some stage prior to the concert.

A few days later we walked into the box office, located immediately to the side of the main theatre entrance, looking down on us were black-and-white portrait photographs of the world's greatest entertainers – Frank Sinatra, Judy Garland, Bing Crosby, Dean Martin etc. – all of whom had performed at this legendary theatre. Shirley was no stranger to the theatre; her *Sunday Night at the London Palladium* television appearance in 1961 had brought her to the attention of many in the early days of her career. Now, however, she was recognised as a 'star' and heading the bill.

We headed to one of the ticket-office attendants from whom we were separated by the glass screen which had a small semicircular opening through which our tickets would be dispensed. First, 'Would you like to see the seating plan?' 'Yes please,' came my dad's reply and the attendant held up the plan, which showed every seat in the theatre – stalls, royal circle, upper circle and boxes. 'Your seats are here,' she said as she pointed with her pencil to three seats in the front row of the royal circle, A24 to A26. She continued, 'they are very good seats.' I couldn't believe it. My dad paid the money, 60 shillings (£3) in total and those lovely green tickets slid through the opening of the glass window. I was over the moon, although the four-week wait seemed a lifetime.

Good Friday, 12 April was upon us and I found it hard to contain my excitement. As we had decided to 'make a day of it', we travelled to London in the morning. Miss Bassey would be giving two performances and we were booked to attend the first, scheduled to commence at 5.30pm. I don't remember what we did prior to arriving at the London Palladium. We must have walked around and gone to eat, those things I can't recall, but once at the theatre the memory cells certainly played the role I required of them.

It was late afternoon when we walked round to the backstage-door entrance of the theatre. There were a number of people waiting by a set of wooden gates, which opened to expose an area large enough in which to park a removal van. At the rear a few steps led down to a dark-red stage door, but there was nothing glamorous about this scene. I had spoken to a few of the people gathered outside but nobody knew for sure if Miss Bassey was inside the theatre or if indeed she was due to arrive. I was just sixteen and although experiencing 'butterflies' got up enough courage to go down the steps and open the stage door. On the other side I immediately faced the stage doorman, sitting inside a very tiny office, and I nervously but politely asked if Miss Bassey was in the theatre.

He easily recognised me as an excited fan and said, 'We are expecting Miss Bassey to arrive shortly.' Thanking him, I retreated as gracefully as I could and took up a position by the edge of the gates. I had come prepared for the moment: I had an 8- by 6-inch black-and-white photograph of Miss Bassey in hand, which I had recently purchased, and my biro was at the ready.

I didn't have long to wait before I heard cries of, 'Here she comes' from the crowd, and moments later a large limousine came to a halt at the very spot where I stood. I glanced through the window, then the car door opened gently against me and I was facing Miss Shirley Bassey. 'Could I please have your autograph Miss Bassey,' I mumbled. She looked at me and for a moment I thought it was to be. Then Miss Bassey said, 'If I sign for one, it will be very disappointing for everyone else', and she was quickly ushered down the steps I had recently trod to the stage door. I know what you are thinking: I must have been disappointed. Well, actually, I was not. I kept thinking about Miss Bassey's words and realised how disappointed I would have been if she had signed an autograph for someone else. To me Miss Bassey had considered all of the fans waiting to greet her and I respected her decision. I knew then that one day I would get her autograph and I would value it all the more. Right now I was on cloud nine, having seen her up close. I remember everyone around me chatting happily; the air seemed filled with excitement. Gradually, the crowd that had gathered slowly started to disperse, the majority heading to the main entrance of the theatre.

The London Palladium dates back to 1910 and in the sixties it was one of the best-known theatres in the country. As I stepped on the red carpet, climbing the stairs to the royal circle, it seemed magical. The atmosphere sent shivers down our spines and we sensed we were about to experience something very special.

The show opened with Woolf Phillips and his Orchestra, featuring several orchestral 'standards' prior to Russ Shepherd, Matt Monro's musical director, taking over the baton. We were then treated to some fine singing by Matt Monro. Matt was enjoying international stardom, having had hits such as 'Portrait of My Love', 'My Kind of Girl' and 'Softly As I Leave You'. However, although my parents and I enjoyed his voice very much, I personally was not 'blown away' by watching him perform live onstage.

When it came to the intermission we went to the bar. I was almost sick with excitement, and then I started to worry. Maybe I was expecting too much – when I saw Miss Bassey, what if it seemed no different to watching her on TV! Thankfully, I didn't have long to consider how I felt; the bell was sounding in the theatre bar indicating it was time to return to our seats. A24, centre front row of the royal circle, placed me directly in line with the microphone which stood centre stage. The orchestra, under the leadership of Shirley's musical director, Raymond Long (no relation), started to play. Suddenly the 2,000-plus audience, which had been rather reserved during the first half of the concert, broke into spontaneous applause, and standing there before me, onstage, was Miss Shirley Bassey in a glittering gown, her hair up high. Immediately she went into song and that incredible voice we now know so well echoed around the auditorium. I was captivated. Between numbers the audience applauded wildly and I could hear the enthusiasm from my mum and dad, but I dared not look at them. My eyes were firmly fixed on Shirley and I didn't want to miss one moment. It was magic, and to coin a modern phase, a 'life changing moment' for me.

I cannot recall every song sung during that performance – the programme listed eleven – but I do remember two numbers in particular, which were not listed. These were, 'If I Were A Bell', which Shirley had recorded with Geoff Love & His Orchestra on the long-playing record, simply entitled *Shirley*, and 'Johnny One Note', which I had never previously heard.

Apart from an incredible voice, Shirley had this unbelievable stage presence. Sometimes criticised for overplaying her arm and hand movements on TV, onstage these movements where highly appropriate and used to perfection. When she sang, 'If I Were a Bell', you have the lyrics 'If I were a bell I'd go ding, dong, ding, dong, ding'. With arms, hands and fingers outstretched, Shirley precisely moved her thumb and forefinger together as she sang 'ding'. The second finger touched the thumb on the 'dong', then the third finger and thumb on the next 'ding', returning to the thumb and forefinger by the time the final 'ding' was sung. It was magical to hear and watch.

Then came 'Johnny One Note', written by Rodgers and Hart in 1937 (the year Shirley was born), for the musical 'Babes in Arms'. I could not recall the song, or if I had, it did not leave a lasting impression upon me. In 1948 it had been recorded by Judy Garland; in 1956 jazz singers Blossom Dearie and Ella Fitzgerald both made recordings, followed in 1960 by Anita O'Day, so 'Johnny' had been around! Right now, before me, however, Miss Bassey was making the song her own. The fast tempo arrangement, the diction which stressed every word of the lyric and that voice, so damn powerful. Yet Shirley had learned the art of control and made it seemed so easy. Although I was only sixteen, I realised it wasn't just Miss Bassey's tremendous natural talent on display: She had worked hard during her early years developing into the 'star', like no other, we now saw before us. Building up towards 'Johnny's' end, Shirley sang, 'sing Johnny one note out loud', holding on to 'loud'... seemingly forever. The audience erupted, almost raising the London Palladium's rafters.

Shirley continued to 'sell' every song, among them, 'What Kind of Fool am I', 'As Long As He Needs Me', 'They Can't Take That Away From Me' and 'What Now My Love', the latter from her recent LP release entitled, *Shirley Bassey with Nelson Riddle and His Orchestra*. It seemed all to soon that Shirley exited the stage, but she returned to acknowledge the audience's ovation, I rose to my feet shouting for more along with my mum and dad and everyone around me. We were rewarded, as I recall, with 'The Party's Over', which made me feel rather sad. More thunderous applause. I am sure if it hadn't been for the fact that Miss Bassey had another performance later that evening, and the theatre had to be cleared, the audience would have remained there all night, transfixed by what they had just experienced. When the curtain finally dropped, the music started to drift away and the applause gradually faded as we were encouraged to leave our seats. I finally looked at my mum and dad and from their expressions it was clear they were as thrilled as I. However, I did wonder if they felt as exalted! I had clapped and cheered for all I was worth and my watch had actually stopped due to the rigorous wrist movements I had made whilst clapping so enthusiastically.

Perhaps now would be an appropriate time to mention something about the audience, since it mainly consisted of middle-aged, smartly dressed couples. Going to the theatre in the 1960s was a special occasion, people wore there 'best frocks', or 'Sunday best' as it was called. It would also be correct to describe the audience that night as generally reserved. Indeed, I was very reserved, and somewhat surprised to find myself standing and shouting out for more. A young girl could be forgiven, but surprisingly I was not alone: the majority of this older reserved audience was acting in the same manner. Importantly though, we only let our feelings of appreciation come into play once each song had ended. This audience of the sixties, and for that matter those in later years, listened to every note. There were often times when you could hear a pin drop. I have to confess, I miss that type of audience nowadays and doubt they will ever return. I wonder, if the opportunity were ever to present itself to see Miss Bassey in concert again, I could live with the audience of today. People seem to feel they must show off their own musical talent, which they believe they have, and sing along with the performer. Is this what reality TV has given us! Let's get back to the sixties, when what we heard was pure Bassey – and I thank God for that!

As we made our way out of the theatre, we found ourselves very near to the spot where we had seen Shirley arrive earlier in the day. The transformation from the Shirley Bassey we had seen stepping out of the car to the 'fabulous' Miss Bassey onstage was magical, yet *both* had me mesmerised. That night I had become one of her ardent fans and somehow I knew I would remain so throughout my life.

Being an only child and a Piscean, it was perhaps not surprising that after 12 April much of my life was spent dreaming. At school the other girls could not quite understand why I was infatuated by Shirley Bassey; after all, they spent their time raving over pop idols, many of whom came and went within a matter of weeks. They didn't seem to realise I was talking about a legend in the making. When they failed to understand, I felt sorry for them for not being able to appreciate the wonderful talent of Miss Bassey, and I just carried on dreaming.

I was considered mature for my years; I think this was because I spent so much of my spare time with my mum and dad. Both my parents were a few years older than most of the other parents, a consequence of my mum having been badly injured towards the latter part of the Second World War. A 'doodlebug' (V1 flying bomb), having decided to cut its motor, had glided down to cause terrible devastation not far from my parents' home. My mum, close to the point of impact, was very badly injured, but she believed she was lucky; others had died. Mum spent nine months in hospital recovering, only to be told when she was finally discharged that she must wait at least two years before trying for a baby. Naturally, when I finally came along, my parents were over the moon and couldn't contain their joy. I remained an only child and maybe some would say a little spoilt. My parents certainly couldn't have loved me more but being loved does not mean you are spoilt. Mum and Dad had started with little, as did many of that generation, working hard to give me the best they could in life, yet more importantly teaching me to respect and recognise life's many treasures in all their shapes and forms. I was a very lucky child.

So, back to Easter 1963... I sat at home looking through the first pages of my Shirley Bassey scrapbook, which I had started to compile a few months previously. It contained a few pictures, reviews and advertising material from the concert we had just seen and now I was copying, in my own handwriting, the notes written by Kenneth Hume that appeared on the sleeve of *Shirley Bassey with Nelson Riddle and His Orchestra*. You may remember I did not have a record player, but nevertheless I had purchased Shirley's LP, partly in preparation for the day when I would have one and partly because I wanted Shirley's record to climb the charts, thus adding to her success. As I wrote out the notes in my best handwriting, still dreaming of Friday's concert, it suddenly occurred to me what I should do next. I would write a letter to Shirley and tell her how much we'd all enjoyed her concert. Why hadn't I thought of it sooner!

I started to draft my letter, choosing the words as best I could to express how much we had enjoyed her singing and wishing her well for the future. I read its contents out loud to my parents who, although encouraging, probably wondered whether my letter would actually get within range of Miss Bassey's voice, let alone be read by her. I, however, had no doubts and the next day went out and bought some lovely writing paper and envelopes onto which I would copy my letter and post it to her, c/o William Victor Productions, Suite 5, 190 Piccadilly, London W1.

Then I was off to the post office to purchase a stamp and, feeling rather proud, I handed over my letter for posting. The postmaster gave me a little smile as he read the name, Miss Shirley Bassey, and I imagine he also wondered whether the lady would read my words.

The days following Easter were very busy for me. On holiday from school for some of that time, I would try to look through the music magazines, *New Musical Express* (*NME*) and *Melody Maker*, as they lay displayed on the counter of the local newsagents. This was quite a difficult task in the 1960s; today it can be achieved more easily, and indeed it seems to be the norm to read half a paper or magazine before purchasing it. However, it didn't take long for the newsagent I regularly called on to understand my needs. He knew if anything featured those three magic words, 'Miss Shirley Bassey', he was on to a winner. As time went by, if I hadn't been to his shop he would actually save me any newspaper or magazine that carried an article about Shirley.

Fortunately, I now had a Saturday job helping out at a local chemist's, which I enjoyed very much. It provided me with a little pocket money, some of which I offered to Mum, but I think she felt I was getting so little for one day's work and so said I should keep it all. She also knew I was starting to save some money for what I called my 'entertainment fund' and I think she was fairly happy to see my money go in this direction. At the end of the day, I needed money to telephone agents, theatres, television companies and record label Columbia if I were to keep up to date with Miss Bassey's performance schedule. These were not the days of the Internet, iPhone and Facebook; to gather my information I needed two 1960s communication tools: the ability to write letters and a telephone. I enjoyed writing letters, so once I had invested in some decent stationery, which I had already done to write to Shirley about the concert, I was ready to begin. First, however, I needed to collect and compile the information I required for the months ahead, and that meant I needed a phone. A private telephone was a relative luxury for a working-class family back then. My aunt had a telephone, as did one or two of the neighbours down our street, but these were only available to me in an emergency. Now, I may have thought booking concert tickets should be classed as an emergency, but I don't think the neighbours would have seen it like that!

So my only option was the good old-fashioned red telephone box, which always smelled of stale tobacco and fish and chips. The secret was, once inside, to press your foot against the glass door sufficiently to allow in some fresh air while making sure you did not let the outside sounds block your ability to hear the person you were talking to on the other end of the line. This required a good deal of left-foot control, something I mastered over the years. Of course, before you could even attempt to do this, you had to be inside the telephone box and this often required a great deal of patience, especially on cold wet days when the person waiting ahead of you in the queue probably wanted to phone his girlfriend.

Eventually my time would come, and with a small notebook and pen placed on the top of the coin box and a plentiful supply of coins, I would lift the receiver, place the coins in the box and dial the number. When you heard the sound of a voice speaking through the earpiece, immediately followed by a series of bleeps, it was time for fast action. Press button A and with luck you were connected. Then you had to state your enquiry, which often meant holding on and inserting more coins into the black box, whilst the person with whom you wished to speak was connected to your phone line. Thankfully, I usually spoke to someone who could give me some information concerning Miss Bassey's engagements; remember, we were living in an age where the level of security was far lower than today. What a joy it was when I was given news of a concert date or a television performance. I would run home excitedly to tell my parents in the hope we might attend.

My bedroom took on the new look of an organised office, with drawers in the dressing table converted to accommodate stationery, notebooks and my scrapbook with its grey and fawn pages. I had covered it in white paper, to which I added a colour photo of Shirley and the words 'The Fabulous Shirley Bassey'. I also had a diary into which I noted any information regarding Shirley's professional engagements, and an address book for retaining useful contact details. Over the coming weeks these two items became very important in my quest to obtain information. To be sure of getting good seats at concerts it was essential to apply for tickets early, preferably before any official announcement was made in the music press. Therefore the more information you had the more likely it was that you could get the best tickets for concert performances.

There wasn't so much block booking by agents then, nor were ticket touts as operational as we know them today. The sixties saw fair play – simply be at the front of the queue or be first to apply meant you could be sure of good seats.

My dad was also collecting information, and being the methodical person he was, he was spending some of his time after Easter researching the latest record players. The postman would arrive at the house with letters addressed to Mr R. F. Pilgrim, all of which contained specifications on the various makes and models. Finally, with my dad's shortlist, we travelled to Romford to visit Wells Music Centre, the town's leading musical store. Inside the store, the salesman, keen to demonstrate the quality of his selection of record players, produced a test LP which contained a variety of recordings, most of which were orchestral or classical. He played several tracks, to our satisfaction, but was rather taken aback when I pulled out Shirley's latest LP, *Let's Face the Music and Dance*, which she had recorded with Nelson Riddle and his Orchestra.

'Could you please play this,' I asked. Rather reluctantly he removed his test record and placed my prized possession onto the record deck, mumbling this was not going to be a very good test. Within moments, rather appropriately, 'There May Be Trouble Ahead' was resounding from the speakers sending tingles down my spine. Dad played with the treble, bass and volume control knobs which were lined up along the top of the Dynatron record player, adjusting each to what he felt was the right sound. The result was pure magic; Shirley's voice was wonderfully reproduced and needless to say we were sold. The recording had even impressed the salesman as well as other customers in the store, who by now were wondering what this was all about. After hearing a few tracks, Mum and Dad agreed to place an order and I was ecstatic. We were told we would have to wait a few weeks before our record player could be delivered but I could easily live with that, since I would soon be able to 'play' Shirley as often as I liked (within reason as my mum reminded me). So life was pretty wonderful, yet unknown to me, it was about to get even better.

It was the third week in May when my mum called out to me, 'You have a letter, it looks a bit special.' It was not often that letters arrived, the envelope neatly typed 'Miss Mary Pilgrim', at our home in Chadwell Heath, yet during the past few weeks I had written to several sources for information, so I assumed this letter had come as a result of one such request. I held the small cream envelope in my hand, inspecting it closely before delicately opening the sealed flap to reveal a folded cream note, which I slowly removed. As I started to open the note, words printed in blue at a 45-degree angle jumped out from the page: *Shirley Bassey.* I screamed out and my mum came running to see what all the excitement was about, as I read aloud:

Dear Mary,

Just a short note to thank you very much for your letter. I am pleased to hear that you enjoyed the show at the London Palladium so much and it was very nice of you to write and tell me so.

With all good wishes,
Sincerely,
Shirley Bassey [hand signed]

I was so delighted. I really hadn't expected to receive any form of an answer to the letter I had sent, yet here it was in my hand and personally signed by Shirley. Mum too was very excited by my receiving such a nice letter and we found it difficult to contain our joy when Dad arrived home later. 'What are you so excited about,' he said as I waved my letter into the air. Later, Dad gave me a special black-leafed photographic album into which I mounted my letter with pride. During the years that followed, several other letters and photographs were added to this album, all of which I still treasure today.

In June, Shirley was scheduled to appear on the leading television show, *Sunday Night at the London Palladium*. I had applied to ATV Television for tickets, requesting specifically to see Shirley Bassey. Normally tickets would be sent to you for a specific Sunday date a couple of weeks prior to the show, but there was never any indication as to who would be appearing on the show, so it was pot luck who you saw. However, knowing Shirley's dates meant it was possible to make a specific date request.

On this occasion I received tickets, but a few days prior to the show Shirley was admitted to hospital and as a consequence, had to pull out from the show. Following news items earlier that year, her legions of fans already knew Shirley was expecting a baby later in the year and so we were more concerned about her wellbeing than the thought of not seeing her perform on TV. When I read the news in the paper I immediately went and bought a get-well card. With a letter enclosed, I sent it off to the hospital where Miss Bassey had been admitted. At the beginning of July, I received another letter from Shirley Bassey, thanking me for my letter and apologising for not appearing on *Sunday Night at the London Palladium* in June. Shirley went on to say she hoped to appear on the TV show once she started working again after the birth of her baby.

I went to the June show, but I have no idea who stepped in for Shirley. What I do remember of the occasion is seeing some of Shirley's fans who, like me, had tickets and so had come along. We enjoyed ourselves by sharing lots of chat, information and discussing Shirley's latest records and performances. To my amazement, one girl, named Valerie, if my memory is correct, said to me, 'I saw you in April and I have a photo of you with Shirley.' 'What!' I replied. I couldn't believe it. Valerie had taken the photo just as I was asking Shirley for her autograph and so I was completely unaware of its existence. Valerie kindly offered to send me a print; we swapped address details and true to her word the photograph arrived.

As might be expected, it went into my special album and rightfully deserves to be the first photograph featured within these pages, so thanks again Valerie.

Throughout the summer we kept in touch and one day made a decision to spend a day in London, hoping to see where Shirley lived. Valerie, who was a few years older than me, had a car and as my parents had immediately taken to her when we first met, they were happy for me to go. Her cheeky chat could win over anyone, as the day's events were about to prove. Knowing Shirley had lived in St John's Wood, this was to be our first place of call, although how we acquired this information I'm not sure. It's possible the details may have been in the press since Shirley featured in the news regularly, partly because, at the time, her marriage to Kenneth Hume was going through some difficulties; however, he continued to act as her manager.

We really had no intention of intruding when we arrived at Shirley's ex-townhouse. A couple of photos of the house were taken for the scrapbook but then our mounting excitement got the better of us and Valerie said, 'I'll just go and knock and see if they know where Shirley has gone', or something similar. Before I had time to respond, Val was climbing up the steps to the front door and about to ring the bell. I waited, rather nervously, at the gate as I watched the door open. Val seemed to chat for several minutes before returning looking excited.

'Shirley's gone to the Mayfair Hotel,' she said. 'However did you find that out?' I asked, to which Val replied, 'I told them we were friends of Shirley's from Cardiff and that Shirley had said if we were ever in London to give her a call.' 'How could you say that?' I replied, but secretively I rather admired her cheekiness.

Back in the car, beaming with excitement, we studied the map and headed off in the direction of Marble Arch before finally locating the famous Mayfair Hotel. Standing outside this impressive establishment I had a bad attack of the butterflies, but we couldn't give up now. As we went to enter the lobby we noticed a tall gentleman heading in our direction. He politely held open the door as we stepped inside and said, 'Hello'. This gentleman was the legendary Nat King Cole.

Although apprehensive, we walked confidently to the reception desk where we boldly asked to see Miss Bassey. 'I am afraid Miss Bassey is no longer staying with us,' came a reply we did not want to hear. Val's quick thinking went into action, and she replied, 'Can you please give us her forwarding address.' I'm thinking to myself, he is not going to do that. The gentleman at reception remained silent as he concentrated his gaze on us, while Val again swung into verbal action. 'You see we use to work with Shirley in Cardiff and she said…' Val, knowing the story had worked once, decided to give it a second chance, and I have to say she told the tale with great conviction. The gentleman walked off into an office while we waited silently, to return a few minutes later.

'Well,' said Val, 'do you have it, we don't have much time, we have to get back to Cardiff tonight.' To our amazement a piece of paper, on which was written Shirley's address, was handed to Val. We thanked the gentleman profusely and hurried out of the hotel. We could hardly control our excitement and it wasn't hard to convince ourselves that it must be our destiny to see Shirley.

Back to the car and off to the exclusive area of Belgravia where we parked in a square close to the private mews where Shirley was reported to be living. We walked onto the cobbled stones, under the arch-shaped entrance that partly hid the mews from the main road. Peering into doorways, we finally reached the door displaying the number we sought. To the side was a doorbell/entryphone. Now we were disheartened. We had come all this way and faced being stopped from seeing Shirley by someone at the end of an entryphone. Val and I looked at each other, not needing to say a thing, and then we pressed the bell. We waited but nothing appeared to happen, so we pressed it again. Almost immediately, to our astonishment, the door opened and for once Val and I were speechless as we gazed directly into the bright brown eyes of Miss Shirley Bassey. Our initial silence was followed by an overexcited apology for disturbing Shirley. We explained we were very keen fans and only wanted to wish her all the very best with the birth of her baby, which Shirley was expecting in a few months. She asked how we managed to get her address and we briefly described our adventure, explaining we had been very persuasive at the Mayfair Hotel, as we didn't want to get anyone into trouble. Shirley gave a smile as we said we were sorry for saying we had worked with her in Cardiff. We chatted a little more and promised we would never 'tell a soul' where she lived, before saying, 'Good evening.'

It was fairly late when I arrived home and I have no doubt my parents would have been apprehensive; however, they sat listening intently as I recalled every detail of our adventure and they were delighted by its outcome.

Around about this time, whilst waiting one day for Shirley to arrive for a concert, we met George Webb. Of my parents' generation, George was a very pleasant man and loyal fan who travelled the length and width of the country to see Shirley in concert. Sometimes George would be accompanied at a concert by his wife and daughter but generally he came alone. He could often be found talking with a group of fans near the backstage area of any theatre where Shirley was appearing, and would willingly share with them any information he had gained regarding Shirley's engagements. He was known by many of Shirley's fans and will feature further on in my story. George continued to be one of a group of fans who have remained loyal to Miss Bassey, throughout their lifetime.

Bournemouth in the sixties could be regarded as a typically English seaside town, famous for its beautiful gardens, beaches and entertainment. A number of shows ran throughout the summer months and Sunday concerts would draw the country's top entertainers to its theatres. We had booked to see Shirley perform at Bournemouth's Winter Gardens theatre and even though the journey by car was far easier then than it is today, it was still a considerable distance from Essex for 'a day out'. Yet when it came to seeing Shirley Bassey in concert, Bournemouth became a second home to us and the reason for this was the Winter Gardens theatre. Built in 1937, coincidentally the same year Shirley was born, it started life as an indoor bowling green. After the war, the building was converted to a concert hall and became famous for its brilliant acoustics. With its wide stage and good seating layout, it was a favourite with fans. On one side of the auditorium were wooden doors which opened prior to the show to expose a large bar and café area. The doors were closed during performances and rehearsals. However, it was possible to sit in the café area on the afternoon of a concert and hear Shirley rehearsing for her show, an experience I can only describe as pure magic. There was little need for amplification here and what you heard was pure Bassey.

The café and bar area extended out onto a long terrace, with views of the pristine gardens, making it a favourite place for anyone with a little time on their hands. Musicians, their wives, girlfriends, stagehands, chauffeurs, managers, musical directors, assistants and fans could all be observed, which added to the fun and excitement of the occasion.

My mum and dad became friendly with the wives of some of the 'gentlemen of the orchestra', several of whom were seconded from the string section of the Bournemouth Symphony Orchestra. These musicians would join the orchestra for the second half of the show, ready for Shirley's orchestral introduction, and together with the musical director, would often transform the sound of the orchestra. The sound of a great orchestra live onstage is sadly not often heard these days and when it is, it is often spoilt by over-amplification and electronically produced sounds in an attempt to replicate the good old double bass and strings. I am probably biased since I married a double-bass player, but to me the sound of the orchestra at the Winter Gardens always seemed wonderful once the overture started.

On our first visit to the theatre we had fairly good seats in the stalls and were much nearer to the stage than we had been at the London Palladium, and I loved it. The first half of the concert, which consisted of five separate acts, seemed to go on and on, but thankfully in the year ahead a better format became established for the first half of Miss Bassey's concerts. Tonight, however, the orchestra opened the show followed by three lads singing in harmony, followed by a third act. The anticipation was getting to me; the butterflies were fluttering again as I sat on the edge of my seat. After the intermission, the interval bell sounded, informing the audience that the performance was about to commence. Now the theatre was packed to the brim and you could feel the excitement mounting.

As the lights began to dim, members of the orchestra came onstage to take up their positions, some warming up with a few notes, before the musical director entered to applause. The moment had arrived, the lights dimmed and a introduction medley, featuring some of

Shirley's hits, began. Over the sound system came the announcement, 'Ladies and gentleman, the Winter Gardens theatre is proud to present the fabulous Miss Shirley Bassey.' Lights went up, members of the audience (including me) rose to their feet and thunderous applause reverberated around the auditorium. Miss Bassey was onstage and the crowd went wild.

I would be lying if I said I remember every number Shirley sang, because I don't, but at that time songs such as 'What Kind of Fool Am I', 'Everything's Coming Up Roses', 'What Now My Love' and 'As Long As He Needs Me' regularly featured in her performances. My mum adored the latter Lionel Bart song and would shed a few tears as Shirley sang, 'If you are lonely then you will know, if someone needs you, your love them so.' Mum was not alone in her feelings; one of Shirley's greatest talents was her ability to extract every drop of emotion from a song's lyrics and it was an essential part of what the audience had come to love. Hearing and watching Shirley perform was like taking a roller-coaster ride to her soul; we suffered the pain and experienced the pleasure and became one. I would watch every gesture, wonder at the power of every note, and inhale the atmosphere. It was an experience like no other and those who were fortunate to be there will know exactly what I mean. Every song received the 'Bassey treatment', making it 'hers', and in doing so sending the original version into extinction. If you need an example, just think about 'Big Spender'. Not yet in the act, it was transformed from its origin in 'Sweet Charity' and well and truly became Bassey's.

One number around at the time was a particular favourite of mine since it brought out Shirley's fun side and was a sort of forerunner to 'Big Spender'. Entitled 'Typically English', the number came from the show *Stop The World I Want To Get Off*, written by Leslie Bricusse and Anthony Newley. The show enjoyed great success both in the UK and USA, where Sammy Davis Jnr starred. The words to 'Typically English' often changed and Shirley had her own adaptation: 'My mother said I never should play with the young men in the wood. If I did she would say, you'll end up in the family way'. Shirley would sing the words in a giggly manner, moving sideways onstage as she used her arm to draw a big bump over her body when she came to the words 'family way'. It always produced a great laugh. Towards the end of the song, after singing about everything 'Typically English', Shirley ended with the lyric, 'And I've never been so ruddy bored!' Much laughter, then cheering broke out from the audience. All too quickly the performance drew towards its climax, often with 'The Party's Over', but the audience was never ready to let it end.

Cheers of 'More, more…' would echo around the theatre as the clapping intensified. Shirley may have left the stage but the audience was not prepared to let her leave the theatre. The applause grew even louder when Shirley came back onstage to acknowledge the audience's response and thank the members of the orchestra, before singing another number. The audience went wild and Shirley took several more standing ovations before the show finally came to an end.

Mum, Dad and I, along with the rest of the audience, left the theatre spellbound. I was overjoyed and went over every moment during our journey home in the car. We had chosen to go to the first performance, mainly because we had a long journey home, but it was also easier to get better seats. When I thought about Shirley going onstage again and giving another performance like the one we had just experienced, I couldn't comprehend how she could do it, but she always did.

Later that year Shirley gave birth to Samantha, and in the summer of 1964 returned twice, in August, to the Winter Gardens. As soon as I had knowledge of the engagements I applied for tickets and was fortunate enough to receive front-row seats for each concert. The format for both concerts had improved, as far as I was concerned, since the first half on both occasions featured a traditional jazz band.

The first concert, on 9 August, featured Acker Bilk and his Paramount Jazz Band. They had become the first British artists in years to reach the number-one spot in the American hit parade with 'Stranger On The Shore'. The second concert, on 30 August, featured Kenny Ball and his Jazzmen, who again were respected jazz musicians. Both acts were introduced by a comedian who then returned to the stage at the start of the second half to tell a few jokes prior to introducing Shirley. With an audience hungry for Miss Bassey, the jokes were not very well received.

On both occasions, however, the jazz bands were well received – this was far better than having to sit through five dismal acts. Kenny Ball won the day and I think I can take a little credit for this. Remember the theatre's lovely café arrangement? Well, during the afternoon of the concert, I had spoken to Kenny Ball in the café and asked if he would be playing 'Samantha', the song from *High Society*, with which Kenny and his Jazzmen had had a hit. He said he hadn't intended to play the number, but when I told him Shirley's new baby daughter had been given the name 'Samantha' he said he would see what they could do.

That evening Kenny Ball and his Jazzmen received a very warm reception from the Bournemouth audience and towards the end of their act, I called out 'Samantha'. Kenny looked down at me, nodded and said to the audience, 'I think you will like this one.' As he started to sing 'I love you, Samantha…' the audience went wild. Kenny gained a few more fans that night.

When Shirley came onstage after the intermission, she looked wonderfully happy. The audience was going wild and I wasn't the only one to jump to their feet. Shirley too had gained a few more fans of her own recently, thanks to her latest hit 'I Who Have Nothing', which had climbed high in the British charts. There I stood almost directly at Shirley's feet, while she acknowledged the audience, then she looked down directly at me and smiled as if to say, 'Sit down now, I'm ready to sing.' Turning to the musical director, Shirley started to give a performance of her life. 'Just One of Those Things', 'Fly Me to the Moon', 'Got A Lot of Living To Do', 'Johnny One Note' and 'All The Things You Are' were probably included. I sat mesmerised, my senses trying to work overtime to record every detail. Shirley's voice was incredible, especially now that I could hear its purity. No microphone was required where I sat; I was hearing pure Bassey. In fact I was so close I could even smell her perfume.

As the concert came to a close, the audience in their appreciation produced a thunderous sound by stamping their feet in unison on the theatre's wooden floorboards. Then I was looking directly into those big brown eyes and shaking hands with the fabulous Miss Shirley Bassey. It's a concert I will always remember.

CHAPTER 2

'S WONDERFUL

Let's just return to 1963 for a moment and I'll let you know a little more about what it was like for me as a fan. Still at school, I wasn't particularly academically minded but showed some talent at art and also enjoyed photography. Encouraged by my dad, a keen amateur photographer, who would develop and print his own black-and-white photographs at home, I shared an interest for black-and-white portraiture. Yet there were times when I wanted to add something more to the photograph. Perhaps I was aiming to capture a little of the subject's soul and I felt this might be possible to achieve through drawing.

It's perhaps not surprising I chose to start on a portrait of Shirley. I especially liked a photograph taken by a famous photographer, Vivienne, so with her photo as my reference I began using a variety of pencils and chalks with which I had been experimenting and developing styles of shading. This would be my first *serious* portrait and after some alterations I was very proud of the finished result. Naturally, my parents thought it was very good, so I decided to send the drawing to Shirley to ask if she would be kind enough to sign it and return it in the stamped addressed envelope I had enclosed. Looking back now at my drawing (yes I still have it), it wasn't that good, but then I was young and had rather a lot of cheek!

After posting the package several weeks went by and I began to wonder if Shirley had seen the drawing; perhaps it had been lost in the post or even worse, what if Shirley didn't like it! Fortunately my fears soon vanished when the postman delivered a recognisable large envelope. I attempted to open the envelope quickly yet carefully. As I gently pulled the drawing out from the envelope I saw, handwritten to one side, the words, 'Best Wishes, Mary, Shirley Bassey' and as if that wasn't enough, enclosed was a letter. 'I think you did a very good job and it must have been extremely difficult,' wrote Shirley. I needed no further encouragement – now I would produce a drawing especially for Shirley.

All I needed was the right photograph from which to work. This was not as easy as it seemed since I wanted to base my drawing on an up-to-date image of Shirley singing. It took several months before I finally found the photo I required and it came to me with help from my dad. He would sometimes set up his camera to take a few photographs of the TV screen whenever Shirley made a television appearance so that I could have some images for my scrapbook. Dad always seemed to get good results, although some experimentation and a tripod were essential to make it possible. I had learned that Shirley was about to make a television 'special' for the launch of the new state-of-the-art, 625 line television station, BBC 2. Not only was I longing to view the show, scheduled for April 1964, but Dad promised he would try to get some good images from the television screen. The show went ahead and was a tremendous success, spotlighting Shirley's exceptional talent. Dad had also produced the goods and I had a lovely photo of Shirley singing.

Most evenings, after dinner, the tablecloth would be removed from the dining table to reveal a heavier protective cloth on which I would place newspaper to protect the cloth from the fine chalk particles that would form as I worked on my drawing. Once I had pencilled in the detail lines, I worked in black-and-white Conté crayons and a range of grey chalks to help give a good tonal range to my larger-than-life drawing. Using what was called a fashion-plate board as my base, I would eventually cover every surface of the board with chalk to achieve the effect I desired. Even when pure white was required, I would still cover the area of white board with the white Conté, which was very hard to apply and could actually burn the paper layer if applied too vigorously.

Mum and Dad were always encouraging, watching, night after night, as the portrait began to emerge. I would draw starting at the top of the head and then gradually work down, not allowing myself to progress further until I was totally happy with the outcome, which meant 'seeing Shirley' before my eyes.

Once finished it was necessary to spray the drawing with a fixative to prevent smudging from the chalks. The fixative, which produced a smell not dissimilar to pear-drop sweets, also required time to dry, so this task was carried out in our back garden. There I was waving a large board back and forth, singing ''S Wonderful', much to the amusement of Mum and our neighbours.

Dad said he would make a frame for the drawing, so the following Saturday we went to an art shop in Ilford to purchase the wooden frame we required. The drawing would be mounted under glass, so once the frame was made, Dad arranged to have a sheet of glass cut to the exact size, which we went to collect from a local supplier. It was a long walk home for Dad, grasping a large piece of glass under his arm, but he didn't complain. That evening we polished the glass free of any marks or dust, and placed it carefully onto the frame. The drawing was then placed onto the glass, followed by hardboard backing which we then secured to the frame. As we lifted our completed work to show to my mum I am sure I saw a few tears in those eyes.

On Sunday Dad drove us to London and there are no prizes for guessing where we were heading. He parked the car near to Shirley's home and carrying the framed drawing, we walked to the house. I remember being nervous, yet wonderfully happy, but when we first called nobody was home. Mum and Dad reassured me by saying we could return again later, and when we did someone answered the door. If it had been Shirley I would have remembered every detail, but it was not, so I can only tell you that I happily left my gift and a note, knowing that Shirley would receive both soon.

That year, 1964, had started with Shirley appearing at the Odeon Leicester Square, London with guest star Matt Monro and John Barry and his Orchestra. The show presented by Vic Lewis, Shirley's manager at the time, was a great success and later toured several leading towns in April and early May. Following on from the tour, Shirley was booked to appear at one of London's finest venues, The Talk of the Town, so life for her was hectic.

Mum, Dad and I had centre front-row seats in the royal circle of the Odeon Theatre for the first performance of what was billed as *The Shirley Bassey Show.* This vast cinema, built in 1937, dominated one side of Leicester Square and I can remember how impressed I was looking up at its frontage. Before entering the vast building we spent time with George Webb and other fans, catching up on news. Some fans would attend both performances, but seeing two almost identical performances so close together never really appealed to me. Cost also had to be considered. The tickets for that night's show were £1/5/- each, or £1.25 if you only understand decimal, but in 1964 that was a lot of money. Doors opened at 5.15pm for the 6.30 show, so we had plenty of time to get some refreshments, although I was always too excited to eat before a performance. We purchased a programme which consisted of sixteen pages and featured a happy casual photo of Shirley taken by Vic Lewis, which I particularly liked, before settling into our seats.

John Barry and his Orchestra opened the first half of the concert. My first impression was that John was younger than I had expected and seemed rather serious. I remember thinking he was rather rude since he would constantly use his forefinger to point at a musician, but in time I realised this was just part of his conducting style. Without doubt he was a very versatile musician and with this performance demonstrated his talents as a composer, arranger and conductor. His programme was entertaining and varied, including bossa nova, jazz and several 'Bond' arrangements. However, 'Goldfinger' had yet to be born. Matt Monro joined the orchestra for the remainder of the first half and gave a polished performance featuring many of his hits, including his latest, 'I Love The Little Things', with which he had taken second prize in the Song For Europe Contest.

When the safety curtain rose following the intermission, magic seemed to fill the air as the audience settled into a silence. The orchestra played an introductory overture, lights dimmed and onto the stage stepped Shirley, looking wonderful in what was probably a Douglas Darnell gown. Fans were cheering, pleased to welcome Shirley back onstage after the birth of her daughter Samantha in November 1963 (her elder daughter, Sharon, was born in 1954). I am not sure whether Shirley began her performance with the Gershwin number ''S Wonderful', or whether it featured in the early part of the show, but with her emphasis of the words 'w-o-n-d-e-r-f-u-l, it's m-a-r-v-e-l-l-o-u-s', she captivated her audience

Other classics such as 'Fly Me To The Moon', 'No Regrets' and 'Just One Of Those Things' were among the fifteen or so numbers Shirley included in her programme, but for many members of the audience one particular song had to be heard: 'I Who Have Nothing'. Shirley had recently climbed the hit parade with her 45 rpm single and was currently enjoying the success, so to see and hear her perform this number was a must for any fan. When Shirley sang 'I' the audience erupted into spontaneous applause, Shirley acknowledging the audience, continued and gave an emotional performance which sent shivers down my spine. It was one of the highlights of the show and proved to be equally successful during the April/May tour.

On 12 April, one year after our first London Palladium concert, my parents and I marked our first anniversary by attending a concert at the Astoria, Finsbury Park, the London venue for the latest tour. Similar in format and content to the show at the Odeon, Shirley included 'My Special Dream' and 'Gone', which Columbia Records had released as singles following the success of 'I Who Have Nothing'. Once again it was 'I' that stole the show and Mum was not alone in shedding a few tears. Lots of fans waited at the stage door that evening and we managed to get a brief glimpse as a smiling Shirley got into her car. As we travelled home I kept thinking to myself this cannot get better, I've seen the best, but as you will discover in these pages, it always did – and that is Shirley's magic.

For a fan it was a very busy time with lots of articles and reviews appearing in the music papers and national press. Any spare time I had was spent playing the latest record release. I would go into our front room, place the record on the turntable and either pretend to conduct the orchestra for Shirley as she sang, or I would simply choose to sing along with her, of course including all the hand and arm movements. I became so good at this, before long I found myself doing Shirley impressions at the family parties. At one Christmas party I took it all very seriously, so when an uncle continued to tease me, I ran 'offstage' upset and into my aunt's kitchen.

With the addition of concert programmes and ticket stubs my scrapbook was filling up rapidly, yet I was unaware that I was about to acquire a very special addition to my photo album. It was one morning in late May when I heard my dad calling to the postman, 'Don't bend the envelope', but the corner of the item was already being squeezed through the letterbox. Dad managed to save the envelope from total destruction, much to my relief, since the package was addressed to

Miss Mary Pilgrim. When I saw the London postmark I began to get excited, but as I withdrew the *Shirley Bassey* letterhead from the large envelope my excitement evaporated slowly when I saw the letter had *only* come from Miss Bassey's secretary. However, it quickly returned when I started to read the letter and discovered my drawing had been put up in the drawing room. The letter went on to say 'it must have taken hours to complete and everyone here thinks it is really good'. Then I read the next paragraph, 'I am enclosing an autographed photograph' and I literally dived into the envelope.

Out came a beautiful full-length photograph of Shirley, wearing a black velvet Douglas Darnell gown with an orchid embellishment of crystals, standing against a white background. Handwritten in black ink across the photograph were the words:

> 'Dear Mary, Many thanks for the Wonderful Sketch, Shirley Bassey.'

My parents were so happy for me and rightly wanted to see my new treasured possession, but I kept holding it close to me; I didn't want to let go of it just yet. When I finally passed the photograph to them I realised how proud they were of me and I was reminded how lucky I was to have such wonderful parents. Finally, the letter stated, 'We may see you at The Talk of the Town, I hope you get a chance to go.'

Over the next few days anyone and everyone at school and work, prepared to listen, was subjected to hearing about the signed photograph and letter I had received from Shirley Bassey. I daydreamed about how wonderful it would be to see Miss Bassey at The Talk of the Town and I am sure I probably drove my parents insane with my pleading to attend this famous theatre restaurant. When Shirley had last appeared at this venue she had broken all attendance records, so naturally I wanted to make my dream a reality and in doing so help her break the attendance record yet again. Having parents who were also great fans meant very little persuasion was necessary; Mum and Dad agreed and the following day made a reservation for Shirley's forthcoming engagement. When I think back now about those days in the sixties I realise money did not come easy to my parents, although we all benefited from Mum working full-time, which meant a little extra money was available for *treats,* as Mum would call them. *Treats* just couldn't get better than the 'Talk'.

The Talk of the Town, at Hippodrome Corner in central London, opened in September 1958 as a theatre restaurant. Regarded as one of the great night spots of the world, it offered outstanding entertainment value with an inclusive charge of 57/6 (£2.88), providing patrons with a three-course dinner, dancing to two famous orchestras, a spectacular floorshow at 10pm and the star cabaret at 11.30pm. All this made it the ideal venue to celebrate an important occasion such as an anniversary or special birthday with family and friends. Primarily, members of the audience were there to have a good night out. Unlike a concert audience, the cabaret audience was not there solely to see the 'star'; the dynamics of this audience could be quite different. Sometimes The Talk of the Town only confirmed the star performer a few weeks prior to the engagement date. This meant if a person wished to book to see a specific performer, they could find it difficult to get a good table since several reservations would have already been taken for that date. We were lucky; we had a reservation, so now we needed to prepare for the big night.

Like Shirley, Mum and I both needed a new frock for this special occasion, so we went to a little shop in Ilford which had been recommended to Mum. The shop was rather like Dr Who's, Tardis; the outside was small and hardly noticeable but once you stepped through the door you were overwhelmed by the quantity of stock held within. The lady who ran the shop greeted us enthusiastically and within minutes of establishing our needs, rushed around the shop gathering up several dresses from the racks. 'Try this on, it looks so much better on,' she said, as she caught my disapproving look. I had to like a dress before I would try it on, plus I preferred something a little more classic than the ones she was holding up.

Soon she began to understand the style I liked and produced a lovely pale blue dress, which had six diamond buttons down the front. I fell in love with it immediately and when I tried it on, it fitted perfectly. Mum had spotted something for herself which was not dissimilar: her dress had several jewelled stones around the neck and partly down the front and was light beige in colour. When Mum tried on the dress and walked out from the changing room, I thought she looked beautiful. I had never seen Mum in anything quite like this before, although she had always looked lovely in everything she wore. Mum loved my dress too, so we were both very happy as we left the shop to travel home and show Dad our new party frocks. When we arrived home it didn't take long for Mum and I to hold our own little fashion parade especially for Dad. One look at his face, as we twirled around the dining room, told us all we needed to know – he would be proud to take us to the ball!

Dad too, had a surprise for us: he had arranged car hire for our evening out. Today when we consider car hire we simply think of just that, hiring a car. Yet back in the sixties car hire incorporated not just the car but also a chauffeur, who would be immaculately dressed in a dark suit and tie, black gloves and peak cap. Dad, knowing Mr Tricker who operated his own car-hire business, appropriately named Ace Car Hire, had hired him to take and collect us from The Talk of the Town on the appointed evening. This very likeable and reliable man was just what we required since it would be around 1am before we would be ready to leave the theatre and head home.

At school my friends, who were often bored by my talk of Shirley Bassey, were happy to hear of the preparations for our special night out. None had been to The Talk of the Town, although many were aware of its existence and its importance in the world of entertainment. As with all teenagers, even today, a few classmates were a little envious.

It was Saturday and our big day had finally arrived. I had found it almost impossible to contain my excitement throughout the week following Shirley's opening night the previous Monday, which received rave reviews in the national press. At 6.30pm Mr Tricker's shining limousine pulled up outside our house. It goes without saying, we were all dressed up and ready and I can remember feeling rather special as I climbed into the car. Turning to look out of the window, I saw our next-door neighbours; they had come out to wish us an enjoyable evening and remained there, waving furiously, until the car pulled away down the street and finally drove out of sight. The drive into London took about forty-five minutes, plus a few more for Mr Tricker to manoeuvre his limousine outside the front entrance to The Talk of the Town. Displayed in the windows at either side of the entrance were large black-and-white photographs of Shirley Bassey.

Suddenly it struck me: this was happening and tonight we were going to witness something very special. The doorman stepped forward and opened the door of our car and I stepped out onto the pavement. As I looked up, my head leaning back as far as it would go, I watched the flashing neon lights spelling out the name of the theatre restaurant. When the doorman lead us into the foyer, I thought I'd entered an Aladdin's Cave, with the deep red carpet, gold fittings and crystal lights. We joined the crowd of people making their way up a few steps to the entrance; to the left was a small bar. As our table had been booked for 8pm and we had arrived early, we were directed to the bar. It was lavishly furnished in deep red velvet and gold; I had never experienced anything quite like this. Ladies sipped at their gin and tonics whilst the gentlemen enjoyed a brandy in between puffing on a cigar. We sat and had a drink while gazing around at the other patrons with whom we would share our evening.

As 8pm drew near we left the comfort of the bar and headed towards the small archway leading into the vast restaurant-theatre area. We could not venture further without checking in with the restaurant manager who presided over a large table plan. Dad gave his name and within a few moments a waiter was summoned to show us to our table. I hardly had time to catch my breath as we followed, dodging other patrons and waiters along the way. Eventually we were shown our table, situated approximately halfway between the stage and the rear of the theatre, then ushered into our seats. Ours provided us with a good view of the stage since our row of tables was positioned on a slightly higher level than the ones in front of us. We were also in a central position, which meant Shirley would be directly ahead – maybe she would see me!

I took in a gulp of air and gazed around; the place looked stunning, red, gold and crystal prominent everywhere. Mum and Dad seemed to share my feelings and we were all smiles when the waiter reappeared to take our food and drink order. I was always too excited to remember anything particular about the food, but I do remember we enjoyed the three-course dinner, my favourite always being course number three. The seating area was vast and I believe it had the capacity to seat approximately 1,000 diners. On three sides, tables surrounded a rectangular dance floor which miraculously rose up about one metre to table level at show time. Slightly further back and above us, rather like the royal circle in a theatre, was another area of seating for diners. During dinner we listened to the orchestra and watched as some members of the audience showed off their dancing skills in front of those gathered around.

Actually, The Talk of the Town had two orchestras: one favoured traditional dance band music whilst the other was known for its Latin American style. The two orchestras would seamlessly rota in an ingenious way as they played 'I Could Have Danced All Night'. One band playing onstage would divide in the middle, the stage moving one half of the seated musicians off to the wings on the left, while the other half were moved into the wings on the right. Simultaneously, the second orchestra, who were seated and playing at the rear of the stage, were moved forward to front of stage. It was a marvellous piece of stage engineering that always fascinated me and I still marvel at it whenever I hear that music today.

'I Could Have Danced All Night' played again, but this time the curtain closed to the audience's applause. It was 10pm and Robert Nesbitt's Roman Holiday revue was about to commence. With an array of dancers, it also featured four principal performers, one of which was Lynda Baron who a decade or so later gained fame in the BBC comedy series *Open All Hours*. The revue showcased Rome and its many facets, with lavish stage sets, colourful costumes and wonderful music. It was also extravagant, featuring fountains which occupied most of the stage area and ran continuously for approximately forty minutes. I can recall thinking this is much more exciting than listening to a comic tell a few jokes!

The revue received a good response from the audience and now, with the stage lowered, couples once again took to the dance floor. The atmosphere was beginning to mount as people seemed to be preparing themselves for the next part of the evening. I began to develop my pre-performance nerves and wondered how Shirley was feeling; knowing she had to walk out onstage and face an audience not entirely formed of fans made me more apprehensive. Yet, I told myself, Shirley has done this before, cabaret is her forte and she will have them in the palm of her hand after her first number.

Suddenly an announcement was made: 'Ladies and Gentleman may we remind you there will be no bar service during Miss Bassey's performance.' Waiters hurried around, fulfilling every order. The orchestra stopped playing, the curtain fell, the stage rose. Suddenly the audience was quiet, no more clinking of wine glasses, as the lights dimmed, the orchestra started to play and the inimitable Miss Shirley Bassey was announced. There were cheers and loud applause, and I rose to my feet as Shirley walked onstage, looked to her new musical director, Kenny Clayton and went straight into 'On A Wonderful Day Like Today'. The combined sounds of the orchestra and her voice were wonderful. When Shirley sang the line 'I will pay the bill', looking towards the gentlemen sitting at a table next to the stage, paused, gave a giggly laugh, and then sang, 'tomorrow', the audience loved it.

The performance continued with a number of Bassey classics, such as 'I Get A Kick Out Of You', 'What Kind Of Fool Am I' and 'With These Hands', all of which confirmed her amazing talent. Then came the dramatic 'I, Who Have Nothing'. As Shirley ended the number she slowly walked offstage, hugging her dress like a matador, as the trumpeter from the orchestra stood tall and blew out those final, memorable notes. The audience was cheering and shouting for more, the applause continuing until Shirley reappeared, which generated an even greater show of appreciation from the audience.

We were offered a few more wonderful numbers, Shirley using the entire stage area during her singing, adjusting her performance to reach every member of her audience. As a fan I was overwhelmed by Shirley's performance and for a moment drawn to look at Eartha Kitt, who sat at a table close to the stage. She certainly seemed to be enjoying Shirley's act, but as a performer herself I wondered if it was possible for Miss Kitt to enjoy the performance, in the same way I was – as a fan!

Fun songs, show songs, dramatic songs, the audience loved them all and as the end of the performance drew near the audience dug deep and produced more applause, with shouts for more, more until finally Shirley returned for a further encore. I just couldn't remain at our table any longer and rushed down the few steps, along the edge of a row of seats, to find myself calling out 'more' as I stood at the edge of the stage. Shirley, having spotted me, came and reached out for my outstretched hand, which I offered together with my thanks for a wonderful evening. With a lovely smile, Shirley thanked me before returning to the microphone for a final number. Making my way back to our table, I was elated.

It took several minutes before any form of normality returned to

The Talk of the Town once Shirley finally left the stage. The orchestra eventually returned, playing 'I Could Have Danced All Night' as the stage lowered to floor level. Someone from a nearby table came up to me to tell me how pleased they were to see me shake hands with Shirley. I wanted to reply, 'Not half as pleased as I was,' but thought better of it, so I simply thanked them. Mum and Dad looked on with their usual pride whilst I continued discussing Shirley's performance. Unfortunately, the party really was coming to a close and we had to think about leaving. Mr Tricker would soon be waiting for us outside, so Dad paid our bill, we gathered up our programmes, collected our coats and joined the crowd emerging from venue. Soon we spotted Mr Tricker and once inside the car, I don't think I stopped talking until we arrived home in the early hours of the morning.

Mum, Dad and I had enjoyed a truly wonderful experience that evening, one of the best during our time together and certainly the best I had experienced up until then. Shirley had been fantastic and seemingly very relaxed and happy at The Talk of the Town, which gave us every confidence in believing she would be back one day soon.

CHAPTER 3

GOLDFINGER

Like every good fan I would be off to the record store whenever I heard or read of a new Shirley Bassey release. As well as singles (45s), record companies also released EPs, an abbreviation for 'extended play', which usually contained four tracks instead of two, on a disc the same size as a single. I did not always buy them because sometimes an EP would be compiled from a combination of previously issued material. One new track, however, was usually sufficient to get me hooked and I would purchase the disc, to the delight of the record company, I'm sure.

Following the success of 'I Who Have Nothing', which put Shirley in the Top Ten of the pop charts, Columbia released 'My Special Dream', soon to be followed by 'Gone', in an attempt to establish another big hit. Unfortunately neither of these songs, in my opinion, was going to be as successful as 'I, Who Had Nothing'. They lacked that something special, in spite of Shirley's excellent performance. However, a fan wants anything ever recorded, so I bought both singles and enjoyed my form of karaoke, prior to its invention. I would sing-along with Shirley, in our front room at home, until I had learned the lyrics and phasing of each tune, to perfection. Personally, I thought we made a great duo but whether Mum, Dad and the neighbours were of the same opinion hearing our free 'concerts' is another matter.

The year 1964 was proving to be a rather topsy-turvy one for Shirley, with illness causing her to spend a short time at The London Clinic. Whenever I read such news in the tabloids, I would be off to the shops to buy a lovely get-well card for Shirley, which I immediately sent. If, after a day or so, no further news was forthcoming from the press, I would phone her management's office to seek information on her progress. Occasionally, I phoned the clinic direct, prompted by my feelings of a need to know that Shirley was well.

I know many, many fans cared and although I recognised the improbability of fans get-well messages reaching Shirley, I do hope Shirley knew, in some way, that we all cared.

Good news soon followed when it was reported in the music press that Shirley would be singing the theme song for the next James Bond movie, to be called *Goldfinger*. The composer, John Barry, who had toured with Shirley earlier in the year, asked Shirley to listen to the music, even though the lyrics had yet to be written. Hearing that haunting introduction and the melody was enough for Shirley to recognise that 'Goldfinger' had that something special and immediately agreed to record the number. John had called upon Anthony Newley and Leslie Bricusse to provide the lyrics, then it was into the studio with Shirley and a mighty sixty-piece orchestra… and the rest is history. Probably not quite as simple as that, but the result was phenomenal. Columbia issued the single, stating 'Goldfinger' from the film of the same name, as if we needed to be told. I remember when I first heard that mighty orchestral introduction and Shirley's first 'G-o-o-o-l-d finger', I shuddered. I longed to hear it at the cinema and when the film finally reached our local cinema, Mum, Dad and I sat in awe as Shirley sang, engulfing the audience with the power of her voice, and transporting them into the mind of Goldfinger.

'Goldfinger' entered the UK charts and sold reasonably well, but it was America where it's greatest success was achieved, selling over one million copies and topping the US charts. This success was instrumental in propelling Shirley to a new level of worldwide-star status, and in doing so generating a new legion of fans spread across the entire face of the globe. I was delighted by Shirley's success, and enjoyed watching the additional guest appearances her popularity had generated on television. However, all this meant we soon had to learn to share Shirley with the world and it was announced she would be embarking on a lengthy tour of America and Australia. But before embarking on a trip across the pond, Shirley had a little shopping to do!

London's Chester Square was, and still is, one of the best addresses in town and according to press reports at the time, Shirley had recently purchased a property there, which was now being decorated to her specifications.

As a family we would sometimes go to London on a Sunday for a day out, often going for a walk through Green Park or Hyde Park, so on our next visit we planned a detour to Chester Square. It required only a little detective work as only one house in the square had scaffolding outside, so it had to be Shirley's new home (later this was confirmed, but that's another part of the story).

I gained a little more information about Shirley's new house, surprisingly, from a girl in my class at school. Celia (or it may have been Cynthia) and I did not usually share much in the way of conversation but on this particular day, Celia enjoyed telling me about her father who had an important job at Harrison Gibson furniture store, in Ilford. The store was very well known for its range of quality furniture as well as for its building, which housed on the top floor, the Room At The Top nightclub. 'My dad is meeting Shirley Bassey today,' said Celia and continued to inform me that he would be advising Shirley about the furniture she would require for her new home. Over the coming days, Celia must have enjoyed watching my face, turning shades of green, as she let out her little snippets of information – the colour of the wallpaper in the drawing room, 'Shirley's bedroom is turquoise' and 'Sharon's room is just fabulous'. To be fair, Celia did not disclose any personal information but during those weeks there were times when I wished it had been my dad working for Harrison Gibson.

One day Dad came home with his own little piece of news. He had spoken to a man who had delivered Shirley's furniture and, he told Dad, Shirley paid £20,000 for the house. Good old Dad had come up trumps! The local newspaper, the *Ilford Recorder*, also supplied me with news when they reported on Miss Shirley Bassey shopping at Harrison Gibson. I had to visit the store for myself, although at sixteen my interest in furniture was minimal. However, my interest developed immediately upon spotting in the store's window a lampshade on which hung a brown label that read: 'Sold to Shirley Bassey'.

Shirley then headed off to America, to be followed by Australia, to capitalise on her well-earned success with 'Goldfinger'. Back in the UK, fans had the pleasure of a new LP entitled *Shirley Stops The Shows*, released in January. One of the pieces of information I had been given by ardent fan George Webb was the existence of Shirley's Record Shop, at West End Lane, Hampstead. The shop, once a book shop owned by Kenneth Hume, had been re-opened by Shirley in 1962. Whenever possible I would order my records through the shop and over time we grew to know the shop's manager, Michael, quite well. *Shirley Stops The Shows* had been due for release on Shirley's birthday but due to a delay in delivery, it didn't arrive at the shop until the following day, Saturday, 9 January. As I had a Saturday job, Mum and Dad said they would travel to Hampstead to collect the record for me, which was great since I was dying to hear the tracks.

When I arrived home in the evening, Mum and Dad were waiting, LP in hand and with a story to tell. Apparently, when they arrived at the shop they had met Shirley's sister, Ella. My mum, who was a lovely, sociable person, always enjoyed having a chat and must have been singing my praises because Ella told her she had seen the drawing I had given to Shirley. This of course delighted Mum and I too was thrilled by their encounter.

As the title suggested, Shirley's latest long player featured show numbers, including, 'He Loves Me', 'The Lady is a Tramp', 'Somewhere' and 'I Could Have Danced All Night', the only track recorded with Kenny Clayton and his Orchestra. The rest of the tracks had all been recorded with Johnnie Spence and his Orchestra; the record's producer was Norman Newell, a master at his art.

One review of the LP, which appeared in the music paper *Disc*, said Shirley sounded like Judy Garland, which prompted me to write to the paper to agree. I'm sure Shirley would have been happy to read the comparison. The record also featured the black-and-white photography of Barry Lategan, which captured Shirley brilliantly. Kenny Clayton became Shirley's musical director, remaining with her for some years and I personally think he was one of the best.

While Shirley was abroad, her fans and the rest of Britain were reading about her divorce from Kenneth Hume in the national press. However, the music press offered happier news for her fans, announcing Shirley would be appearing on ATV's *Sunday Night at the London Palladium* in April. Now we could look forward to seeing Shirley again, so I immediately sent a letter to ATV to request tickets for Shirley's appearance, scheduled for 25 April. During February I received tickets from ATV, but when I looked at them I noticed they were for a show only a week or so away. I managed to telephone ATV and they told me to keep the tickets they had sent and promised to add my name to the list for Shirley's April appearance. Each ticket issued by ATV permitted entry for two people and specified the area of the theatre you would be allocated – stalls, royal circle or upper circle. It was a considerable task for ATV to transform the London Palladium from a theatre into a television studio in one day, which is basically what it had to achieve. With the Palladium's current production running all week, the TV cameras were set up on Sunday morning, with rehearsals following on during the day. In the side streets at the rear of the theatre, mobile control units were parked and, if a door was left open, you just might catch a glimpse on one of the monitors of what was happening onstage. In the evening, the show would be broadcast to the nation.

Once rehearsals had finished, the theatre was made ready to seat the invited audience, some of whom had already started to queue behind the appropriate bus-stop-style signs, which read either stalls, royal circle or upper circle. Tickets did not have an allocated seat number, so it was a case of first come, first served, which meant it was possible to get front-row seats if you were at the front of the queue.

We loved going to the London Palladium, so in February we joined the queue to see the televised show which featured Kenny Ball and his Jazzmen, Frank Ifield and Petula Clark. It was an enjoyable show and I should have been grateful I guess, but I kept thinking, I just hope we will be here in April to see Shirley.

During early April, I visited Shirley's Record Shop and bought the EP *Live at the Café de Paris*, which had printed across its cover the word 'CENSORED'. Recorded in 1957, it is early Shirley and captures a wonderful moment in her career. I think it's a fabulous record and I was so delighted I was able to get a copy. I also bought Shirley's new single release, 'No Regrets', which received very good reviews and sold reasonably well. The shop manager, Michael, had also applied for tickets to the Palladium TV show and said if he was allocated some, he would give me one. A few weeks later I received a ticket for two from ATV and fortunately Michael was also able to provide me with a ticket, which meant Mum, Dad and I would all be there so support Shirley on her return to London's most famous stage.

News of Shirley's return home came during the second week of April along with an announcement in the *New Musical Express* that

S.V.B. Ltd was presenting a series of concerts featuring Shirley Bassey. No prizes for guessing what S.V.B. stood for, but I'll give you a clue: the V is for Veronica! A list of venues and dates were supplied, so I immediately took out my Parker 51 pen (a recent birthday present from Mum and Dad) and wrote to the Guildhall, Portsmouth, requesting tickets for the concert scheduled for 30 May.

A few days before the London Palladium appearance, I went to Romford to buy a special box of chocolates, which I was hoping I could give to Shirley when she arrived at the theatre on Sunday, and naturally I had to buy gold wrapping paper for my gift.

On Saturday, a lovely colour photo of Shirley appeared in 'TV Times', a weekly television magazine, which I immediately transferred to my scrapbook. As you can imagine, I was very excited about the next day as the London Palladium offered a good opportunity to see Shirley prior to the show. The big day arrived and after a hearty breakfast, Dad drove us to London, parking the car fairly near to the theatre, a feat that would be impossible today. In the sixties, the streets of London were normally quiet on a Sunday, and even the famous street opposite the backstage entrance to the Palladium, Carnaby Street, was relatively quiet. As we walked towards the stage-door area, where a small group of people had gathered, we recognised some of the faces, fans of Shirley we had seen at previous concerts. There were other unknown faces, some of which belonged to the 'autograph hunters', who were solely there for the purpose of collecting an autograph to add to the trophy list. I never had a great deal of respect for the latter group mainly because some were demanding and showed little respect for the artist.

We spotted George Webb, who told us they were expecting Shirley for rehearsals soon. It was good to know other fans, especially on these sorts of occasions when one of us would act as a 'lookout' at the corner of the street, shouting out to the others when they saw Shirley's car approach. Soon the call came and the small group of loyal fans surrounded her car as it drew up to the edge of the pavement.

Shirley looked radiant in a full-length,V-neck coat, to which had been fastened a gold brooch depicting two cats seated side by side. Shirley's secretary, Hazel, carried Shirley's dresses, which were protected in suitable covers.

To our great delight, there was another passenger in the car – Shirley's daughter, Sharon, who seemed a little shy when we first said hello. I am sure the day must have been just as thrilling for Sharon, going to see her mum rehearse at the London Palladium, as it was for us. Then we spoke to Shirley and I told her how nice it was to see her again, gave her my gift and added, 'We shall be at the show tonight.' After thanking me for the gift Shirley said, 'That's good, we will see you later', then they all made their way into the theatre. We went off, ecstatic, to the nearby café for a cuppa and to chat with other fans. We would talk about future concerts we planned to attend, record releases and television performances; in fact we would chat about anything as long as it was linked to Shirley Bassey.

Always the true professional, it never usually took Shirley long to rehearse, but for a television appearance a few additional aspects had to be considered, for example the colour of the dress or whether it would reflect too much sparkle under the television lights. While we waited outside the theatre fans would often speculate about the dress Shirley would wear – would it be gold, silver, or maybe pink? One thing was fairly certain: it would be a Douglas Darnell. Douglas was born in London in 1933. Although self-taught, he became a successful couturier and was the man behind the 'Darnell of London' label. Stars flocked to seek his creations. For more than fifty years he created stunning stage gowns for Dame Shirley, who later described his talent as 'magic'.

We returned to the backstage area mid-afternoon and were pleased to learn that Shirley had not left the theatre. It was a lovely sunny afternoon and we waited for signs of movement from the stage door. Then slowly the door began to open and Shirley walked out into the small group of people waiting to catch a glimpse or looking for an autograph. Sharon and Hazel followed closely and I was delighted to see Sharon carrying the chocolates I had given to Shirley earlier. A few people obtained Shirley's autograph and Dad asked if he could take some photos, to which Shirley agreed. He took a few shots while Mum chatted and wished Shirley all the very best for her evening performance. Shirley seemed very happy chatting with us and I like to think she recognised she was amongst people who were solely there to express their love and appreciation of her.

In a few hours we would be able to show our appreciation by offering our greatest gift, applause, but first we had to queue behind the sign marked,'Royal Circle', which had been positioned outside the front of the theatre. To be at the front of the queue meant excellent seats, but we would need to remain in the queue for an hour to an hour and a half before the doors opened. Of course it was worth it.

The theatre doors opened and we were directed up the staircase to the royal circle where we headed towards our seats at the front. With the television camera nearby, the seats didn't get much better than this and I was reminded of the first time I had seen Shirley, from these very same seats. We knew that even if Shirley didn't see us, when the lights went up, without a doubt she would hear us. It took a little time for everyone to be seated and then the initial warm-up with the audience began, during which those butterflies of mine took off for their journey. I find all shows drag a little when you are waiting to see the last act, but we enjoyed playing 'Beat-the-Clock'. This was a game that took place in the middle of the show, in which members of the audience were selected to take part. They were given a task which they had to complete within an allocated time, which ticked away on a large clock, hence the name. Thinking back, it all seems a little silly now but the game was a fundamental part of a show which, at its peak, achieved TV audiences of 20 million viewers.

Once 'Beat the Clock' had finished the curtain closed in preparation for the finale. If you were sitting at home watching the show on television, the adverts would appear before the cameras finally switched back to the London Palladium. The show's compère, who I believe on this occasion was Norman Vaughan, took to the stage and probably told a few jokes before introducing Britain's very own international singing star, Miss Shirley Bassey. I have forgotten the introductions over the years, but the sound of the audience welcoming Shirley home has remained with me. Like me, the audience just wanted to hear Shirley sing and be a part of the magical experience her performance could generate.

We were treated to five songs that evening, one, 'The Name Game', about a game of variations with a name, had been a big success for Shirley Ellis, who wrote the song with Lincoln Chase. This unusual choice showed Shirley's sense of fun along with her ability to make any song her own. The audience loved her cheeky interpretation, rewarding her with laughter and loud applause. My favourite song that evening was the fast tempo number, 'You Better Love Me While You May' and although I had told myself I should remain seated as we were on television, I rose to give Shirley a standing ovation. I was not alone; other members of the audience, including Mum and Dad, joined in the cheering. The lights went up, lighting the entire audience, as Shirley looked towards us and acknowledged our applause. We were convinced she had recognised us and cheered even louder as the curtain finally fell. It had been a fabulous day and, yes, Shirley wore a lovely pink dress!

I should have stopped dreaming during the weeks ahead as I had exams to take at college, but I didn't. My results weren't very good but this was partly expected since I had chosen to study sciences, subjects not taught at the girls' school I had attended. However, I must have acquired some information during my college course, because I made an impression at an interview held in the physics department of Queen

Mary College, University of London. The next day I was offered the full-time position of junior laboratory technician, although one day a week I would be attending Paddington Technical College, in London, to study for job qualifications. I was delighted to accept the offer and looked forward to starting work in September.

Back in May, work had not been on my mind as I waited for the postman every morning, hoping our tickets for the Portsmouth concert would soon arrive. After a few days an envelope dropped on the mat, which I hastily opened to discover three tickets, numbered A13–A15, had been reserved for us. 'Front row, front row,' I called out. What magic.

The day finally arrived. Dad found driving along the A3 to Portsmouth on a Sunday a pleasure. Although we didn't know the route very well, I had become a fairly good navigator during the last year, so armed with my road map, Dad happily trusted me when I called out the necessary directions. However, on our journey down to Portsmouth, neither of us realised how important map reading and my directions would become during our journey home.

The Guildhall at Portsmouth, an impressive building in Guildhall Square, was probably Hampshire's biggest concert venue and is still used today for a wide variety of performances. I remember the stage-door entrance, accessed by climbing a few steps, as very tiny. I found the rear of the building rather cold, preferring the 'backstage atmosphere' of the Winter Gardens, Bournemouth. Yet even today, when I find myself on a train to Portsmouth Harbour and I spot the stage-door entrance shortly after the train leaves Portsmouth main station, the memories of those wonderful concerts Shirley performed at the Guildhall come flooding back.

That Sunday in May, we waited to welcome Shirley on arrival. During our wait we had spoken with fans then, following Shirley's arrival, Dad spoke with her chauffeur about the journey from London. I remember feeling it a little odd when I heard him ask Dad what make of car we owned. He then said jokingly, 'I'll look out for you in my mirror on the way home, and then you can follow me.' I assumed this related to Dad not being sure about the route through London and thought no more about it.

As we entered the theatre that evening, I was feeling very excited and rather special as I took my seat in the front row of the stalls. Trying to control my excitement didn't get any easier even with Mum and Dad by my side. Seating so close to the stage probably made my nerves even worse but I wouldn't have changed my seat for the world. The first half of the show featured Cyril Stapleton and his Showband, with vocalists Ray Merrell and Peter Wynne. The band, compiled of well-established musicians who frequently played on radio and TV, presented a good programme of music ideally suited for the first half of the concert.

During the interval you could feel the atmosphere building as people returned to their seats. Lights dimmed, the orchestra started to play and someone offstage was heard to say through the speakers, 'Ladies and Gentlemen, please welcome the Fabulous, Miss Shirley Bassey'. Maybe not the exact words, but I am sure you get the picture! The spotlights rained down and suddenly right in front of me in a gorgeous, sparkling gown, stood Shirley. Smiling, acknowledging the applause, she looked directly at me and went into song. 'You'd Better Love Me While You May', 'Please Mr Brown', 'If Ever I Would Leave You', interspersed with heart-rending ballads like 'Fools Rush In', 'Who Can I Turn To' and her new single release, 'No Regrets'. I, along with the rest of the audience, was under her spell and remained captivated throughout the evening. People rushed closer to show their appreciation; nobody wanted Shirley to leave the stage. At that moment, her right arm was reaching out towards my applauding hands; I reached forward and held her hand gently with both hands, quite overwhelmed with emotion. Sitting back in my seat for the final number, I watched and listened in awe, then reminded myself, again and again, that I had just shaken hands with the Fabulous Shirley Bassey.

The journey home turned into a dream when half an hour into our journey we were overtaken by a black limousine. 'It's Shirley, Dad, follow her,' I cried out. Fortunately at that time on a Sunday, there was very little traffic, so Dad followed at a safe distance, although I don't think he was as positive as I that Shirley was in the car. As we approached the city I thought it unlikely we could stay close but the gods were good, traffic lights stayed green when we needed them and surprisingly both cars seemed to catch the red lights together as well. Once or twice Dad said we would probably have to let them go, yet somehow we remained joined right up to the door of Shirley's new home in Chester Square. The limo pulled up outside and Shirley and her assistant exited the car just as we passed. Unwinding our passenger windows, Mum and I waved and quietly called out, 'Goodnight Shirley and thank you for a lovely concert.' Shirley, who didn't seem surprised, turned and waved, before saying 'Goodnight.'

As we drove home, Mum and Dad said they were sure the chauffeur must have told Shirley we were following, but knowing who we were, we think she may have enjoyed being part of our little adventure. After all, we were living in the world of James Bond and Goldfinger.

CHAPTER 4

THE SECOND TIME AROUND

Whether Kenneth Hume had the Midas touch is debatable, but there is no doubt he worked hard for Shirley and she, in return, worked hard for him. As Shirley's manager, we saw him during 1965 at the London Palladium and again at the August Bank Holiday concert in Bournemouth, where Shirley sang one of Kenneth's favourite songs, 'Black Is The Colour of My True Love's Hair', the lyrics written by Nina Simone. The newspaper headlines that followed her opening at the Pigalle Club later in the year didn't come as a great surprise to anyone who had witnessed that performance.

Mum and Dad had celebrated their silver wedding anniversary in August 1965 at The Talk of the Town and and needless to say I'd hoped their day might coincide with an engagement for Shirley at the venue, but that was not to be. Instead we were entertained by American singer and pianist Buddy Greco, a fine performer, who was also watched by the record producer Norman Newell and concert promoter Vic Lewis in the audience that evening. That evening I heard Shirley would be opening at the 'Talk' in September, for an eight-week engagement, so we made a booking for October since we would be on holiday for opening night. However, plans changed at the end of August, and it was announced Shirley would not be appearing at the 'Talk' but instead an eight-week engagement had been booked at the Pigalle theatre restaurant in London's Piccadilly, to commence on 13 September.

Although the Pigalle was housed in the basement of 190–196 Piccadilly, it was advertised as London's Premier Theatre restaurant and offered a similar experience to The Talk of the Town but without the floorshow. Shirley's engagement was billed as follows: dancing to the Jack Nathan Orchestra and the Jerry Day Four, a three-course dinner and the 'exciting Shirley Bassey' supported by Alyn Ainsworth and his eighteen-piece TV orchestra, all for 57/6 (£2.88).

Only a few days after the August Bank Holiday concert we booked for the Pigalle. As we were going to be away for opening night, we booked for the first Saturday following our holiday, 25 September, as well as Shirley's final night on 6 November, determined to be at the Pigalle for her final performance after missing her opening night. Unlike The Talk of the Town, the Pigalle presented two shows on a Saturday, so we had to choose between the 7.30pm and 11pm sitting. We opted for the earlier show on 25 September, mainly to get a better table, booking for the 11pm show on the final night.

Of course I sent Shirley a card with our best wishes for her opening night. Although on holiday on the Isle of Wight, we still spent time thinking about her cabaret engagement and wondering how her performance would be received by the theatre critics in attendance. I knew several fans that would be in the audience that night, so it would not be long before I would hear about their evening. As it happened I heard the news sooner than I expected. The morning following opening night, Shirley was pictured with Kenneth Hume on the front pages of most daily newspapers. Shirley had announced during her act, 'I am now going to sing a song to the man I am going to marry. He is in the audience this evening and he also happens to be my ex-husband' to huge applause, and with Alyn Ainsworth's orchestra behind her, Shirley began 'The Second Time Around'.

I had gone to the local newsagents and on seeing Shirley Bassey on the front pages, bought several newspapers which had covered the story. Lots for the scrapbook and off went another card to Shirley offering our congratulations. For the fans there was great joy because the evening's performance had been recorded and was later released as an LP entitled, *Shirley Bassey at the Pigalle*, her first live album. I laugh whenever I view the LP cover because printed at the bottom are the words 'in person'. Could Shirley have done it any other way, I ask myself! It is a fabulous recording that captures the atmosphere of cabaret, a wonderful experience, which sadly can rarely be experienced today.

Although we had a wonderful holiday, when we returned home we were looking forward to going to the Pigalle the following Saturday evening. Our taxi had been arranged and the excitement was mounting, especially after reading the reviews which appeared in the music press later that week. Several extracts appear on the LP cover, confirming Shirley's triumph and international-star status. The Pigalle, because of its downstairs location and elongated cabaret room, never appealed to me in the same way as The Talk of the Town. Although the stage rose to table level in a similar manner to the stage at the Talk, it offered a rather small stage area. However, if you were lucky enough, as we were, to have a table near to the stage, then it was hard to experience a better cabaret. It was as though you had invited Shirley home and she was singing just for you, as she sang her way through a range of material, varying the mood and tempo. On the upbeat 'La Bamba', Shirley's dance routine resulted in a pearl from her dress, propelling itself across the stage, where it then gently rolled to a stop. Shirley seemed unaware of the escaping bead.

Throughout her performance the packed audience applauded, cheered, and shouted for more. She had given a wonderful performance and her final number confirmed what her audience was feeling, it was indeed 'A Lovely Way To Spend An Evening'. Shirley took her final exit and a few moments later the stage began to lower slowly for dancing to resume, but I had not forgotten the pearl, waiting to roll across the floor to be lost forever. Quickly I grabbed a waiter's arm and pleaded with him to retrieve the pearl, which I am delighted to say, he did. His action was almost as good as a real pearl diver, as he dived onto the rolling pearl. When we left the Pigalle that evening I had my own very special memento.

The next morning I found a small jewelry box in which to keep my pearl, although naturally it is not a real pearl. I have kept it all my life and to me it is priceless. There was one occasion, in 2003, when I did consider parting with my gem. Dame Shirley Bassey 50 Years of Glittering Gowns was a gala charity auction held at Christie's, London, with proceeds going to the Dame Shirley Bassey Music Scholarship and the Noah's Ark Appeal. Several of Shirley's gowns were going under the hammer including dresses worn at the Pigalle, so I wrote to Christie's telling them the story of the pearl and offering it up for auction since I felt the story could add an extra dimension. I did receive a nice reply in which they said they did not require the pearl and thought I should keep it since it was a lovely story and souvenir.

The weeks that followed our first visit to the Pigalle were extremely busy for me. I had started work my work at Queen Mary College, working in the teaching laboratories, and I was enjoying the role very much. One great asset for me, as I had no telephone at home, was being able to use the telephone as long as I asked permission. My boss was very understanding when I felt it necessary to contact a theatre box office, management or record company's office but I only did so when it really was urgent, which was how I saw it!

I was also busy at home working on another drawing of Shirley as well as a portrait which a neighbour had asked me to do. And I had my scrapbook to maintain, especially as so much news was appearing in the press about Shirley's two engagements, to Kenneth and at the Pigalle. As the weeks went by fans were expecting to read news of Shirley's marriage, but nothing appeared in the press.

At the Pigalle Shirley was breaking all attendance records and I was writing to the establishment to see if we could be seated at the same table, where we'd sat on our first visit, for our final night booking. They replied stating the table I had requested seated four persons and as demand was so great for the final night, we would need, on this occasion, to book for four persons to reserve the table. Working meant I could now contribute more to the expense, so we amended our booking and the Pigalle wrote back to confirm we had Table 50 booked for the late final-night performance.

On 6 November my cousin Anne joined us for 'An Evening with Shirley Bassey'; the second seating at the Pigalle did not commence until 11pm, with Shirley appearing onstage at midnight. Customers could choose to dine prior to or after Shirley's performance, as no service took place during Shirley's act, but I have no recollection what time we ate. Now as I sit and write about this event I have become far more aware of how hard an eight-week engagement of this type must have been. Performing for at least an hour, sometimes longer, for six days a week, with two shows on Saturday, as well as fulfilling TV, recording and press engagements, was a demanding schedule, especially for a mum, yet Shirley gave it her all.

As midnight approached my cousin was feeling the excitement. The place was packed to capacity, several members of the audience choosing to take their seats immediately prior to midnight. It was obvious to all we were here for one reason only, to share 'An Evening with Shirley Bassey'. Then the lights dimmed, the music began and Shirley boldly entered the stage. A thunderous roar went up and I jumped up from my seat, clapping wildly. Everyone, it seemed, had joined me, and Shirley was happily acknowledging a standing ovation before even singing a note. The audience already loved her and clearly wanted her to feel the presence of their love as the orchestra played, 'A Lovely Way To Spend An Evening'. Shirley seemingly understood and delighted everyone by appropriately opening with the song from the musical *The Roar of the Greasepaint – The Smell of the Crowd*, 'On A Wonderful Day Like Today'. The orchestra, which seemed vast, filling the back of the small stage, played wonderfully as if showing their appreciation for the artistry Shirley had delivered during the previous eight weeks. She had truly established herself and tonight Shirley sang with a feeling that told her audience, this is how it's meant to be. Her programme included past hits, saucy numbers, fun numbers, songs of love and songs of sorrow, each one delivered in the unique Bassey style. We loved it and the more we applauded the more Shirley gave. We were witness to a perfect performance, when performer, orchestra and audience join as one to create an unforgettable experience.

When Shirley announced 'The Second Time Around' the applause was deafening. It was a beautiful song enhanced further, I believe, by the Nelson Riddle arrangement and Shirley's interpretation. At the end of the number whistling, cheering and loud applause reverberated around the room. Shirley, coming to the end of her performance, once more thanked the audience but they were not prepared to let her go just yet. To shouts of 'Bravo' and 'More, more', Shirley returned, taking several standing ovations before the sounds of the orchestra playing 'This Is A Lovely Way To Spend An Evening' made us all aware that it was over. Shirley had broken all box-office records during her engagement at the Pigalle, the venue would never experience anything like it again.

There was no time to relax; Shirley had been invited to perform at the Royal Variety Show on 8 November. The line-up included Tony Bennett, the legendary Jack Benny, folk group Peter, Paul and Mary, and the popular comedy duo Peter Cook and Dudley Moore, to name just a few. Shirley followed this with an engagement in Beirut before returning home to fulfil more concert bookings and an appearance on the *Eamonn Andrews Show*.

I had made two separate applications to ATV for complimentary tickets, one for the *Eamonn Andrews Show* in December, the other for *The New Palladium Show,* where Shirley was scheduled to appear in January 1966. Fortunately we were lucky to receive tickets for both appearance,s although the *Eamonn Andrews Show* was a little disappointing for me. Eamonn Andrews had recently swopped from the BBC to ATV where he hosted one of television's first chat shows, and I was looking forward to watching him 'chat' with Shirley. It had been a long journey to Elstree Studios at Borehamwood but once inside the studio we were allocated good seats in the front row, near to the seating area where the 'guests' were to be interviewed. This was lovely for seeing Charlton Heston, a handsome hunk of a man who starred in the epic movie *Ben Hur*, but unfortunately when Shirley was introduced she took up a position to sing her one number, at the opposite end of the studio. We enjoyed her singing immensely and cheered loudly, along with some other fans, but in truth we were too far away for Shirley to have known who was cheering. I was a bit disappointed at being so far away, having been spoilt by the intimacy of the Pigalle.

It was only a few weeks later, 2 January, when we returned to the London Palladium to see Shirley introduced by that cheeky young comic, Jimmy Tarbuck. We had seen Shirley arrive for rehearsals and my dad had taken a few photos, although Shirley had seemed a little stressed. The agent Tony Lewis accompanied Shirley and as usual her performance that evening was wonderful. Days later, shortly after Shirley's twenty-ninth birthday, the press reported that Shirley had been taken ill and admitted to the London Clinic.

At about this time I received from BBC Light Entertainment tickets to attend a show entitled, *This Is The Sound Of Shirley Bassey*, to be recorded on Tuesday, 25 January. I was concerned for Shirley's health and sent off a get well card immediately. Within a few days Shirley had left the London Clinic and her engagement for the BBC was confirmed in the press.

We had been lucky in getting three tickets, which meant Mum, Dad and I would be able to attend the BBC's Television Centre at Shepherds Bush, where the recording took place. It was lovely watching Shirley perform with such an enthusiastic audience in front of the television cameras since I had been critical of some of her TV appearances in the past. Frequently, cameramen had filmed down from above and I felt this camera angle did little to show Shirley at her best. It appeared to exaggerate her hand and arm movements, making Shirley's perfectly appropriate actions seem overly dramatic. Previously, as a true fan, I had written to Shirley expressing this opinion and it came as no surprise when I never received an answer! However, as we watched Shirley's performance this time, we were delighted by what we witnessed and later left the Television Centre convinced the BBC had done a great job in capturing her talent. I was certain the show would become a TV classic.

The very next day, Shirley flew off to Australia.

Mum, Dad and I were excited by the prospect of seeing the show on television. We had never experienced seeing a show 'on the box' where we had been in the audience, as the other television shows we had attended had all been transmitted live. BBC2 transmitted *This Is The Sound Of Shirley Bassey* in February, one month after the recording. That night we sat at home, warm and comfortable in our dining room, our eyes focused on the television in the corner of the room. The screen, smaller than many computer screens today, sent out its images and we were intoxicated. Miss Bassey was casting her spell in our home.

CHAPTER 5

THE PARTY'S OVER

Within a few days of Shirley flying to Australia the press was reporting 'It's Off'. It seemed that Shirley and Kenneth Hume would not remarry for the second time around. They had decided they were far better at being friends than man and wife. Shirley confirmed Kenneth would continue as her manager. Engagements had been booked for Melbourne and Sidney, to be followed by a tour of Australia and New Zealand, in March. April's schedule was just as hectic with Shirley flying to Manila to perform in cabaret, before heading off to the States.

Like me, Shirley's fans were sorry to hear the news from Australia; we all wished her happiness. I was getting to know some of Shirley's fans quite well, regularly meeting up with George Webb at a number of venues and also becoming friendly with a young guy named Derek, who was about the same age as myself. We met originally at the London Palladium, which he had attended with his Mum. Derek and I got on well together; both of us would continually talk about Shirley, and his mum and my mum always enjoyed chatting with each other while we waited for Shirley to arrive. Following on from the London Palladium engagement I kept in touch with Derek, as I had done with George, so we could exchange any photographs we had taken and generally keep ourselves updated with any news regarding Shirley. Keeping in contact with other fans helped to pass the time while Shirley was away and soon news came of Shirley's visit to America.

Following on from Manila, in April Shirley headed for New York where she appeared at the Royal Box club in the Americana Hotel. It was a great triumph and the setting for Shirley to announce she would now be recording exclusively for United Artists Records. I wrote to the Americana Hotel, part of the Loews' hotel group, requesting any information they might have relating to Shirley.

In May that year, I was so excited when the postman knocked at our door, holding a large envelope with a New York postmark. Inside, along with a letter and advertising material from the Americana Hotel, were two 10- by 8-inch photographs of Shirley, one of which had been taken during a recording session. America, it seemed, knew how to look after the fans!

Shirley had flown on to Las Vegas where she was now appearing, twice nightly, at the famous Sahara Hotel. It was here that Ralph Burns, well known for his arranging and orchestrating of major Broadway shows, prepared and rehearsed the numbers with Shirley for a forthcoming debut album with United Artists Records. On completing her successful engagement on the famous Las Vegas Strip, Shirley, Kenneth Hume and Ralph Burns headed back to New York and into United Artists recording studios. With Kenneth Hume producing, the appropriately named album *I've Got A Song For You*, was recorded within one week.

Shirley immediately headed home and news of a fortnight engagement at the Prince of Wales Theatre, London, in July, was great news for her fans. We immediately sent for tickets and fortunately obtained front-row seats for both the opening and final nights. Derek also managed to get a front-row seat, next to mine, for opening night (I may have obtained the ticket for him). Later I booked for one other performance during the second week but had to console myself with second row! How lucky we were in those days when it was possible to get such good seats. Our good luck may have been due to footballs biggest event taking place at the same time. The World Cup was held from 11–30 July and that famous final, when England beat West Germany 4–2, took place on 30 July, Shirley's final night at the Prince of Wales Theatre, but more about that later.

Another engagement had been organised for 29 July when Shirley would be opening a record shop in Soho's Dean Street. The event was to coincide with the release of her new album, which was eagerly awaited, plus an opportunity to see Shirley 'offstage' was a rare event, one that I certainly did not want to miss. At work I arranged a day's holiday leave and looked forward to the shows, television, live appearances and a new album. July was going to be a dream!

Tuesday, 19 July finally arrived and I was looking up at the frontage of the Prince of Wales Theatre. The twenty-foot-plus sign, above the entrance, was impressive and read: 'Kenneth Hume presents SHIRLEY BASSEY ENTERTAINS'. At street level the billboards displayed glamorous life-size photographs of Shirley, which had been commissioned by United Artists, and informed the passing public that Shirley would be entertaining for 'two weeks only'.

Being a weekday, we had been to work, although Mum and I must have arranged to leave work early so that we could get ready for the show. Dad had a little more flexibility in his work as a credit collector and so was home on time to get ready for our night out. Dad drove us into town early in the evening and we went for a meal prior to the show at a restaurant near the theatre. Mum and Dad always tried to make these occasions extra special in any way they could, but they had also brought me up to appreciate and be grateful for all the things we receive in life. They enjoyed seeing Shirley as much as me and we were all delightfully happy as we approached the theatre.

The foyer was bustling with people as they headed for their seats. We walked down towards the front of the stalls, having purchased, at a cost of 2/6 (12½p), a souvenir programme which contained several fantastic photographs of Shirley, taken by New York celebrity photographer Milton H. Greene. I also purchased the theatre's programme, called *Playbill* (not to be confused with *Playboy* magazine) for 1/- (5p), which gave information about the show and a short biography of each performer. We reached the stage and were shown to our seats located on the right side as you looked to the stage. Don't ask me why but I always preferred to be sitting on the right and I felt Shirley played more to that side of the audience, but that is only my opinion. Derek sat next to me and we looked through the programme. A comedy act, an all-round musician/entertainer and a vocal/instrumental group made up the first half of the show. To be honest we didn't really want to see any of them, but we sat through these mediocre acts and offered as much applause as we could muster. The problem was these acts were average and we were there to see a superstar, so average just didn't tick the box! As we sat so close to the stage, I am sure Mum and Dad felt a sense of duty to the acts appearing on the bill with Shirley, believing they needed support and appreciation from the audience, and they were always encouraging towards them.

The interval was announced and new arrivals took to their seats, others hurried back from the bars and the fans, of which there were many tonight, sat on the edge of their seats in anticipation. A warm applause welcomed Kenny Clayton, now established in the role of Shirley's musical director. Kenny had accompanied Shirley throughout the year and I was delighted he was now permanently with Shirley. He seemed to read Shirley very well, and I greatly admired his musical ability and the general politeness he always showed to fans.

It only took a few notes from the orchestra and the audience was on its feet. Shirley arrived onstage to cheers and huge applause as Kenny directed the orchestra to continue with a few more bars from the opening number. Then we were treated to a performance that can only be described as unbelievable. The chosen programme offered ballads, performed with tenderness and emotion, showstoppers, Bassey classics and new numbers from her debut album. One number, an old hit reinvented with the help of Kenny, 'Kiss Me Honey, Honey', lead to Derek and I providing the words that followed the line, 'don't care even if I blow my top, but honey, honey'. The response, 'Ha, ha', was called out by Kenny Clayton and I quickly suggested to Derek that he and I should call out 'Ha, Ha' in response to Shirley, next time round. Shirley sang her line and perfectly in time and in tune, Derek and I called out, 'Ha, ha'. Shirley and Kenny both looked at us and fortunately enjoyed the joke. If you know the number you will be aware of the line 'I'd like to play a little game with you'. Well, Shirley did just that. She waltzed to where we were sitting and sang the song to us as we continued to reply, with our 'Ha, ha' in all the appropriate places. At the end the audience went wild and Derek and I were overwhelmed when Shirley came over and shook hands with both of us. With the applause and whistles still ringing out, she stood at the microphone and announced, 'By the way, they aren't part of the act', then blew us a kiss. Kenny was smiling and then led Shirley into another number. Everything she sang was wonderful; to me she just got better and better and it seemed the audience felt the same. It ended with 'The Party's Over' and I could have cried, the evening had completely drained me emotionally. Ovation followed ovation, then it really was over. Still, how lucky was I – in one week's time I would be enjoying the performance again.

During the week ahead I purchased any newspaper which carried a review, pasting them into the most recent scrapbook. Soon it would be necessary to rearrange my bedroom in order to accommodate the growing number of magazines, photographs, records and programmes that I seemed to have rapidly accumulated during the past months. Again, I was fortunate being an only child, since my bedroom was my own.

At nineteen I was living my dream and although I had been blessed with a good deal of common sense, I was, shall we stay, naive. *New Musical Express* wrote snippets on the last page of their music paper reporting, 'There were more queens at Shirley Bassey's opening night than at a royal wedding'. Believe it or not, at the time I did not fully understand the statement and asked my parents about the strange comment. They explained, casting no judgement, as I remembered we had seen some men, who seemed a little different, in the theatre foyer. It didn't bother me and I thought nothing further on the subject until one day I phoned Derek. I walked to the phone box and dialled his number, expecting him to answer the phone, but I was greeted by an answerphone message. The words of longing and love that echoed through the earpiece had clearly not been intended for my ears; I had discovered Derek was gay. Quickly, I put down the receiver. Derek had left a heart-rending message for the man he loved and I, purely by accident, had stumbled upon it. I never told Derek of my discovery and he never confided to me his feelings. My new-found knowledge never affected our friendship and we continued to meet regularly at Shirley's concerts.

On the Saturday following opening night, I returned to the Prince of Wales Theatre, this time to wait at the stage door in the hope of seeing Shirley and to tell her how much we had enjoyed her opening-night performance. I loved seeing Shirley arrive as it presented me with a brief opportunity to say, 'Thanks', the simple thing I believe loyal fans want to do. The stage door always attracts the most ardent of fans and I have always enjoyed the time I have spent in the company of them whilst waiting. As well as some of the regular fans I knew, on this occasion I met two girls who had travelled down from Birkenhead especially to see the show. Like me they were loyal fans and regularly travelled miles to see Shirley in concert at such venues in Blackpool, Manchester and Cardiff. We instantly became friends, promised to write to each other and exchanged addresses. There were two performances scheduled for a Saturday and Shirley would normally arrive shortly after the first show had commenced.

Following on from the very first time I saw Shirley live, I routinely asked at concerts whether I could briefly see Shirley backstage. The reason was to say 'thanks', but my requests were never granted. Sometimes I was given a reason why this was not possible, 'Miss Bassey has to rush off after the show', Miss Bassey is busy', and on other occasions, there would be no reply. I didn't take me long to realise that fans did not go backstage and I have never met a fan, by my definition, who did! Over the years I realised the imaginary line, Shirley had drawn, whether consciously or not, was not intended to be crossed by fans and indeed probably contributed to her mystic charm, which we adored.

So, as Shirley arrived, smiling as she approached the stage door, we excitedly conveyed our good wishes. Some may have gained an autograph, others fired their flash guns, and then it was over as Shirley entered her world, backstage. We were all delighted to have seen her, but now it was time for me to head for home, along with Derek. Joyce and Reon, the girls from Birkenhead, would soon be entering the foyer to be shown to their seats. They had promised to write and tell me all about the concert and I, in reply, would write about the concerts and record-store opening I planned to attend the coming week. Now I was heading home and looking forward to telling Mum and Dad about my adventure.

I was always in a dream during the the journey home after a concert, but travelling by train I had to be careful not to miss my stop. I had a good twenty-minute walk home from the station, at Chadwell Heath, and I probably sang all the way. Mum and Dad, as ever, wanted to know about the day's activities and after first telling them about Shirley, I went on to talk about my new friends, Joyce and Reon. Mum, in her usual way, said, 'They sound very nice girls. I hope we shall get to meet them.'

The following Tuesday, Dad and I went back to the Prince of Wales Theatre, where we sat in the second row and enjoyed another remarkable performance. Kenny Clayton nodded towards us as he saw me rise to my feet the moment Shirley walked onstage. The audience, slightly tamer than opening night, nevertheless gave Shirley a wonderful welcome before Kenny led Shirley into her opening number. We watched and listened in silence, hanging on to every word, sung with such deep emotion that it etched into your soul. Then a change of tempo and Shirley would dance along the edge of the stage, catching the eye of a loyal fan to whom she would direct the lyrics. All too soon she was acknowledging the cheering and ovations from the audience and finally, she ran offstage and the curtain fell. What is it they say? Time travels fast when you are enjoying yourself. How true.

And Shirley always gave great value for money, her performances usually ran for well over an hour and featured at least a dozen songs. No time for idle chit-chat between numbers, what you got was pure, beautiful music. Later in life I saw another singer adopting a similar approach onstage to his music: his name was Frank Sinatra.

The following Friday Shirley walked, with her luncheon companions, the short distance from the nearby Italian restaurant to the record shop, which she was opening in Dean Street. Crowds had gathered along the street but I managed to stay close to Shirley as she was led to the shop's entrance. She looked stunning in a navy dress with matching navy-and-white fully brimmed hat decorated with a large diamond brooch. Prior to her being led into the store, I took a few photos of her beaming happily. The door was then closed before us, after being reassured that this was only a temporary measure while Shirley was introduced to the official guests and enjoyed a glass of champagne. Behind Dad and I, the crowds gathered, but fortunately we were able to witness the event through the glass door.

It was lovely just watching Shirley being a person. We watched as she cut the ribbon, officially announcing the shop open for business, while the press photographers took appropriate shots. The occasion also marked the release of Shirley's new debut album for United Artists

Records. Entitled *I've Got A Song For You*, it was produced by Kenneth Hume who, with Shirley, selected the songs. This record would signal a change in Shirley's recording career, showing a new aspect of her musical talent with up-tempo songs, and the fans couldn't wait to get a copy. We didn't have to wait long before the front door of the shop opened and we were directed, in an orderly fashion, to the counter where we could purchase records. Then we moved along the counter towards Shirley, who was sitting behind another counter. My new album in hand, I waited with Dad for our turn as Shirley asked each fan their name before autographing their record. Then I was standing directly in front of Shirley. I don't know what made me say it, but I heard myself saying, 'You must know my name now.' Shirley smiled and said, 'I do', and taking my album wrote, 'Best Wishes Mary, Shirley Bassey'. As she handed the album back she must have noticed my look of amazement and added, 'I told you I knew your name.' Dad asked if he could take a photo and Shirley happily agreed. The photograph he took appears within these pages and I am sure you will agree he captured a very relaxed and happy Shirley, holding my personally signed copy of her new album.

I must have driven my dad mad on the way home. 'Shirley knows my name,' I kept telling him and he smiled back proudly. Early that evening I went to meet Mum at the hairdresser's where she had gone to have her hair set. Most of the customers were regulars and knew we were going to see Shirley's final night performance the following evening. I expect Mum had also told the ladies where I had been that day, because when I arrived at the salon they all wanted to know if I had seen Shirley Bassey. Everyone was delighted as I conveyed my story and Mum, as proud as ever, was holding back the tears of joy.

The next morning the air was filled with 'The Sound Of Music', along with the other eleven tracks from *I've Got A Song For You*. I was delighted with 'Johnny One Note' and especially liked 'The Shadow Of Your Smile' and 'Shirley', a new light-hearted number. No time now to learn the lyrics; we had to get ready for our night on the town, so the album was carefully placed back into its extra-special cover.

Today was also a very special day for every English football fan. England were through to the final and faced playing West Germany for the World Cup. The atmosphere in London was terrific and prior to entering the Prince of Wales Theatre, I think every man in the audience had tried to find out the score. Remember, in the sixties we were not living with mobile phones and the Internet.

The theatre was fairly empty for the first half of the show, but following the interval, it filled to capacity and there was a tremendous buzz in the air. We had seen several other regular fans and Michael, who had managed Shirley's Record Shop, had returned for Shirley's final night performance. We settled into our front-row seats, and the orchestra began. The audience cheered loudly as Shirley walked onstage acknowledging the applause before going straight into song. Following her first number she stood in front of the microphone and announced to the audience, 'The score is 4–2, England has won the World Cup'. The audience went wild, cheering and stamping broke out and the party atmosphere continued through the night.

Shirley could do no wrong and I believe it was here that she first performed 'Big Spender', a fun number from the Broadway musical *Sweet Charity*. The musical opened in London, at the Prince of Wales Theatre, the following year, when Shirley's single was also released. Shirley's version of 'Big Spender' was much more upbeat than the original stage version and went on to become legendary.

All too soon the party really was over. Shirley had sung her heart out and could not have given any more. The audience responded with its usual thunderous applause and shouts for 'more'. Shirley's final number said it all, 'The Party's Over, My Friend', and what a party the last two weeks had been.

We went home that evening, exhausted and very, very happy. In my diary I wrote the words, 'Two weeks I shall never forget'.

CHAPTER 6

I'LL BE YOUR AUDIENCE

Life had been a dream but I knew I would not have the opportunity to see Shirley in concert again for some time. I had written to Joyce and Reon, telling them about the record-store opening and enclosed a few photos. Joyce quickly replied, saying they had booked to see Shirley at the Blackpool Opera House, on Sunday, 11 September. As I would be on holiday with my parents at the Isle of Wight, Joyce promised to write to me there, since she knew I would want to know immediately every detail of the show. Joyce writes wonderful letters and I kept the one she sent to me following the Blackpool concert. It expresses just what it was like to be a fan in the 1960s and how we loved being Shirley's audience. The letter, dated 12 September 1966, reads as follows:

Dear Mary,

What can I say? It was a 'fab','fab','fab', show. Shirley was at her best, she was in great voice . . . For the first performance we were on the front row, during the interval we met George [Webb], he was in the circle but came down to the stalls to look for us.

When Shirley came on, there were great cheers and applause, the theatre was full, she was in a red dress and gown, it was the one she wore at the Pigalle the night we were there. She started the performance with 'I've Got A Song For You' then she said that her recording manager had named a song after her, 'Shirley', and that she would like to say that it just wasn't true but she would sing it as she liked it, then she sang 'The Shadow Of Your Smile'. I remember them as the first three, after that I can't remember the order, but they included 'Kiss Me Honey, Honey', 'Strangers In The Night', 'Burn The Candle' and 'BIG SPENDER', that was once again absolutely great, the audience loved it as she was being witty as well.

'What Now My Love', which she finished with the terrific high note, the same way she recorded it. . . . she was really in tremendous voice . . . The applause was fantastic . . . after several curtains, she sang 'The Party's Over' and nearly brought the house down . . . a really terrific performance as usual.

We went to the second performance . . . Once again Shirley came on to a grand applause and thunderous cheers. Once again she was great, just great. It was very similar to the first performance, she had a few extra witty remarks and 'Big Spender' went down a treat. The fellows sitting behind us were terrific, cheering and shouting, it was marvellous. At the end she was on and off to thunderous applause and one young girl presented her with a bouquet of carnations. Shirley sang 'The Party's Over' once again as an encore. . . . She held on to the last note; you know the last line is 'It's all over my friend', well she held 'friend' on loud and long, then went into a hum and repeated the last few lines. When she came up to the last line again she sang 'it's all over' stopped and there was a hush in the theatre . . . nobody coughed, moved or anything. Then in the silence one piece of the orchestra came in with a sound like the stroke of midnight, it was marvellous and then with all she had, Shirley came in with 'my friend' in the highest, loudest way possible, she was great. Once again the National Anthem was played very quickly, and once again it was all over.

When we got outside the fellows who had been sitting behind us told us they would show us where Shirley would come out. It wasn't the stage door, piles of people were waiting there, but we went behind a garage you would never have guessed, there were two Rolls-Royce, two men brought out a pile of luggage, Mr Simmons [Leslie Simmons, director of SVB Ltd] was there . . . When [Shirley] came out she looked lovely, she was in a gorgeous grey suit. She said she was in a hurry as she had to catch a plane. I think she was as she had all her luggage with her. Reon and I ran after the car and she waved to us until she got to the end of the road . . .

Well as I say, it's all over once again. The next day it always seems too good to have been true. We had to be up at 4.40am so as to get back to work for 9am. We made it anyway and getting up was well worthwhile to see Shirley.

Well Mary, I have writer's cramp so will say cheerio for now . . . Shirley's off to France next . . . to make the film which will be on TV sometime.

Cheers for now, Joyce.'

I was sitting in the lovely warm sun when I received Joyce's letter, but as soon as I began to read the opening lines, I was quickly transported to the Opera House, Blackpool. It was lovely to read about Shirley's performance and the fantastic response given to her by the audience that evening. Joyce's letter helps to illustrate the excitement we experienced as fans during the sixties and expresses the affection we felt towards Shirley.

It would be several months before we would have another opportunity to see Shirley in concert again. Now Shirley was heading for Paris, where she was due to record a television show. Then she would be flying off to the States for a string of cabaret, concert and television engagements, which would include Hollywood's Coconut Grove, the Sahara Hotels at Lake Tahoe and Las Vegas, the Eden Rock Hotel, Miami and then off to Boston. The American fans did her proud and they were increasing in number by the minute as Shirley's success continued.

Guest appearances with Dean Martin and Andy Williams on their respective television shows signalled to all that Shirley had conquered America. Years later, in Shirley's 25th Anniversary Tour programme, a lovely signed photo of Dean Martin with Shirley was reproduced. I've always admired Mr Martin's inscription, which read: 'To Shirley, who makes every note sound like a rainbow'. So true.

In March 1967 Shirley was back in the recording studios for United Artists before heading home to her British audience who eagerly awaited her return. It was around about this time that George Webb discussed with me the idea of running a fan club and indeed he wrote to Shirley regarding the matter. I remember George had acquired a number of letters from various fans, which he brought to show me, and although I would have loved to help run a fan club, I was rather concerned by the small percentage of correspondence that seemed to be directed more towards sexual innuendo than to Shirley's singing talents. I clearly remember one remark, 'I love the body that fills that dress', which shocked me at the time. When George received a reply from Shirley's management saying she felt she could not devote enough time, which we all thought necessary, to an official fan club, we gave up on the idea. Looking back, I think that was the right decision, although today I think it would be nice to have a reliable point of contact. The Internet is full of sources of information, and I respect Dame Shirley wanting to protect her privacy, perhaps now even more than then, with the world we live in. Yet we, her old fans, only want to know if she is well and happy.

As I reflect back to the times when we were her audience, it's sad to think those days have gone for good.

CHAPTER 7

AS LONG AS HE NEEDS ME

Early March 1967, Shirley was home, and by the tenth both Joyce and I had received tickets for her forthcoming appearance on ATV's *London Palladium Show*, scheduled for Sunday, 19 March. For me, things couldn't get better as the date in question happened to be my birthday, so Mum and Dad suggested I invite Joyce and Reon to stay for the weekend. To add to all of this, Shirley's new LP, *And We Were Lovers*, was about to be released.

When the girls arrived, Mum and Dad made them most welcome and thinking back I realise Dad had to sleep in his armchair the couple of nights they were with us. That wasn't considered unusual then, but I'm not sure people today would be so willing to give up their beds! On the Saturday, Joyce, Reon and I made our way into London to visit Shirley's Record Shop and we had a great time. Shirley's new record had just been released so we each bought a copy. In addition, the girls bought a few other records that they hadn't been able to get locally and the shop's manager supplied us with a supply of photos issued by United Artists.

We left the shop absolutely delighted, with so many records we could have set up a small stall ourselves. There was only one place to head – Chester Square – although we had previously agreed we would not knock at the door. Well you know how things are, especially if you've been a fan yourself. Once outside the impressive house it seemed silly not to knock, or to be precise, press the intercom. A voice answered (we believe it was Shirley) and Joyce replied by telling, in thirty seconds flat, how she and Reon had travelled from Liverpool, were staying with me, that we'd been to her record shop and bought some records and we would all be at the London Palladium tomorrow, when it was my birthday – and, oh, could she please sign our records. Well, I was out of breath just listening, and then I heard a voice from the intercom reply, 'One moment'.

That one moment seemed like a lifetime while we waited on the doorstep, then the door slowly opened and a lady asked us to put our name on each of the bags in which we carried our records. We just about managed to do this in our excitement, and then handed over the bags. 'Just wait here,' we were told, as she went upstairs, but she had left the door wide open so we were able to get a view inside. It was wonderful and we couldn't believe how lucky we were. We waited ages for our bags to be returned, thinking, How long does it take to sign your name on three LPs? Eventually the lady returned with the bags and we asked her to thank Miss Bassey profusely. She replied, 'Miss Bassey didn't know what ones you wanted signed so she has done them all.' We again expressed our thanks and said goodbye before darting quickly around the corner to examine our prizes. Sure enough, Shirley had not only autographed every record we had purchased but had also signed every photo given to us at the record shop. No wonder we had been waiting so long at her door. Finally, we took out her latest LP and our mouths dropped open as we read the words written on each individual record: 'To Mary, To Joyce, To Reon', followed by, 'Affectionately, Shirley Bassey.' We were on cloud nine.

I remember how happy we were as we headed back home to Chadwell Heath, sitting in a line on a red double-decker bus. We sat with our LPs on our laps, facing them outwards so that everyone who boarded the bus could see. Some people asked us who we were, others asked where had we been, to which Joyce proudly replied, 'To Shirley Bassey's House'– well, it was the truth!

When we arrived home Mum had dinner waiting for us and as we told the story of the day's adventure I think my dad though we might have been exaggerating the facts a little, until we showed him our LPs and photos. They were so excited for us, and we spent the rest of the evening singing along to the new album, before finally heading off for bed. Tomorrow promised to be another exciting day.

And what a birthday it was. Mum and Dad had bought me a small portable reel-to-reel tape recorder, very stylist, with a carrying handle that gave it the appearance of a small travel bag. On one side, a lead plugged in for recording, connected to a small square-shaped microphone. The microphone had an individual on/off switch and the compactness of the unit, which operated from mains or batteries, made it rather stylish for its day. More importantly, Dad, who had practised recording with the machine over the past few days, now considered himself a 'skilled operator', ready to record Shirley if an opportunity arose. I joked with Dad that he would 'have his work cut out' since he also had to be our photographer.

At the London Palladium we met up with George Webb, who had also managed to get tickets for the show. Shirley had not yet arrived for rehearsals, so we waited eagerly near the stage-door entrance. Soon she arrived looking lovely in a white fur jacket, with a scarf covering her hair, but she was quickly ushered through the stage door. We were reassured, however, that Shirley would not be too long in rehearsal and then she would have time to chat. There were only a few other fans waiting with us and we were all excited by the prospect, Dad ready with the tape recorder and camera, and me determined to ask Shirley if Joyce, Reon and I could have a photograph taken with her. All I had to do was 'get some courage', like the lion in the Wizard of Oz. But, after all, this was Miss Shirley Bassey I was going to ask – and she was definitely no witch.

Later, when Shirley emerged from the stage door, a few fans approached and asked for her autograph. Shirley happily signed as Mum and Dad chatted, Dad almost acting like a roving reporter with my new tape recorder. Shirley just took it in her stride. She knew the fans around her; Mum chatted in her usually natural way and Shirley seemed very happy and relaxed. Then I asked, a little nervously, 'Miss Bassey, could we please have a photograph taken with you?' 'Yes, of course,' came the reply. No further encouragement was necessary, Joyce and Reon stood to Shirley's right and I stood on her left, looking rather serious it has to be said, although I can tell you I was bursting with pride. Dad took the photo and we thanked Shirley. We seemed to chat for several minutes, while Dad took several more photos, before Miss Bassey eventually started to make her way towards the awaiting limo. I remember just how excited and happy everyone was, then, as Shirley was about to step into her limo, she turned to me and said, 'Oh, by the way, Happy Birthday.' I was knocked-out speechless for a few moments but recovered in time to say, 'Thank you, thank you.' As Shirley drove away we stood on the pavement spellbound. Dad rewound the tape recorder and my very own recording of Shirley Bassey saying 'Happy Birthday' to me was played, and played, and played.

Only a few days before, Shirley had hit the headlines with news that she would be starring in a new musical, to be especially written for her, entitled *Josephine*. The musical, based on the lives of Napoleon and Josephine, would be produced by Kenneth Hume.

Shirley had longed to become an actress for some time and her disappointment was certainly felt by her fans when news broke that she had been rejected for the role of Nancy in the film version of *Oliver*. I could not understand at the time how Shirley, who'd had a tremendous hit with her recording of the title song, 'As Long As He Needs Me', could lose the part to Shani Wallis.[1]

With all this recent news in the music and national press, we had lots to talk about as we waited at the front of the queue, ready to enter the London Palladium for the evening's televised broadcast performance. During the day we had seen and spoken to Kenneth Hume, and Dad took another of his great photos of Joyce, Reon and I standing beside Kenneth's Ford Mustang, with its personalised number plate.

When the doors of the theatre eventually opened, we made our way to the front row of the royal circle. Here we were, George Webb, Joyce, Reon, my mum and dad and I, a finer more loyal group of fans you could not find, sitting waiting for the star of the show to appear. Shirley sang five numbers that evening, although I can't remember the actual songs she sang. It's quite possible she introduced 'Big Spender' to the viewing TV public because she wore a spectacular silver cutaway dress, which provoked a good deal of press coverage the next morning.

One thing I do remember is that Shirley's performance was sensational. Audiences made up from people who'd applied to the television companies for free tickets sometimes lacked enthusiasm, mainly because they consisted of members of the public who weren't really concerned about who they were going to see and often didn't really care; after all, they had a free night's entertainment. Fortunately, that night some of Shirley's loyal fans where in the house and we were certainly going to make ourselves heard when Shirley entered the stage.

When that moment finally did arrived, we stood up and cheered, as Shirley took centre stage and went into her first number. She ignited the audience with her voice, phasing and a cheeky interpretation of the lyrics. Only a few bars of Bassey magic was necessary, then the audience was in the palm of her hand. Somehow we could tell Shirley

1 John L. Williams in his book *Miss Shirley Bassey* offers an explanation as to why Shirley was not offered the role of Nancy in *Oliver*, which I, rather naively, would not have considered at the time.

was loving the performance as much as we were and clearly enjoying herself. At the end, the audience cheered and cheered as the show was 'wrapped up' quickly in its usual manner to accommodate the TV schedule. It had been a wonderful performance and as we left the theatre I was thinking my birthday could not have been bettered.

We made our way to the stage-door area, now packed with people hoping to get a glance of Shirley as she left the theatre. Our 'fan' intelligence lead us to watch for Shirley's limo, which we sighted turning into a back alley, leading to a dead end behind the theatre. Her chauffeur parked in the only available space in the alley, so we realised that Shirley would be leaving the theatre via a small doorway exit located at the end of the alley. We quickly made our way to the door to find it firmly closed. Within a few minutes one of the other artistswho had been in the show came out of the door, saying, 'Good Night' to us as he made his way out. No showbiz glamour waited at this exit; it was simply an easy exit for the performers and stage hands alike. I have to admit that even though we knew the chauffeur was waiting at the far end, we did wonder if it was all a big bluff. A few other fans waited with us and soon our fears were dismissed as the door opened and standing in front of us was Shirley dressed in a white fur coat and carrying a stylish oval make-up case. Joyce immediately positioned herself on Shirley's left and with me to Shirley's right, we bacame her self-appointed escorts, walking her down the alley towards her waiting limo. I am very fortunate to have a photo of the moment. George Webb was next to Joyce, and Shirley is smiling, looking up at me, while I am waving my hand in true Bassey fashion, whilst obviously singing out praises to Shirley about her performance. We arrived at the limo and finally said good night before heading our separate ways. The day had been unreal and very special for me, sharing it with Mum, Dad, Joyce, Reon, George and, of course, Shirley. I genuinely believe it was an enjoyable day for her, a day when she was comfortable being herself, Miss Shirley, international star.

The next morning the national press was full of praise regarding her performance and describing her dress as 'sexy'. One paper featured a photo of Shirley in the silvery dress, taken backstage at the London Palladium prior to her going onstage, which became one of Douglas Darnell's classics. Rave reviews later appeared in the *NME*, *Record Mirror* and *The Stage* as Shirley prepared for a visit to Stockholm where she was due to open at the Berns theatre restaurant on 1 April. I had managed to find out that Shirley was flying out to Stockholm on 29 March and since I had taken annual leave that week, I decided to go to the airport to see Shirley fly out. Looking back it seems hard to believe how easy it was to obtain flight information, but things were so different then and security at the level we need today, just wasn't necessary. As fans we often obtained Shirley's flight dates from her management, then a couple of telephone calls to the airlines would give us the flight times. With far less flights in the 1960s, it was possible to predict with a high degree of accuracy the actual flight Shirley would take. Once at the airport, I sometimes met George Webb, then we would simply watch and wait for Shirley's limo to arrive. Often the airline had a representative available to assist press reporters and photographers and this proved beneficial to us, since once we saw him appear on the concourse we knew Shirley wouldn't be far away. The photograph I have featured here I believe was taken as she arrived for her flight to Stockholm and it is one of several I took that day.

Over the years ahead I was to visit London Airport (Heathrow) on several occasions and Shirley always seemed happy to see me. I would always ask her for her permission to take a photograph, and Shirley always gave it! There would be many more Bon Voyages and Welcome Homes (more about those later), but right now I was waving goodbye to flight BE 758, bound for Stockholm.

There was no doubt Kenneth Hume's plans were taking shape and Shirley seemed happy with the heavy work schedule arranged for her. The months ahead looked optimistic as we waited for further news regarding her starring role in *Josephine*. While plans were being established, Shirley would return to the UK to complete a two-week engagement at the Alhambra Theatre, Glasgow. When Shirley poured out 'As Long As He Needs Me', her fans knew the 'he' to whom she referred was Kenneth.

A week after Glasgow, Mum, Dad and I decided to spend a day in London enjoying the early June sunshine in the parks, as well as a little window shopping along the King's Road, Chelsea. I had expected to hear news that Shirley would again be appearing at The Talk of the Town, since this was becoming an established regular engagement for her, but no announcement had been forthcoming. I had made several phone calls to the venue's booking office, only to be told they didn't know who would be appearing in July, yet they could confirm the artists for August onwards. So, if Shirley was going to appear at the Talk that summer, then it had to happen in July. I had also had a letter from Theo Cowan Ltd suggesting Shirley would be appearing at the Talk in July. We decided, therefore, to make a reservation, but first we were heading for the King's Road.

This was the place to go and be seen and it was not uncommon to see a famous face amongst the shoppers. Of course I always looked out for one face in particular, wishing it would appear in the crowd. Suddenly a white mini drew my attention and I looked at its driver, almost unrecongnisable in dark sunglasses. It was Shirley, I couldn't believe it! The car turned off the King's Road into a side street a little way ahead of where we stood and I quickly called to my parents, 'It's Shirley, I've got to see her' and I was off in a flash. I sprinted along the road and turned the corner so fast I'm sure my rubber soles were burning as I almost collided into the back of the white mini, which Shirley had just parked. As Shirley emerged from the car, she said, 'Hello' and I told her we were visiting King's Road and planned to book for The Talk of the Town. 'Will you be there?' I asked. Shirley replied, 'Yes, I haven't signed the contract yet, but I will be there.' I thanked her and told her we would book to see her and after saying goodbye, left her to make her way along the King's Road, surprisingly without anyone realising who was walking beside them. Mum and Dad had caught up with me by now and we continued to watch Shirley until she was lost in the crowd.

No prizes for guessing where we would be heading next. Upon arrival at The Talk of the Town, we made a reservation for Monday, 3 July, which would be Shirley's opening night, as well as Saturday 29 July, final night. On our way to the venue Mum and Dad suggested inviting Joyce and Reon to stay with us; this would mean they would attend the final night with us. And so we made our reservation for a table for five.

When I contacted Joyce, naturally she was thrilled with the news. Being given confirmation from Shirley, before any press announcement about the engagement, meant our reservations were amongst the first and this would present us with a good table on opening night, even with an audience consisting of a number of showbiz celebrities. Containing my excitement at the thought of going to see Shirley again at The Talk of the Town was very difficult, but within a few days news appeared in the press regarding the engagement. The article stated it would be Shirley's last cabaret appearance before going into rehearsals for *Josephine*. I had already been aware of the news regarding the show since in May, Howard Kent, a director of Theo Cowan Ltd, the company handling publicity, had replied to my letter enquiring about the musical.

'It looks at present as though Miss Bassey will go into rehearsal for the part of Josephine around the end of August,' he wrote. 'As she has never done any straight acting before, the rehearsal period would be rather longer than usual, and it looks as though the show may open out of town around October. This would mean a West End opening probably in November.

'As I'm sure you understand, big productions of this sort are often subject to changes of schedule and these are, therefore, only dates we are working on at present. I am hopeful, however, that we shall be keeping pretty closely to this schedule…'

As fans we were looking forward to an exciting year ahead. On Sunday, 18 June, we were given our first glance of Josephine when Shirley made a guest appearance on the television special *Secombe and Friends*. With the popular Harry Secombe, Jimmy Tarbuck and Dudley Moore, all dressed as Napoleon, Shirley joined them, as Josephine, in a hilarious sketch. One week later tragedy struck.

CHAPTER 8

I WISH YOU LOVE

'Kenneth Hume has been found dead' are words I will always remember hearing. My dad had been watching the news on television; Mum and I were in the kitchen when Dad entered looking very upset. When he told us the tragic news it seemed beyond belief since Kenneth was only in his early forties and had seemed well. Later we learned he had been suffering from depression for some time and had sadly died from an overdose. We could only imagine the grief Shirley was experiencing, and wanted so much to be able to offer some sort of help, yet we realised there was no way we could. As a family we hugged each other and shed a few tears for Kenneth and for Shirley's loss. The next day I sent a letter to Shirley, not to her home address but via the SVB Ltd office, which somehow seemed more appropriate.

The press reported Kenneth's death in its usual manner. Headlines like 'Shirley's ex-husband dies from overdose' sold newspapers, Shirley's feelings weren't considered. I felt terrible when I thought about what she must be going through. I wondered what would happen about The Talk of the Town engagement – surely it would be rescheduled to a later date. Yet in the grand show-business tradition, 'the show must go on', and it was confirmed Miss Bassey would open at the Talk on Monday, 3 July 1967, only eight days after Kenneth's death. I am sure it's what Kenneth would have wanted. When all was said and done, he had helped Shirley prepare for the engagement and had been instrumental in choosing much of her material. But how would she cope!

The fans, although shaken by Kenneth's death, rallied round Shirley. We consoled ourselves knowing that we would be in the audience on opening night to give Shirley all the support and encouragement she might need. Most importantly, we wanted her to know how much she was loved by her fans.

Several months previously I had seen the comedians Mike and Bernie Winters present Shirley with a bouquet of roses following her performance on their television show. I remember thinking at the time, what a lovely gesture, and wondering why I had only seen it happen on a regular basis to ballet and opera stars. I told myself, one day I will present Shirley with flowers at the end of her performance.

I am a great lover of flowers and would regularly buy flowers for my mum on my way home from work on a Friday evening. It didn't take long for the owner of the flower shop, located near Chadwell Heath train station, to become aware of my admiration for Shirley Bassey; after all, I would talk about Shirley to anyone who would listen. So when I called in to the shop to make enquiries concerning a very special bouquet, which I would need to collect late one afternoon but which I insisted should look its best at midnight, she had a good idea who would be on the receiving end. Actually the florist was delighted to prepare the flowers for me and so I arranged to collect the bouquet at 4pm on Monday, 3 July, opening night.

Now I am certainly not claiming to be the first to present flowers to Shirley Bassey at the end of her performance, but I do claim to be one of the first. I am delighted to say it gave me tremendous pleasure and I continued to repeat the practice for many years. Over time, more fans would approach the stage at the end of a performance to offer flowers or gifts. I will go so far to suggest this form of appreciation by fans probably prompted the gesture, later adopted by Miss Bassey, of throwing carnations into the audience at the finale of her act. More about carnations later; now, back to the roses.

As we travelled to The Talk of the Town our excitement about seeing Shirley was surpassed by our concern. We could only begin to imagine the pain she must have been experiencing, yet somehow we all felt the performance would be a tribute to Kenneth and Shirley would pull through.

Once inside the theatre restaurant, I deposited my flowers with the cloakroom attendant, who promised to take good care of them, leaving instructions that I would be back to collect them just prior to the commencement of Miss Bassey's act. Shortly after, we were taken to our table, which to our delight was fairly near the stage. This meant in order to hand my bouquet to Shirley I would only have to walk down a few steps and then along between two tables, which were next to the stage. Being a rather shy person, I was concerned that I would trip up in the dim lighting and make a complete fool of myself!

As we settled at our table, the venue already seemed packed, the atmosphere reserved. We soon spotted George Webb, who came over to chat, along with a few other regular fans, but tonight the audience near to the stage consisted mainly of show-business celebrities, including the world's greatest entertainer, Mr Sammy Davis Jr. I'll never forget how intensely he watched and listened to Shirley – the look of a keen fan – and I was delighted when he signed his autograph in my diary following Shirley's performance. Little did I know then that later in my life, Sammy would come and sit next to me, during rehearsals for a Royal Command Performance held at the London Palladium, and we would talk about photography!

The diners, who had enjoyed a three-course meal and watched the revue, now sat silently in anticipation. I had collected my bouquet from the cloakroom and placed it on the empty chair beside me. It was looking perfect. The lights dimmed, the audience fell silent and the orchestra began. Suddenly the place erupted, as the Fabulous Miss Shirley Bassey walked out onstage to be greeted by an audience that had completely risen to its feet to give her a standing ovation. The applause and the cheering almost drowned out the notes coming from the orchestra and clearly Shirley was already beginning to feel the emotion within the room. How she got through that performance I shall never know but I am sure that knowing she was, in a sense, performing Kenneth's act, helped give her the strength she needed.

Highlights from the act included 'Big Spender', which although not yet released on vinyl, already had become a big hit with Shirley's audiences. I particularly enjoyed the number 'French Foreign Legion', which, at the time, was a new number to me, and I made the assumption that it was going to be featured by Shirley in *Josephine* since the lyrics made it an ideal choice. It was a fun number, which Shirley performed extremely well under the circumstances and raised laughter in the audience. It was several decades later when I next heard that tune and rather to my surprise, it was being sung by Frank Sinatra. However, tonight at The Talk of the Town it was really about seeing, hearing and feeling the emotion. Nobody could sing a song with more feeling than Shirley and, in my opinion, nobody has since. When Shirley closed her act with the song, 'I Wish You Love' – 'and so when snowflakes fall, I wish you love' – there wasn't a dry eye in the house as Shirley left the stage. The love was for Kenneth.

Cheering, shouts for more and thunderous applause were coming from every direction as I approached the stage. I don't remember speaking as I handed the flowers to Shirley; I was too choked up with emotion. I don't think Shirley spoke either. As I looked into her big brown eyes, no words were necessary.

The reviews were wonderful acclaiming, once again, Shirley as an international star, the likes of which Britain had never seen before (and will probably never see again). As fans we were delighted by the success we read about in the press but we also recognised how difficult it must have been for Shirley. We made an effort to ensure some fans, every night, would be at the stage door of The Talk of the Town to welcome Shirley when she arrive for her engagement. We saw it as a way to offer our support.

As we waited near the backstage entrance, we were frequently exposed to a lesson of life, since the backstage entrance was situated in the heart of London's Soho area, known for its sex and striptease. In fact that very word, 'striptease', appeared as a backdrop in several photographs I took, including the one featured here, but thank God for Photoshop! During this particular season at the Talk, I waited at the stage-door area on a few evenings, usually accompanied by my dad, since it was often late evening before Shirley arrived. Poor Dad even got propositioned by a 'lady of the street' one evening, which he found rather embarrassing, but I'm pleased to say he didn't take up the offer.

On one occasion while we were waiting, a taxi pulled up and we were a little taken by surprise to see Shirley step out from the taxi, closely followed by Norman Newell, the EMI record producer and lyricist. Norman had already written the lyrics to 'Reach For The Stars' and went on to write a string of hits for Shirley, which included 'This Is My Life', 'Natalie', and 'Never, Never, Never'. He was also responsible for producing some of her best recordings. On this occasion Shirley and Norman had come directly from a theatre where they had been part of the audience; now Shirley was about to get ready for her own performance but we managed to capture a photograph, shown here, which she later signed. Norman Newell was a great fan and I suspect he was also a very good friend to Shirley over the years. I saw him on several occasions at concerts, always the gentleman who would stop to have a quick chat whenever he spotted me.

All too soon Shirley's month-long season at The Talk of the Town would be coming to an end, but we had final night to look forward to. Joyce and Reon travelled down from Birkenhead to stay with us and I ordered another bouquet of flowers. Final nights were always special at the Talk, attracting celebrities who wanted to see and hear Shirley perform. Shirley gave so much, every ounce of emotion poured out onto that stage as each performance got better. After watching a performance, I always told myself, You will never see Shirley perform better than she did tonight, but then I'd go to another performance and guess what, it was always better. It's was hard to imagine just how she managed to achieve that all her life, but she did. That night there would be no opening-night nerves, for neither artist nor fans; it was an occasion to be enjoyed. We were lead to our table and finally arrived at the appointed place, almost speechless. Our table literally joined the front of the stage. We could hardly contain our excitement as 11pm approached. Like champagne bottles, we were ready to pop. 'I Could Have Danced All Night' was the music to which the orchestras changed over, or ended their particular session, so when those familiar notes from *My Fair Lady* were heard, the audience began to fall silent apart from the sound of slight movement from chairs as the audience positioned themselves to face forwards, centre stage.

Joyce, Reon and I were on the edge of our seats, whilst my mum and dad showed a little more restrain, but only a little! Suddenly we jumped to our feet and I swear the entire audience seemed to follow our lead. The cheering and applause seemed endless until finally Shirley managed to launch into song. This was to be one of the finest performances I had ever experienced and when it came to an end, one hour, thirty minutes later, Shirley received seven standing ovations. Whilst acknowledging one of the ovations Joyce, Reon and I were able to present Shirley with our bouquet. This time, when we each shook her hand and looked into her eyes, we saw a happier Shirley and we were so delighted that somehow the roar of the crowd had helped her through.

Her act had included all the emotion and dynamics we had come to expect, but now her audience also had the opportunity to experience Shirley's humour with her 'Big Spender' routine and they loved it. As she crossed the stage to select an appropriate gentleman in the audience, to whom she would perform the number, the audience roared its approval. Every cheeky movement bought cheers and needless to say the chosen gentlemen were delighted, especially when the audience cheered for more. Shirley offered each gentleman an encore, which probably caused their blood pressure to rise.

Ovation after ovation we cheered and clapped until our hands were stinging. Finally, when Shirley left the stage, a quietness descended as members of the audience resumed their seats and we were left to ponder at what we had seen and heard. I can only describe it as pure magic and I, for one, remained under the spell for several days following this performance.

In fact I would always be 'spellbound' after seeing any Shirley performance, whether it be a live performance or a recorded TV show. Over the years I expected the 'magic' to fade – after all, I was an adult, and sensible – but happily the magic always returned. Over time I learned the magic was actually Shirley Bassey, a singer who could weave a spell during her performance!

Later that year, 'Big Spender' was released as a single and I remember going to her record shop on the day of release to collect my copy. The very next day Shirley was due to appear on the television game show *The Golden Shot* to promote her record, and succeeded in scoring a bull's eye. The following day, Sunday, I travelled to Heathrow Airport to see her fly out to New York. It was wonderful to be able to wish her well for her engagement at the Waldorf Astoria and offer my congratulations with regard to the 'Big Spender' release. What a fabulous weekend it had been for me.

As the weeks flew by, the success of 'Big Spender' only increased, resulting in Shirley 'guesting' on various television variety and chat shows, including the BBC's Simon Dee's show, *Dee Time*, which could be described as a sort of forerunner to *Parkinson*. Chat shows usually involved the host chatting with the 'guest' artiste, followed by the artiste performing their latest hit. I don't think Shirley ever seemed comfortable chatting to chat-show hosts.

Guest appearances on the *Engelbert Humperdinck Show* and *Dave Allen At Large* followed. I especially enjoyed hearing Shirley duet with Engelbert and I regret she never recorded duets in her later years, as so many other artists did.

As the months passed, following The Talk of the Town engagement, her fans gradually began to realise that *Josephine* was not to be. Why, we never really knew. Perhaps for Shirley to play Josephine she needed her Napoleon at her side and now he was no longer there.

CHAPTER 9

BIG SPENDER

Monday morning and although the words from 'Big Spender' were running through my brain, I had to bring myself back down to earth as I walked the streets to the railway station, a walk that took about twenty minutes. There I would wait for the train, stopping at all stations to Liverpool Street, which I took to Stratford before joining the underground tube to Mile End. The journey took just over an hour and I was nearly always late; getting up on time was not one of my strong points but somehow I always managed to get away with it. I had been working at Queen Mary College for a while now and really loved my work as a science technician, but it was work and as such didn't compete with the world of a fan of Shirley Bassey. However, working meant I was earning money, and I had also even managed to earn a little extra from my portrait drawing over the previous months.

Friends had seen the drawings I had done of Shirley and some had asked if I would do a portrait of them. I was a little reluctant at first because, I'm sorry to admit, I wasn't very interested. However, I did attempt a few and they were happy with the results, so I thought I would advertise, in *The Stage* newspaper. The advert went something like this:

> 'Hey, Big Spender… why not have a portrait drawing done from your favourite photograph.

I actually gained a few commissions and more importantly, people liked my work, so I started to spend more of my time drawing, but it always came second to my devotion of anything connected with Shirley Bassey

It was in fact through the *The Stage* that I first became aware of another 'Big Spender' by the name of James Corrigan. *The Stage and Television Today*, to give it its full title, a weekly newspaper serving the business of living entertainment, had reported earlier in the year, 1967, on the opening of James Corrigan's Batley Variety Club in Yorkshire. In the late sixties, a working-men's club was the place where a man could take his family, to socialise and have a drink, or two, with his mates. Entertainment would sometimes be provided by a resident trio/band and, if you were lucky, a compère would introduce a 'star' act, which often performed against the backdrop of continual chatter and the clinking of pint glasses. No wonder these institutions became the training ground for so many top entertainers. If your act could survive a club 'Up North', then it could survive anywhere, such was their reputation.

James Corrigan knew what the people of Yorkshire wanted, a working-man's club that attracted STARS. To his credit he attracted the best from both sides of the pond, so when I discovered Shirley was to open at Batley on New Year's Eve, well, we just had to go; after all, Batley Variety Club was described as the 'Vegas of the North'! We booked, thankfully, to stay at the Queens Hotel, Leeds, where I was told Shirley would be in residence. Booking for Shirley's opening proved more complicated than we had expected since we had to be a member of the club, but we managed to make arrangements and longed for our adventure to Leeds. However, before our anticipated trip, we happily made another visit, in December, to the London Palladium.

The cold weather didn't seem to bother us as we waited for Shirley to arrive for rehearsals; once again our 'fan look-out' technique paid dividends and we spotted Shirley's limo heading for the front entrance. I remember this particular visit to the London Palladium for two reasons: first, Shirley's performance of 'Big Spender', which was sensational, and second, because of the photograph I took of Shirley, as she sat in her limo, dressed in a white hat, polo-neck sweater and fur coat to protect her from the cold. The photograph captured an 'off guard' Shirley, looking a little apprehensive as she arrived at the steps of the famous theatre. It's a moment captured before the 'star' emerges and it became one of my favourite photographs of her. During 1969 I used the photo as a reference for a drawing of Shirley that I produced for my first exhibition. My mum carried a small copy of the drawing in her handbag and would proudly take it out to show friends whenever an opportunity arose.

Christmas was always a wonderful time for family gatherings, when we would all laugh, joke, sing and enjoy making our own entertainment. At these parties, although I was fairly shy, I could easily be encouraged to mime to one of Shirley's records and this particular Christmas, 'Big Spender' became my speciality act. I knew every movement, and the family laughed hysterically as I focused my attentions on an uncle whilst singing 'wouldn't you like to have fun', not really fully understanding what the fun was all about. My reward for my appearance, one that I treasure to this day, was one of Shirley's first 78 rpm recordings, which an aunt brought to the party and gave to me.

A few days later we were travelling to Leeds. I have no recollection of the journey to the city but we must have travelled by train to the Queens Hotel, one of those beautiful art-deco railway hotels located in City Square near to the main train station. I do remember being impressed as I entered the imposing building and I am sure my parents had similar thoughts as they gazed at the spectacular decor. We had never stayed in such a posh hotel before but we rose to the occasion; at the end of the day, we had travelled all this way to see the Fabulous Miss Shirley Bassey open at Batley Variety Club. It was New Year's Eve and fortunately we had arranged, prior to arriving in Leeds, for a taxi to collect us from the hotel and take us to the club. We had also booked the taxi to collect us from the club, after Shirley's performance, to take us back to the hotel, a distance of approximately nine miles.

If you had to pick a colour to describe Batley, it would be grey, dark grey. I remember the taxi pulling up outside the club and thinking to myself, Is this it? From the outside, the building seemed to resemble a large carpet warehouse, distinguished only by the six neon stars that twinkled above the words, 'Batley Variety Club'. Inside, Mr Corrigan had done his best to imitate a Las Vegas nightclub, but sadly it fell short when it came to glitz. However, members could have a good night out for a fraction of the cost of Vegas and certainly seemed happy to accept the basket-meal menu and preferred pint glasses. I remember joining the line of ladies queuing to deposit coats in the cloakroom, when a man headed straight to the front of the queue and attempted to deposit his coat on the counter. The women looked disapprovingly but said nothing, except for me of course. I may have been rather naive, but I had been taught good manners and was somewhat taken aback by the gentleman's behaviour. I stepped forward and politely told him there was a queue for the cloakroom and suggested he joined it... at the back. Well, the place fell into silence, I had clearly shocked this 'Big Spender' and my audience of ladies, some of whom gave me a smile, but he retreated to the back of the queue without saying a word.

As we were shown to our seats my heart dropped as we found ourselves located some distance from the stage, but it would have been wrong to have expected anything better, we had to accept we were in unknown territory. I always loved to be close to the stage but finding ourselves further back from the stage than usual was not going to stop us from enjoying Shirley's performance, assuming I could see her through the smoke! Before the smoking ban, a night club's atmosphere was created mainly from the fog of cigarette smoke and although many clubs had air conditioning, it really wasn't very effective. If Shirley had opened her act with 'A Foggy Day In London Town', it certainly would have raised a laugh from me, but whether the Batley audience would have seen the joke, I'm not so sure. Smoking was very much part of the culture.

We dined on our chicken and chips, served in a plastic basket, and watched the resident compère trying to entertain the audience. Fortunately, the tiered seating did offer us a good view of the stage, but as with the first act in a theatre show, nobody was really interested. We had always tried to encourage these acts and showed respect by trying to listen to them, but unfortunately the audience at Batley must have heard it all before, since several members walked around, pint glass in hand, visiting the bar and chatting with their companions during the entertainment. Although my heart was pounding with excitement at the prospect of seeing Shirley, I was becoming apprehensive and began to wonder why she was appearing here. The answer, of course, was money. When Shirley 'opened' tonight she would become the highest-paid entertainer to appear at Batley. She would also establish another first: there was to be NO bar service during her act. This fact didn'tt go down well with some of the club's members at the time but I was delighted it had been imposed. The thought of trying to listen to Shirley while bar service continued would have been unthinkable.

I had sent a 'best wishes' card backstage to Shirley and was happy to see other fans in the audience, some of whom I knew, including George Webb. At the very least Shirley would receive a rousing cheer from us. However, I remained a little on edge; this was a working-men's club where some artists had been known to struggle keeping an audience happy.

It wasn't long before an announcement was made reminding the audience that the bars were about to close, which seemed to generate a purge of activity. Tonight Batley Variety Club was packed to capacity (it could hold 1,600 people). The orchestra started up with the overture, the house lights dimmed as the spots aimed for centre stage. 'The Fabulous Miss Shirley Bassey,' was announced through the speaker system, immediately followed by rapturous applause as Shirley walked out onstage.

It only took Shirley a few notes to mesmerise each and every one of us with her voice. Every number ended with cheering and thunderous applause as Shirley sang her heart out. 'Big Spender' probably added cracks to the building but who cared – the folks from Batley were having the time of their lives watching Britain's top female entertainer. The hour or so seemed to flash by like a comet leaving a trail of stardust in its wake. The audience fell silent again, this time holding their breath as Shirley performed 'The Party's Over'.

The entire audience was overwhelmed by Shirley's performance; Batley had done her proud. Mum, Dad and I settled back into our seats, drained by the emotion Shirley had created. 'Happy New Year' was ringing out around the auditorium as we privately raised our glasses and toasted to Shirley, wishing her a very happy 1968.

As we slowly emerged from Batley Variety Club onto the cold street, we found ourselves amongst a mass of people all looking for their taxis. We scanned every direction but our driver was nowhere to be seen. I wasn't worried, the sound of Shirley was still ringing in my head, but clearly after a while Mum and Dad began to get anxious. I spotted a police car and had a great idea. Leaving my parents to wait by the club exit, I ran along the road to the parked vehicle, pressing my head inside the front window to greet the policeman with my request. 'Our taxi hasn't arrived, do you think you could please drive us back to the Queens Hotel?' I asked. The policeman took one look at me and said, 'Clear off, I've met your sort before.' Somewhat surprised, I went back to my parents who, by now, had found our driver. He had been delayed by the mass of traffic, but did he laugh when I told him my story, repeating the policeman's words to me.

It was a New Year when we entered the hotel and made our way to our bedrooms on the third floor. Mum and Dad, in spite of some early reservations about the Batley Variety Club, had totally enjoyed the evening and knew only too well that I too had again been captivated by Shirley's performance. As we stood by our bedroom doors, we wished each other a Happy New Year and kissed one another goodnight. 'Sweet dreams,' my mum said.

I probably lay awake for several hours, far too awake to sleep, reliving the evening, running through every song Shirley had sang and listening as fellow residents arrived back at the hotel. Could the noise of that car door possibly be Shirley returning to the hotel, I thought to myself. Eventually I must have fallen asleep, although it didn't seem long before I awoke to find it was morning. The chicken and chips from the night before had worn off and I was ready for breakfast. The restaurant in which we sat was vast and glamorous. We ordered a full English breakfast in preparation for the long journey home and as we waited I constantly eyed the entrance in the hope that Miss Bassey would come down for breakfast. Of course I didn't realise at the time that anyone booked into a suite would have breakfast delivered to their room, so I almost expected Shirley to walk into the restaurant as if walking onstage. It didn't happen but I wasn't too disappointed.

Before we departed from Leeds I'm sure we met up with George Webb to chat about Shirley's performance as well as the latest news regarding her engagements. There was talk of a new LP release from Columbia, so we had that to look forward to, but we were also aware that Shirley had a number of engagements to fulfil aboard. However, within a week Shirley would be celebrating her thirty-first birthday and I wanted to buy her a small present to wish her a Happy Birthday and thank her for the previous night's wonderful performance.

Returning home seemed a very long journey, even today it would be quite a task. But once the kettle was on and our record player piping out Shirley's songs, Mum, Dad and I were soon revitalised. Christmas and the New Year had been wonderful and we reflected on the events that had made it so special. The next day we would all be back at work, something I looked forward to as my work mates would be wanting to hear about my Batley adventure.

The next morning, during the coffee break at work, I entertained many and probably bored a few with every detail of Shirley's Batley Variety Club performance. I also told them about the grandeur of the Queens Hotel and Batley's chicken and chips, and for some in my audience it was a world away from the Christmas and New Year they had experienced.

When the following weekend arrived I awoke early on Saturday morning ready for my shopping trip to Leytonstone, a suburb of London which marked the terminal for several bus routes, one of which was route sixty-six; the bus stop was a five-minute walk from my home. Leytonstone was also famous for a wonderful department store, Bearman's, which could match any of the famous London stores; it even had an arcade which ran along one side of the building, leading to a cinema. I loved this store and often spent hours within its walls and only a few weeks earlier had looked for Christmas presents for the family. Today, however, I was seeking a present for Miss Shirley Bassey's birthday.

Can you ever buy something for someone who can have anything they require? I don't really know, but as a fan who had returned from seeing Shirley give a performance which utterly thrilled and gave my family so much enjoyment, I just wanted to buy something as a token of thanks. I spent hours looking for something that I thought would be appropriate. Eventually I spotted a glass clown, from Italy, which seemed appealing and appropriate since I had seen a recent photo of Shirley taken at her home with several stuffed clowns. On closer inspection, I was delighted with my choice and purchased my gift along with some lovely wrapping paper and a specially selected birthday card. Proudly, goods in hand, I walked in the direction of the bus terminal where, after a cold wait, I eventually boarded the bus for home.

Mum and Dad were eager to see my purchase, expressing their delight at my choice, as I carefully wrapped it in a layer of tissue. Then covering the glass clown with a layer of gift-wrapping paper, I precisely cut the Sellotape to the desired length and secured the paper in place. I added a small gift card with a few words that expressed our best wishes.

The next day we travelled to London, which we occasionally did on a Sunday, to walk in Hyde Park and see the sights, often indulging in a pot of tea and cakes. Today, however, was extra special, because I would also deliver Shirley's birthday card and present to her home. Mum and Dad stayed out of sight as I, feeling both excited and a little scared, rang the doorbell. I was rather relieved when someone other than Shirley answered the door and graciously offered to take my gift. From the very beginning I have always believed Shirley should be entitled to her privacy (as should anyone), but there were times when I probably crossed that invisible line which separated 'star' from 'fan'. On those rare occasions I called at her home, I always tried to show consideration and respect and I'm sure that was understood and appreciated. The very last thing I would have wanted would have been to upset Shirley.

Happy that Shirley would be receiving my birthday card and present in time for her birthday (the next day), I retreated for tea and cakes with Mum and Dad, a great finale to our day.

CHAPTER 10

THIS IS MY LIFE

Towards the latter part of January 1968 I received a letter from Shirley's Record Shop informing me of her pending LP and single release, which I naturally rushed to order. Within days I received Shirley's new LP, released by Columbia, entitled *12 of Those Songs*. Following the tremendous success Shirley was experiencing with 'Goldfinger', it seemed appropriate for James Bond (Sean Connery) to write the sleeve notes for the album. Clearly he was an ardent fan: 'Every time I hear Shirley Bassey sing – and that includes the playing and re-playing of the same record – I am always thrilled and surprised by her extraordinary vocal range. There are notes on these tracks which catch at your heart…'

These words echoed my thoughts exactly as I played through the tracks, 'Come Back To Me', 'If Love Were All', 'A House Is Not A Home' and the haunting 'I Wish You Love'. Of this track Mr Connery and I again agreed, for we both knew Shirley had to 'feel' to allow herself to put the song across so beautifully. It is with this ability that she reaches out to others through her music, drawing in her fans like moths to a flame. The album was produced by Norman Newell who was highly regarded both as a record producer and lyricist, and this could not have been better demonstrated than with this album and Shirley's latest single release, 'This Is My Life'. Norman Newell had written English lyrics to the Italian song known as 'La Vita' by Bruno Canfora and Antonio Amurri. It was aired on television to the British public just prior to Shirley performing the number at the Sanremo Music Festival, where the song unfortunately was not selected by the judges for the finals. Shirley's performance at the festival, however, melted the hearts of the Italian public. Later this would lead to concert tours throughout Italy, and United Artist releases recorded by Shirley in Italian.

Immediately following the Sanremo Festival, Shirley flew back to Britain. I went to London Airport to meet her flight and give a little support, if required. I was delighted to see a happy Shirley making her way through the airport lounge and, as if I needed an extra bonus, Norman Newell escorting her. While cases were being collected, I rather excitedly said hello and even managed to have a little chat about 'La Vita/This Is My Life'. I was thrilled. Looking back now, I realise again and again how lucky I was and I treasure the memories I have of these occasions. Wishing Shirley every success for her forthcoming engagements in Australia and New Zealand and then the States, we said our goodbyes and went our separate ways. I found the parting sad since I knew from Shirley's schedule that she would be away for several months, but as I made my way home I began to feel excited at the prospect of sharing the day's adventure with Mum and Dad.

Mum had loved the single from the very first moment she'd heard Shirley perform it on television and it remained her favourite number throughout her life. The song, of course, became very successful for Shirley who often chose to perform it at the closing of her act. Whenever I watched Shirley onstage, rarely was there a moment when I would take my eyes off her, except when she sang 'This Is My Life'. I would watch her sing the first few lines of that song, then quickly turn to my mum to see tears, highlighted by the stage lights, running down her cheeks. On every occasion, once Shirley had ended her last note, Mum would jump out of her seat and give Shirley a rousing cheer, always to Shirley's delight. They shared that song!

When I woke up the next morning, reality soon set in as I started to get ready to go to work. Mum and I always took the fifteen-minute walk from home to Chadwell Heath's High Street together, where Mum would wait for her bus to Manor Park and I would continue on to the train station, a few minutes away. We chatted all the way and the topic of conversation nearly always included Shirley; on occasion her ears must have been burning!

Work was the tonic which brought me back down to earth and now Shirley was away, I knew I had to dedicate more of my spare time to my studies. I was attending a day-release course, linked to my work as a lab technician, so I needed to make an effort. The trouble was, I wasn't really the brainy type, but I persevered and eventually achieved my educational goals.

Mounting the press cuttings, listening to my records and corresponding with a few of Shirley's fans, occupied some of my time and, it goes without saying, as the months passed, we all longed to know when Shirley would return to British shores. I had hoped in the summer there would be another engagement at The Talk of the Town, but this did not materialise. A little disappointed, I learned Shirley would be appearing at Las Vegas in August. I always scanned *The Stage*, *New Musical Express* and the national press for any news of Shirley but apart from record reviews, any other information was lacking – and I longed to hear something! Then early one evening, on 12 August, as we watched the news on television, I jumped for joy as the newsreader announced, 'singer Shirley Bassey married hotel manager Sergio Novak at 2.40am this morning, in Las Vegas'. I was so surprised and excited. Dad managed to set up his camera ready for a later edition of the news and took some of his TV shots, which showed a photo of Shirley and Sergio at the chapel. The next morning I bought almost every daily paper to read about the wedding and later pasted the reports in my scrapbooks. Shirley and Sergio looked to happy and we were so delighted that I had to send a card of congratulations and a letter to the hotel in Las Vegas where Shirley was appearing, although I had doubts as to whether it would ever reach her.

A few weeks later, having been unwell for a few days, I was feeling rather sorry for myself when Mum bought a cup of tea up to my bedroom. 'Oh, there is a letter for you,' she said, with her cheeky smile on her face. Looking at the 'via air mail' envelope and the Los Angeles postmark, you didn't need to be a detective. My spirits rose as I quickly opened the envelope to expose a letter with the words 'Shirley Bassey' printed in blue at a 45-degree angle cross the left corner of the page. The letter, dated 4 September 1968, read as follows:

> Dear Mary,
>
> Thank you very much for your letter. I hope to be coming back to England next April – that seems a long way away, but the time will soon go and until then I have a full schedule of work both on the continent and here in America. In spite of the fact that I will be living in Switzerland I shall be coming back to England as often as I can, but at the moment we are still finalising my engagements for next year and until this is finished it is difficult to be precise with dates.
>
> With all good wishes,
> Affectionately,
>
> SHIRLEY BASSEY [signed]

I simply couldn't believe my eyes and kept reading the letter over and over again until I had memorised every word.

It didn't take too long for me to recover now my spirits were high. Soon I was contacting George, Joyce and Reon with the news. How we all looked forward to Shirley's return, even though we now knew it was several months away. During that time, we consoled ourselves with news which we managed to obtain via United Artists Records, music magazines and the press. Further record releases, which Shirley had recorded in the United States, also brought us joy.

My life was also changing and with a little more time on my hands, I spent more time concentrating on my portrait drawing. Dad had been told about a library in Whitechapel, East London, located next to the Whitechapel Art Gallery and near the Sir John Cass College of Arts. Apparently, if an artist's work was considered acceptable, the art department at the library would offer the opportunity for the artist to hold an exhibition of their work. Somebody had suggested to my dad that I should apply to have my work considered, but he was also told the waiting list to exhibit was long. The thought of waiting several months was of little concern to me, since at the time I only had a couple of completed drawings to show; however, the thought of having to be accepted to exhibit was daunting. It took a lot of encouragement from family and friends before I started to believe in myself, but eventually, I picked up my pen and wrote to the librarian. Soon I received a reply asking me to take some examples of my work to the library for him to view. I nervously phoned and arranged a convenient date. Dad would accompany me as the drawings were large and fairly heavy once framed.

I had already started to experiment with a variety of chalks and paper surfaces, seeking a balance which would then allow me to create a smooth texture and establish a form of continuity in my style of portraiture. I made regular visits to a well-stocked art shop, located near Cranbrook Park in Ilford, where I soaked up information and advice offered by friendly, knowledgeable staff. I wanted my drawings to be more than photographs and I am pleased to say, this I managed to achieve.

When the day came to take a few examples of my work to Whitechapel Library to see the area librarian, Mr Lewis, I was both excited and nervous. I think I took about four framed examples and of course one of the portraits was of Shirley. I remember Mr Lewis as a very pleasant man who immediately put me at ease. He loved the drawings and was happy to offer me an exhibition as long as I could supply sufficient portraits to warrant it. I happily assured him that I could meet the requirements and Dad confirmed he would prepare all the frames. In January 1969 I received a letter to confirm my exhibition of 'Portrait Drawings of Show Business Personalities' had been accepted and would take place 6–25 October. I was delighted, but it took some time to sink in. I had to keep telling myself, My work is going to be put on display. Then suddenly it dawned on me there was lots to do – approximately a dozen drawings to be completed and framed in eight months.

I worked from photographs, mainly my own, but sometimes I spotted an image in the press of someone famous which appealed to me for various reasons. In these circumstances I would make contact with the newspaper or magazine in which the photograph appeared, and arrange to purchase a print and pay an additional fee, known then as 'artist's reference', which granted me permission to use the photograph as a reference for my drawing. Since each drawing took between thirty and forty hours to complete, I usually spent most evenings, often to the sounds of Shirley's latest LP playing in the background, happily drawing.

In July 1969, the BBC televised *Show of the Week – Shirley Bassey at the Berns Restaurant, Stockholm*. It was a wonderful show with Shirley performing before an audience of 2,000 diners at this famous century-old restaurant. It was lovely to see her perform again, even though it was only on our twelve-inch television screen and in black and white!

Shirley appeared in a simple white gown and looked stunning, so I contacted the BBC to see if I could get a print taken from the show. This I managed to achieve, gaining artist's reference to permit me to complete a further drawing of Shirley and one which would take pride of place in my forthcoming exhibition.

As the year progressed Shirley's fans began to realise that Shirley, having set up home in Lugano, Switzerland, would not be returning to England just yet, but the release by United Artists of the album, appropriately named *Does Anybody Miss Me*, offered a welcome interlude.

October arrived and my first exhibition was about to commence. My parents were immensely proud when they saw all of my drawings, now framed, displayed on the art department's library walls. Portraits of show-business personalities, many of which were larger-than-life size, looked down on anyone who cared to come and view. It would be fair to say that it came as a shock to some people that the exhibition drew in the crowds. Generally speaking the art world frowned upon the use of photographs, but I must have shown some talent since I was invited to join the nearby art college, only to discover they wanted to change my style. I remember somebody telling me at the time, when talking about a stage school, 'It [a stage school] will produce a chorus but seldom does it produce a star.' Although a dreamer, dreams of being a star never entered my mind but I knew I didn't want to be the chorus, so even though I greatly appreciated the offer to attend the college's classes, I declined. My artistic ability had been self-taught and I wanted to retain the individuality people had seen in my work.

Sometime during those three weeks my work was viewed by a London gallery owner who invited me to exhibit my drawings at his gallery. I was thrilled to be offered the opportunity to display my drawings again, particularly as the gallery was located close to the London Palladium and offered me the possibility of attracting some publicity. A date was set for the following summer.

Shortly after the library exhibition ended, my head still in the clouds, I received a lovely letter from the area librarian telling me the total attendance figures for the exhibition had been 1,134, a record for any of their exhibitions. I was thrilled. How I laughed with my parents when I told them that, like Shirley, I had broken 'box office' records. So for a time, with more portraits to produce, my drawing took centre stage in my life – well, almost.

Boyfriends also began to feature more frequently in my life, although none lasted for very long. One or two were very fond of me. Actually, one proposed marriage but in the same breath told me he wasn't really sure if he loved me! That was the big problem, for me it had to be love, the kind Shirley sang about and romantics dreamed of; sometimes I wondered if perhaps it would always evade me.

Time passed and soon I received the news every fan had been longing to hear, Miss Shirley Bassey would be returning to the The Talk of the Town, next spring

After an absence of two years, Shirley was coming home and there was nothing I dreamed about more than to be at the airport to welcome her home.

CHAPTER 11

DOES ANYBODY MISS ME

The title track from Shirley's recent album posed the question, 'Does Anybody Miss Me?' It wouldn't be long before Miss Bassey would have her answer and it would be a resounding, YES. Every fan in the country wanted to demonstrate just how much they had missed Miss Bassey and our first opportunity came when I went to London Airport one spring morning in 1970 to welcome Shirley back.

George Webb and myself had probably driven Shirley's agent, Tony Lewis, and Noel Rogers at United Artists crazy with requests for information, but what did we care as we waited at the arrival lounge along with the airline's press representative and an array of press photographers. Fortunately, my dad had a job which allowed for some flexibility in his working hours, so he was able to come along, but sadly Mum had to work. I was glad Dad was with me since I had bought my 35mm camera in the hope of taking a photo of my own. I was also juggling with a 'welcome home' card and a large bouquet of red roses which I planned to give to Shirley, so Dad's extra pair of hands would be needed.

I was almost bursting with excitement, but would Shirley remember me! Then the press representative came over to speak to us and I was suddenly afraid he was going to tell us to leave! Luckily, he realised we were sincere; he was just asking us to show consideration since the press photographers needed to get some photographs for publication in tomorrow's papers to announce Shirley's arrival back in Britain.

The press, the airline representative, George, Dad and I periodically scanned each other for any sign of movement as we waited. Suddenly the glass doors opened and we were looking at a smiling Shirley as she emerged with her husband, Sergio Novak, at her side. We all rushed to greet her and I couldn't wait to hand Shirley her bouquet of roses and tell her how wonderful it was to see her and offer our congratulations on her marriage. Shirley thanked me and said it was nice to see us and asked how we were. She had remembered me. Suddenly, quite shocked, I heard myself saying, 'He is gorgeous, does he have a brother?' referring of course to her tall Italian husband. Shirley laughed and then turned to Sergio, speaking to him in Italian, and it was obvious she was telling him what I had just said. Sergio looked over to me and offered a broad smile.

As we all headed for the exit and Shirley's waiting limousine, the press pack were anxious to get a suitable photograph. Stepping forward, the airline representative spoke to Shirley and Sergio and then arranged for the couple to be photographed sitting on a luggage trolley. I worked by my own set of rules and always asked Shirley if I could take a photo. I did this and she happily agreed. As Shirley and Sergio positioned themselves, directed by the press, Sergio lovingly placed his arm around Shirley as she laid my bouquet of roses in front of her. I was so proud and shaking slightly with excitement, but fortunately I managed to get a good picture. We were not in the age of digital cameras and iPhones; taking photographs then required a little more technique than is needed today. Framing the picture, trying to avoid camera shake, considering the amount of light were things you had to think about and then you could only see the result after the film had been developed.

Having taken the required shots, the majority of the press photographers went on their way. Shirley walked over to the limo while Sergio went in search of the luggage. Fortunately for us, it took some time for all the pieces to arrive, so we were given a golden opportunity to take some more photos, as Shirley posed and chatted willingly. It was lovely to see her so happy and we were delighted to have the opportunity to spend a little more time in her company. Eventually Sergio returned with the luggage and soon we were waving goodbye, but this time we knew it would not be long before we would be watching her homecoming performance at The Talk of the Town.

What a day we'd had. I couldn't wait to get home to tell Mum all about it. Dad, too, was excited and offered to develop my film almost as soon as we arrived home. He would develop his black-and-white film using a blackout changing bag which allowed him to remove the film from the cassette before transferring it onto a spiral holder, which fitted into the developing tank. This procedure had to be done in complete darkness, since any unwanted trace of light reaching the film spelled disaster. It took practice to master how to load a film successfully but once achieved and the lid secured, the rest of the process could be done in the light.

Dad would keep his photographic 'bits and pieces' in the box room of our house, what we would today call the study. That evening Dad went upstairs to the box room and did his magic, preparing the chemicals to process the film. Within an hour or so the film was sufficiently dry for us to hold it by its edges and squint at the negative images which appearing before us. It was a thrilling moment, seeing the images I had taken that day as well as a relief that I had captured the moment successfully.

While Dad had been kept busy in the box room, Mum and I cleared up the dinner things whilst I chatted continually about Shirley and

Sergio's homecoming. 'It will be in the papers tomorrow,' I told Mum. 'That's good', was her ever-encouraging reply.

The next morning was one of those rare days that I got up early. I had to call into the newsagents to scan the papers for reports on Shirley's arrival. That morning the newsagent made a good sale and I felt wonderful reading the reports and gazing at photos of Shirley and Sergio, with my roses.

At work, colleagues having seen Shirley's photo in the papers, asked if I had been to see Shirley at the airport. When I told them I had, most wanted to hear my tale, but a few gave me a doubtful glance! I didn't mind; soon I would be printing my photographs and then there would be no doubts! I was very lucky that my employer allowed me to use the dark-room facilities in the laboratory, providing it was in my own time and at my expense. This was a great asset since I could develop and print my photographs to my liking, at a faction of the cost I would have paid to a professional printing firm. The process was similar in many ways to developing the film, but you did not require complete darkness for the entire procedure. Once the film had been 'exposed' onto photographic paper using an enlarger, the next stage could be carried out under the darkroom's specially equipped red lighting. Systematically, the photographic paper would be placed through trays of developer, water and fixer before finally being washed and dried. For me, the magic moment occurred when the exposed paper lay floating in the tray of developer. Slowly, as the chemicals did their job, you witnessed the images you had taken materialise before your eyes. It was a wonderful experience, sadly missed when film and printing declined in the digital age.

A few hours spent in the darkroom and I was rewarded with a couple of dozen 8- by 10-inch black-and-white photographs. I also produced some smaller copies that I sent to other fans, retaining the original prints, which I still have today.

Around the same time as I was printing my photos, Shirley and

Sergio were being photographed on the Roof Terrace of the Dorchester Hotel in London. During the following few days several pictures and reports appeared in newspapers and one photograph in particular drew my attention. It was a lovely portrait of Shirley and Sergio, looking lovingly at each other. It had been taken by a *Daily Express* photographer and after making several enquiries, I paid the artist's reference fee and purchased a print. During the coming weeks I worked on the portrait of Shirley with Sergio, producing a drawing I would exhibit at my next exhibition and later present to the couple.

Suddenly, there didn't seem to be enough time in the day. Letters to write, drawings to complete, theatre reservations to make and naturally I had to buy a new frock! There had been one positive thing during Shirley's two-year absence: my 'entertainment fund' had grown in leaps and bounds, and so as soon as we became aware of Shirley's pending Talk of the Town engagement, we made reservations. Unfortunately, due to other commitments, Joyce and Reon were unable to join us but their dedication to Shirley was still as strong as ever. We booked for three separate performances, opening night, the following Saturday and final night a week later. Now Mum and I had to find time to revisit our favourite dress shop in Ilford. Shirley was back and the excitement was already building up inside us as opening night, 13 April, drew near

Taking place only a few days before my mum's birthday, I wanted the opening night to be very special for us. I had collected a bouquet of red roses to present to Shirley and now I was trying hard to contain my excitement as we waited for our taxi to arrive. I have no recollection of the journey to London, but I do remember my heart pumping extra loudly as we stepped out of the taxi and walked into the theatre. The atmosphere was electric and it seemed as though everyone wanted to be part of it. We made our way through the crowds lining the entrance and entered the restaurant, joining a queue to enquire about table allocation. I expected ours to be good since we had booked early, but I also knew opening night brought out the 'stars', all of whom would expect a good table. Although only early in the evening, it seemed the restaurant manager was already experiencing the stress. 'I've come to check our table,' I asked politely. He looked at his list, said the table number and pointed in the direction of the stage. I was happy with that but then he uttered the words, 'but it might change'.

'Might change, how can it change?' I replied rather naively. I pointed to another table next to the one he had offered: 'We could sit there.'

'Shirley Bassey's family will be seating there and I have been told if they aren't sitting there Shirley will not sing.'

I don't know where I gained the nerve but I heard myself saying, 'Well, if we are not sitting at the table next to them [the table that evening we had originally been offered] Shirley still won't sing.'

He really couldn't argue since I was only asking for what was rightfully ours, having been one of the first to book. 'All right, all right, but you can't give her those [looking at my bouquet] during the act.'

'OK. I will give them to her at the *end* of her act.'

He threw his arms in the air in desperation and summoned a waiter to take my bouquet. I wondered if I would ever see my roses again but I couldn't stop him.

Later that evening, we were shown to the table of our choice and shortly before Shirley was due to appear, the waiter returned my bouquet to our table. I was most grateful since the roses had been placed in a refrigerator allowing them to remain at their best.

Earlier we had dined and watched as show-business celebrities and sports personalities joined the audience. I never regarded myself as an autograph hunter, however that evening I did ask two of Shirley's greatest admirers, who were seated near to the stage, if they would be kind enough to sign my programme. They happily agreed and after I had thanked them, I walked back to our table with a programme that had written across the cover, 'With love Danny La Rue and Liberace, Love'!

At 9.30pm Robert Nesbitt's latest diamond-studded revue, 'Jet Set

70', took to the stage, jetting the audience off to Paris, Greece, Las Vegas and Venice. Then it was the turn of the dance bands, which played until a few minutes before 11pm. Waiters now hurried around from table to table, desperately trying to fulfil bar orders. The sounds of laughter and chatter diminished as the audience began to fall into silence. Applause was followed by cheers as Brian Fahey, Shirley's musical director for the past three years, took to the stage. The orchestra began to play the overture and then, in an instant, the audience erupted. The two-year wait was over and Miss Shirley Bassey was standing, at centre stage, there before our eyes. Cheers and whistles resounded through the theatre before Shirley could sing a note. Eventually the audience went silent and Shirley began to sing in a way we had never heard her sing before, 'Does Anybody Miss Me', to which the audience cried 'Yes, yes'. If Shirley had had any doubts as to whether we missed her, they were now firmly cast aside as the audience poured out its love for her. In response Shirley sang a heartfelt rendering, 'As I Love You'.

For over an hour love flowed back and forth between audience and star as we enjoyed 'oldies' like 'The Lady is a Tramp' and new offerings such as 'I'll Never Fall In Love Again'. When Shirley removed her flowing outer cape/gown to reveal a stunning creation by Douglas Darnell, announcing it was time for 'Big Spender', I'm sure I was not alone in wondering how her dress[2] would stay up. Fortunately it did, but we were left in no doubt: Shirley's 'Big Spender', and that dress, could bring down any house!

Our table was in a fantastic position, to Shirley's left, and located just behind the first line of tables joining the edge of the stage. As this was opening night I wasn't sure which number Shirley would choose to close her act. I hoped it would be 'This Is My Life' since, during Shirley's absence, the song had become my mum's particular favourite. As soon as the orchestra played those opening chords it was obvious

2 Douglas Darnell named this particular creation the Harlem Dress, and talks about it in an interview in 2003, published by Christie's for a Gala Charity Auction, *Dame Shirley Bassey: 50 Years of Glittering Gowns*.

Mum was not alone in her choice. The audience screamed out its approval as Shirley gently began to pour out her heart, building to a rapturous finish... 'This Is My Life'.

Shortly after finishing the number and Shirley ran offstage, thunderous applause was ringing out from the audience as they rose on mass to their feet. The orchestra continued playing and I couldn't wait any longer. I scooped up my bouquet and headed for the stage. Within seconds I found myself wedged between two tables adjacent to the stage as Shirley came back out. Heading towards the opposite side of the stage, she began shaking the outstretched hands reaching up to her in appreciation. Slowly she made her way around the edge of the stage as the orchestra continued to play and the audience cheered. The applause was deafening, but I could not clap as my hands were full, so I cheered at loud as I could. The people on either side didn't seem to mind; they were cheering, too.

Several people, including George Webb, offered Shirley gifts ranging from champagne to daffodils, everyone just wanted to express their love and appreciation. It seemed forever but finally Shirley, having deposited her collection of gifts with her musical director, was heading towards me. I thought I was in heaven, I had never been happier than I was at that moment when, bending slightly, she shook my hand and I handed her the bouquet. Then I was back in my seat as Shirley prepared to perform an encore. The standing ovation which followed was followed by another, which was followed by another, they just kept coming. This was a party nobody wanted to end. Eventually Shirley took her final exit and the music ended. The stage was lowered and a small group of musicians started to play for anyone wanting to take to the dance floor.

After watching a performance I am in my zone, trying to memorise every moment and simultaneously trying to recharge my batteries, so to speak. I'm always drained, in the nicest possible way. A visit to the ladies cloakroom was essential and for some strange reason I vividly remember the buzz of all the ladies around me. Every conversation seemed like a script being read over and over again. Words like fabulous, marvellous, thrilling, powerful, exciting, bewitching, mesmerising, wonderful, magic, were constantly being repeated. Everybody was talking at once and they were all talking about one thing, Shirley Bassey. Had they caught my bug? I thought!

As we were about to leave, the restaurant manager called out to me and asked if I had enjoyed the show. Naturally, I responded with great excitement and he said that he hoped to see us again, but his enthusiasm seemed to dim slightly when I replied we would be back on Saturday. 'I suppose you will want the same table' he said, to which I replied, 'That would be wonderful.'

The following Saturday, when we arrived at the Talk, we did not expect to get the same table since we knew we were further down the booking list. To our delight the restaurant manager greeted us warmly, and then said 'I'll take you to your table.' I feared the worst, but he led us directly to the lovely table we had occupied on opening night. 'I hope this is satisfactory madam,' he said with a big grin. I later learned, he told my parents I had a lovely personality and 'I could get away with anything.' Well, I'm not so sure about that, but I did get the table that night.

That same evening I managed to speak with Shirley's husband. I had spotted him standing discreetly at the back of the restaurant, but when you're as tall as Sergio it's difficult to avoid being seen. I went over and he said hello. Although he had only seen me on a few occasions, he recognised me and we had a nice chat. I told him I was with my parents and pointed our table out to him before ending by asking him to give Shirley our best wishes, which he said he would do. When I returned to our table, Mum and Dad wanted to know about our chat. It wasn't long after when a waiter came to our table and said, 'I have something for you.' He handed me a Talk of the Town programme, only this one had been personally signed by Shirley. Wow, was I delighted.

When Shirley took to the stage that evening she gave another unbelievable performance and once again the packed house rose to its feet. Mum enjoyed yet another birthday celebration, although 'This Is My Life' brought a few tears. As we left I said to the restaurant manager, 'See you next Saturday.' He laughed, threw his hands in the air and replied, 'Oh no!'

Over the previous few days I had gathered together the reviews from newspapers and musical publications. Everybody sang from the same hymn sheet – Shirley had been fabulous and truly showed she was one of the world's leading cabaret artists. Not that I needed any convincing!

The following Saturday Mum, Dad and I again made the journey to The Talk of the Town. Although we did not know it at the time, it was to be our last visit together to the venue, but what a finale it would turn out to be. George and I had spoken on the phone earlier in the week and he had told me he heard Shirley's performance at the Talk was going to be recorded, but that was all he knew. At that time it wasn't unusual to hear such things, and then for nothing to happen, so we hadn't thought anymore of it. As it was final night I again bought a bouquet of red roses to give to Shirley.

That evening, as we entered the 'Talk', the restaurant manager came directly up to me and took the roses from my arm, saying, 'We will look after them for you and bring them to you later.' He then added, 'We have a surprise for you. Miss Bassey is extending her performance tonight as it is being recorded.' I immediately thought, Oh no, he is going to tell me I won't be permitted to give her my bouquet, but nothing further was said. I prayed we would have a reasonable table although I knew we were down the pecking order. 'Now, let's see,' he muttered as he looked at his table plan, then smiling he said, 'I don't have to take you to *your table*, do I? You know where it is.' I thanked him profusely before heading off in the direction of *our table*, Mum and Dad proudly following behind. After settling into our seats we ordered a bottle of Lanson Black Label champagne, for Mum's third birthday celebration; at the end of the day, this one was going to be an even greater night to remember.

The place was packed to capacity; any direction you cared to look, you could spot a showbiz or sports personality. On the table next to us was the British boxing heavyweight champion, Henry Cooper, with his Italian-born wife, Albina. Affectionately known as 'Our 'Enry', he chatted with Mum, Dad and myself throughout the evening and when my bouquet of roses appeared at our table Albina told me she thought it was wonderful that I was going to give them to Shirley. I secretly thought to myself, Nobody will try to stop me with Our 'Enry so near.

The atmosphere was electric as the lights dimmed and the orchestra began to play. Cheers rang out as Shirley walked onstage in her flowing gown to receive a standing ovation. She gave an unbelievable performance which lasted over an hour and a half and when the final number came, she received seven standing ovations. Somewhere between the ovations I made my way to the edge of the stage and presented her bouquet. Thanking me, we shook hands and I just couldn't thank her enough for the fabulous two weeks, but I think she understood what I was trying to express. When I returned to our table Albina said, 'I'm so pleased you did that.' It was a magical evening and a fitting end to Shirley's engagement, which broke all previous attendance records. Fortunately for all her fans, the performance was recorded and the following June, forty-six minutes and forty seconds were released by United Artists on an LP entitled, *Shirley Bassey Live at Talk of the Town*. The record sold well, entering the album charts, and when I play it today I can still recognise my shouts of 'more' and am transported back to that unforgettable evening.

CHAPTER 12

SOMETHING

In the months leading up to summer 1970 I was extremely busy completing my drawings. With my exhibition opening at the Woodstock Galleries, close to London's Oxford Street, I had contacted someone at Syndication International, who allowed me to go and view some photographic files for suitable photographs. What an eye-opener that proved to be, but I did source some good material on which to base some drawings. Needless to say, I particularly wanted to see Shirley's file and miraculously came across a photo which had been taken during her recent Talk of the Town engagement. What was special was that I appeared in the photo, standing there at the side of the stage with my bouquet, mouth wide open, obviously shouting for 'more'. Well, I had to purchase a copy of that!

Dad had worked hard making frames for all of my drawings and must have felt a little proud when he finally saw them displayed at the gallery. The owner had worked hard to try and get me some press coverage. Some art reviewers had promised to attend the exhibition and possibly write a review, but he managed to get a reporter from the

Daily Mirror interested in my work. I was shocked when one day, while at work, I received a phone call from the reporter asking if I could go and meet up with him at a pub near the newspaper's offices. A bit risky, I thought, but I arranged to meet him for an interview.

A day or so later, as I travelled to work on the Underground, I casually looked over someone's shoulder as something had caught my eye. The man was reading the 'Inside Page' in the *Daily Mirror* and near the centre of the page was a photo of Barbra Streisand, except the photo was actually my drawing of Barbra and had been taken from the cover of my exhibition catalogue. My initial casual glance resulted in my eyes nearly popping out of my head; the reporter had told me he would try to print something, but I really hadn't held much hope. Once off the train and out of the station I headed for a newsagents and purchased several copies of the *Daily Mirror* and although I arrived a little late for work, everyone wanted to read *my news*. As you can imagine when I arrived home that evening and showed the paper to Mum and Dad, they were over the moon to think that I had made the national press.

Whilst I was kept busy with my exhibition, Shirley was on the other side of the world performing in Australia and New Zealand where she had become enormously popular, partly due to the success of her album *And We Were Lovers*, for which she received a gold disc, the first awarded to a female artist in Australia. Today, we can access news instantly from almost anywhere in the world, but back in the seventies it was rare to hear any news relating to Shirley's performances abroad and therefore I don't think I fully appreciated, at the time, the extent of Shirley's popularity abroad. I guess I always saw her as a star but never stopped to think about the size of her fan base.

It was a lovely summer's day when Shirley returned to London to record a television special for the BBC. Seizing the opportunity to go to the airport, I took with me a 'welcome home' card in which I had enclosed my exhibition catalogue (there were three drawings of Shirley in the exhibition), along with my *Daily Mirror* press cutting. Walking with Shirley from the arrival lounge to her limo, it seemed I was the only fan around. Shirley, wearing large framed sunglasses, a lovely summer dress and lots of jewellery, let me take several photos, before settling into the back seat of the limo. I expected her to close the door as she waited for her luggage to arrive but to my surprise she kept her door open and then proceeded to open the envelope I had just given her. Upon seeing my Daily Mirror press cutting, Shirley immediately turned to me and said, 'Oh, congratulations, I read this in Australia.' Well, I was shocked. I stood there speechless; I tried to say something sensible but nothing came out. Here I was with my idol, Shirley Bassey, and she had just told me she had read my press cutting whilst on the other side of the world. More importantly, Shirley had recognised it related to one of her fans and had made the connection with me. Eventually, the luggage arrived and I managed to speak, thanking Shirley before she waved goodbye and her limo drove off. That day, I felt very special indeed.

My summer continued to be special. I gained promotion at work and received two further offers to exhibit my drawings. I was very happy with life but my success was microscopic in comparison to Shirley's. Her latest single release, 'Something', was climbing up the charts and in so doing she was gaining recognition as a pop idol. Her interpretation of the George Harrison number was stunning and, over time, Shirley made history by becoming the only artist ever to have achieved greater success with a Beatles number than the Beatles themselves.

Shirley's television special screened in August, along with further TV guest appearances, added to her popularity, leading to an announcement of a British tour in November. News like this prompted a flurry of letter writing on my part, resulting in the booking of concert tickets. In the meantime Shirley had flown to the States to fulfil a cabaret engagement at the Sahara Hotel, Las Vegas. An engagement at the famous Empire Room, within the Waldorf Astoria Hotel, New York, immediately followed. Both engagements received outstanding reviews in the American press. How I would have loved to have been there, but in the early seventies visiting New York was an impossible dream. Not that I was complaining, I was content to dream about 'sunny' Bournemouth in November and the Royal Festival Hall, London.

There was more excitement that summer concerning our family holiday. During the pervious couple of years we had spent our summer holiday in the lovely town of Interlaken, Switzerland, enjoying the beautiful scenery and Swiss mountain air. Initially Mum and Dad had been apprehensive about flying, but once they had experienced their first flight they loved the idea of flying again. This year, to my delight, they had suggested a two-centre holiday, spending one week in Interlaken, to be followed by a second in Lugano, a beautiful Swiss resort where Shirley and Sergio had decided to settle. So that's where we were heading.

Although I knew Shirley's Lugano address, I had every respect for her privacy and had no intention of intruding, but as a fan I naturally wanted to see where she lived. It's hard to explain, but seeing where she was living seemed to offer me some kind of reassurance that she was fine. It may seem silly but that's how it felt at the time. When we arrived at our Lugano hotel, which coincidentally was located not far from Shirley's apartment, it didn't take long for me to decide to go and take a walk to see the sights! Next day Mum and Dad joined me and Dad captured a photograph of me for the holiday album, with the apartment forming the backdrop.

We loved Lugano and the surrounding area, returning on a couple of other occasions. Surprisingly, I had acquired Shirley's phone number on our first visit, simply by looking in a Swiss phone directory which had been placed in our hotel room. I looked up S. Novak and there it was... The next day I just had to phone and nervously dialled the number. 'Pronto' came the reply and I instantly knew it was Sergio.

I apologised for disturbing him, explained we were on holiday in Lugano and asked if it would be possibly to just say hello to Shirley. Sergio told me Shirley was at the hairdressers adding, 'You know what you women are like. I don't know when she will be back.' I thanked him and said I would not trouble him again but asked if he would pass on our good wishes, which he said he would, adding he hoped we had a lovely holiday.

To go into Lugano's town centre we usually took the funicular railway, which runs from the railway station. The railcars always seemed packed to capacity in the morning as residents and tourists alike headed down the hillside. One morning we found ourselves at the front of the queue and so could get seats. Looking out at the line of passengers also hoping to board, I suddenly noticed a young child who seemed to be getting a little impatient. Her little legs were stamping up and down in her excitement to board the railcar. She was holding onto the hand of a lady in conversation with another lady and as they boarded and moved along the car, the little girl stopped in front of me. I looked down and immediately knew who it was. I had seen photos of Shirley as a child and this little girl was her double; it had to be Samantha, Shirley's younger daughter. I obviously didn't want to draw attention to the child but glancing at my parents it was obvious they too had seen the likeness. I looked at the child and said, 'Hello Samantha.' She looked up at me with an expression that said, 'Do I know you'? and the lady whose hand she held looked at me slightly anxiously. I turned to her and said, 'It's all right, I know her mother.' 'I see,' she replied. I explained we were on holiday and I guess she realised we were fans. The journey on the funicular only took a few minutes but when we left the railcar to head for the shops, Samantha waved goodbye. Then she was gently led in the opposite direction, to school. Giving her a wave, we couldn't believe our luck. We were so thrilled to have seen her, but more importantly we felt that here in Lugano Shirley had an opportunity to live a normal life, at least until the footlights beckoned her once more.

On another occasion, while strolling through the town, we saw Sergio heading towards us. On seeing us, he immediately came and shook hands with Mum and Dad and asked if we were enjoying our holiday. We chatted for a while before he said he had to get to the bank, which made us laugh!

Our holiday was over only to soon but we came home with lovely memories. Soon we were thinking about Shirley's forthcoming British tour. As I've already mentioned, the Winter Gardens theatre at Bournemouth was always a favourite with us because we were able to see Shirley when she arrived at the theatre and if we were lucky, sometimes hear her rehearse. Sitting in the café area on the afternoon of a concert was pure heaven for me. Just hearing Shirley sing a few lines, often without any amplification and sometimes without the full orchestra, I grew to truly appreciate the power and quality of her voice. It's also one of the reason why I loved to be seated near to the stage: you heard pure Bassey.

The 1970 tour marked the first in a series of concert tours undertaken during the seventies. I loved the format of these concerts, the orchestra performing a selection of pieces during a fairly short first half, followed by an interval and then Shirley taking to the stage for the entire second half of the show, which usually lasted for an hour, sometimes longer when an audience continued to demand encores. That November the Bournemouth audience, now expanded by the new fans enlisted since the release of 'Something', joined the regulars. What a treat they had in store, for I knew that seeing Shirley perform live would be a mesmerising experience for them.

The first half of the show was well received, the audience appreciating the talented musicians which Brian Fahey had assembled within his orchestra. Brian was a well-respected conductor, arranger and composer who, having worked with Shirley during the last few years, had now established a great rapport.

When that announcement was made, requesting the audience to

return to their seats, and the words 'tonight's performance is about to continue', every nerve in my body switched to overdrive. At times I even thought I might be sick! Then the orchestra played, the audience cheered and Shirley, wrapped in feathers and sparkling cape, walked onstage – and I was cured.

Jumping to my feet, those around me followed, cheering and applauding Shirley as she appeared to acknowledge each and every one of us personally. Tonight was, after all, the first opportunity for many fans to welcome Shirley back to Britain and they were determined to let her see just how much they had missed her.

Shirley's range of material featured some of the old favourites along with the expected 'Big Spender', 'Goldfinger', and her recent success 'Something', which created an eruption of applause when the opening notes sounded through the auditorium. Numbers from her newly released LPs, *What Are You Doing The Rest Of Your Life?* and *Yesterday I Heard The Rain* showed off more of Shirley's range and talent. We shouted for more and she continued to sing until finally the introduction to 'This Is My Life' confirmed that the end was near. Shirley sang her heart out and Mum shed a few tears as was usual, along with several others in the audience. As Miss Bassey left the stage the audience again rose to its feet in a fury of excitement, seemingly mesmerised by the whole experience. Shirley's return to the stage only intensified the applause and many fans, myself included, approached the stage with our hands outstretched hoping to shake her hand. The orchestra continued to play as Shirley walked along the edge of the stage, shaking the line of hands before her in the spotlight. When she finally left the stage, the applause still continued for several minutes before the audience accepted the concert had ended and it was time for us to leave. I always found it difficult to believe that Shirley had given a similar performance a few hours earlier to the first house audience. I really did not know at the time how she did it, but I did appreciate that it only happened because of all her hard work, dedication and professionalism, as well as her remarkable talent.

During that tour, Mum, Dad and I were also booked to attend a concert at the impressive Royal Festival Hall, on the South Bank in London. Along with some friends, who shared a musical taste more classical than Bassey, we climbed the stairs up to the terrace seats we'd booked. It was our family's first visit to this famous concert hall renowned for its excellent acoustics and I was told our seats were in a prime location, but when I discovered how far they were from the stage, my heart dropped. How could Shirley know I was here!

Our friends, however, were delighted with the seats which offered a good view of the stage. I told myself, Now I will experience what it is like to be *in* the audience with a view of the whole auditorium, but as I was with friends perhaps I should try to show a little more reserve. Well, that was the plan I made as I looked around at the audience sitting near to us during the first half of the concert. They certainly looked reserved, in fact some appeared quite dull. I was beginning to get nervous; this was an audience unlike any other I had sat with previously. Perhaps some of them were tourists, happy to see any show, others may have come to the concert out of curiosity, but somewhere there had to be some fans, like me, trying to contain their excitement.

Second half and the overture began, then suddenly it seemed as though I had been transported to another world. As Shirley walked onto the stage, those dull individuals transformed into excitable men and woman, rising to their feet in appreciation. In no time at all Shirley had captivated her entire audience and the Royal Festival Hall came alive.

Although I tried to show some reserve it just wasn't going to happen. Soon I found myself shouting for more between numbers and then, after 'Something', I could no longer remain at my seat. At the end of the number, as the applause rang out, I quickly walked down the gangway stairs, heading in the direction of the stage and praying that nobody would stop me. It seemed to take forever but once there, I felt at home. Hand outstretched I took Shirley's hand and we exchanged greetings. Our friends had said to Mum, on seeing me leave my seat, 'Mary's gone.' They hadn't seen me in the dim light heading for the stage, so were totally surprised when they saw me shaking Shirley's hand. As Shirley began her next number, I quietly, and more slowly, happily returned to my seat.

It had been a wonderful concert, Shirley's world-class status more than justified. After the concert, our friends told us they had never witnessed anything like it – we loved her, she really was 'Something'.

CHAPTER 13

TILL LOVE TOUCHES YOUR LIFE

It seemed, as we entered 1971, everyone wanted to see and hear Shirley and demand resulted in a further British tour with Brian Fahey and his Orchestra in April. Early in the year, Shirley had released the single 'Fool On The Hill' and this was quickly followed with the theme 'Where Do I Begin' from the film *Love Story*. Her LP sales reached new heights with *Live at The Talk of The Town* and *Something* and her engagement diary read like a travelogue to the world's most glamorous places.

In April we were lucky enough to see her perform at the Guildhall, Portsmouth on Friday 23rd, the Winter Gardens, Bournemouth on Saturday 24th, before finally attending the Royal Albert Hall, London, on Sunday 25th, where we had arena, row A, seats 1–3. It couldn't get any better than that! During those three days it seemed as though Mum, Dad and I were 'on tour', with Dad driving us to the venues and back home each night. What fun we had!

We had taken the decision to attend all three concerts since my parents were planning to retire the following year, to the Isle of Wight, and we knew living on the island would restrict our opportunities to see Shirley performing live. I intended to change jobs and relocate but it proved far more difficult to find work on the island than I expected. Actually, I did find suitable employment but the pay offered was significantly less than I was currently earning. So, in 1972 I took a bedsit in Wanstead, London, where I continued to live until I married in the latter seventies. During those years I travelled home to the island most weekends, but this lifestyle meant I had little spare time available to collect press cuttings or pursue my portrait drawing. The pattern to my life was changing significantly but one aspect was certain, being a fan of Shirley Bassey was always going to play a prominent part. Every concert that April was wonderful and as we left each theatre we embraced Shirley's performance. She had given her all and the public loved it.

Following that, after a tremendously successful year appearing in the States, Europe and the UK, Shirley returned to Britain in November to star in the Royal Variety Performance, to be held at the London Palladium in the presence of Her Majesty the Queen. I immediately contacted the theatre as soon as I heard the news and managed to purchase three tickets, although these were without doubt the worst seats I had ever had, at £2 each in the upper circle, but at least we would be part of the audience on Shirley's very special night.

The tickets arrived by post together with detailed instructions relating to 'setting down', 'parking' and 'picking up', printed on a large sheet of paper on the reverse of which was printed a large red 'P' and above which was stated 'Royal Variety Performance'. This apparently was to be placed in the window of the vehicle in which you would travel in order to gain access to the theatre. We were instructed to arrive by 7.30pm, be seated by 7.45pm, and our tickets stated we were required to wear evening dress. Finally, we were expected to remain in our seats at the end of the performance until the Royal Party had left the theatre.

Above left: Face to face with Miss Bassey at the London Palladium, April 1963. Photo taken by Valerie.

Above right: Shirley at London Airport (now Heathrow), prior to departing for Stockholm, late 1960s.

Below left: Miss Shirley Bassey at the opening of a record store in Dean Street, London, and the launch of her first United Artists LP.

Below right: My drawing of Shirley Bassey, which became my mum's favourite, completed in 1969 for my first exhibition, based on a photograph I took of the star in 1967.

Above: Reon, Joyce, Shirley and me at the stage-door entrance to the London Palladium, 19 March 1967.

Below: Shirley Bassey, with Norman Newell behind her, arriving at The Talk of the Town in the late 1960s. Shirley signed the photograph.

Above and below left: Shirley Bassey at the Winter Gardens Theatre, Bournemouth, in 1976.

Below right: My drawing of Shirley Bassey performing before an audience of 2,000 diners, based on a BBC photo taken at the Berns Restaurant, Stockholm. The performance was recorded for BBC 2's Show of the Week, May 1969.

Above left: Shirley Bassey sings her heart out as Michael Alexander conducts the orchestra at the Bournemouth International Centre (BIC), 1986.

Below left: Shirley Bassey in concert at the BIC in 1986 . . .

Below right: . . . and at the same venue in the 1980s.

One of three photographs, framed in crystal, presented at Fort Regent, Jersey, 1995.

Top: Shirley Bassey in concert at the BIC, 1989.

Below left: Shirley Bassey at Jersey's airport prior to boarding *our* flight back to London.

Below right: Shirley Bassey performing 'Hey Jude', 1986.

Shirley Bassey wearing a three-piece stage outfit by Zandra Rhodes.

Shirley, at the last concert we attended as a family – BIC Bournemouth.

Dad arranged the car hire with Mr Tricker, who was excited at the prospect of driving us to the theatre on this special night, and our own eagerness increased as the performance approached. Eventually, Monday, 15 November 1971 arrived and soon we were entering the doors of the great London Palladium, but on this occasion crowds were lining the street outside in readiness to see Her Majesty's arrival.

Climbing the stairs to 'the gods' seemed to take for ever and when we finally entered the upper circle, I remember feeling rather unsteady. The rows of seating rose steeply and as I was uncomfortable with heights, I needed a little time to adjust. Once seated, things improved and I thumbed my way through the beautifully embossed white-covered programme. Soon I had enough courage to lean down and see the beautifully dressed people below in the stalls as the orchestra played.

Moments later we rose as Her Majesty the Queen entered the Royal Box – it was magical – then as the orchestra played the National Anthem, the audience sang, 'God Save The Queen'.

The first of the show featured approximately eight acts, introduced by compère Bruce Forsyth, and closed in a blaze of colour when the 'Little Angels of Korea' performed. Intermission, when we would normally be preparing for Shirley but on this occasion there were still several acts to perform before Shirley would take to the stage, including The New Seekers, Sacha Distel, Stéphane Grappelli and Tommy Cooper. Although some of the acts were very good, especially Tommy Cooper, I just longed for them to end. Finally it happened, the orchestra, now assembled onstage and lead by Brian Fahey, started to play. Shirley entered, looking stunning in a revealing white diamanté gown, and quickly began a beautiful song, 'Till Love Touches Your Life', from her latest album. 'Where Do I Begin', 'Yesterday When I Was Young', 'For All We Know' and finally 'Something' followed. Her performance was electric and although she appeared rather small, seen from our great height, she commanded the stage and intoxicated the audience, who rose to give her a standing ovation. Mum, Dad and I stood cheering for more but we knew this would not happen, as Shirley finally left the stage. The show's finale immediately followed and when Shirley joined the line-up the audience erupted, before the entire company turned to the Royal Box to again sing 'God Save The Queen'.

We understood that everyone was to remain seated until the Royal Party had left the theatre but somehow the audience in the upper circle was permitted to leave. I believe this may have been because we could exit via the rear of the theatre without having to use the main entrance. Anyway, I know I needed the toilet and Mum and I were directed down some stairs. Dad came down with us and waited nearby until we rejoined him. It seemed surprisingly quiet and nobody seemed to be around, so we continued to make our way down the stairs. Suddenly someone appeared and quietly asked us to stay just where we were. I turned to look over the staircase, gasping as I saw below me some of the stars of the night's performance lined up below, and the nearest to us was Shirley. I couldn't believe it and I don't think Shirley could either when she looked up and gave us a smile. Then she turned to Tommy Cooper, who was at her side, and said something to him. He then looked up to us and started waving to us to come down and join him, but I froze. I didn't want to end up in the tower. They then all walked away, Shirley giving us a wave as she departed. I could only assume Shirley and Tommy Cooper had been presented to Her Majesty literally moments before we arrived at the staircase. Now that Her Majesty had left the theatre, the stars were permitted to return backstage and we were 'shown the door', so to speak.

We continued down the stairs and emerged from the theatre as the crowds, waiting outside, looked on. Bubbling with excitement I chatted furiously with my parents as we looked around for Mr Tricker. What a surprise it had been to see Shirley after the show, fate had placed us there at that precise moment and we could not believe our luck. As we headed home, the events of the evening just kept spinning around in my head, for it had been one of the most thrilling nights of my life.

The next morning the daily newspapers reported Shirley's success, several featuring photos taken of her as she was introduced to HM the Queen. There was one beautiful photograph I particularly liked so I contacted the paper and immediately ordered a 12- by 10-inch print, which arrived a week or so later. I purchased a lovely gold and white frame in which to display the photo that we later displayed upon the piano in my parents new bungalow.

More triumphs for Shirley followed, with the release of her latest recording, the title song from the new Bond movie *Diamonds Are Forever*, and a sell-out concert tour in the States.

In May we were heading again to the Winter Gardens, Bournemouth where we had front-row seats for the last night of her 1972 British tour. The format of this tour was slightly different to those presented by Robert Paterson: the first half of this show would solely feature the Maynard Ferguson Orchestra who would then accompany Shirley, under the musical direction of Brian Fahey, during the second half. Billed as the world's most exciting trumpet sound, Maynard Ferguson had played with Jimmy Dorsey and Stan Kenton before forming his own band with the best of New York's session men.

I found this band brassy and loud when I first heard it, sitting in the café adjacent to the auditorium during rehearsals. There were a few other fans present and we all looked at each other in horror. It sounded so loud that when the drummer came into the seating area, I couldn't stop myself from saying to him that I hoped he would play more quietly for Shirley. I have never forgotten his reply: 'I'm trying to kill the gipsies', a reference to the string section, most of which were members of the Bournemouth Symphony Orchestra.

As it was the final night of the tour, I had ordered a bouquet of red roses to present to Shirley at the end of the show and deposited these safely with the ladies in the cloakroom, arranging to collect the bouquet during the interval. Then I went to purchase a programme before settling into my seat, prime position almost centre in the front row, just feet away from Shirley's microphone. When I looked around there appeared to be more empty seats than usual; this sometimes happened if people had previously seen the show at another venue and had disliked the first half. The lights dimmed, the orchestra took to the stage and Maynard led his band into their first number.

To say it was brassy is about as kind as I can be and after a couple of numbers it was clear, from the lukewarm reception, that the audience was not in tune with his type of music. Between numbers there seemed to be some movement behind us but I had no idea what was happening. Then the band just seemed to play louder and louder, as though competing with each other, until finally I thought my ear drums would burst. Eventually I turned to Dad and said, 'I've got to go out otherwise I won't be able to listen to Shirley.' Dad and I stood up, in the middle of a number, leaving my mum in her seat, and walked out. Expecting to be leaving on our own, we were shocked to see several other members of the audience join us. At the end of the number, my mum also left the auditorium to join us in the bar where she found me talking to Brian Fahey and Norman Newell. When both men had seen me walk into the bar, Brian immediately said, 'Mary, I never thought I would see the day when you would walk out of a Shirley Bassey concert.' We all laughed and I told them I would have gone deaf had I continued to remain in my seat during the first half of the show. I was surprised and delighted, however, that they had called me by my name.

Norman Newell had travelled down from London for Shirley's last night partly because it also marked the end of Brian's time as Shirley's musical director, a position which he'd held for six years. It had recently been announced that Brian had been appointed musical director of the New Scottish Radio Orchestra, which would regularly feature on BBC Radio 2 and TV. Although extremely sorry to see Brian leave,

Shirley was very happy for him and wished him every possible success. Although we had laughed about my concerns, regarding the orchestra, Brian did offer reassurance when he told me 'it will be fine in the second half.'

Returning to our seats I laid the bouquet of roses in front of me, next to the stage, hoping that neither I nor any other enthusiastic fan would step on them. The auditorium was now full to capacity and although the audience seemed a little reserved whilst waiting for the show to commence, they suddenly came to life when Brian Fahey took to the stage. Cheers rang out and the orchestra started to play the overture. If I hadn't heard it for myself, I never would have believed the same musicians, with the addition of a string section (the lovable gipsies), could produce a sound so wonderful and different from what we had endured during the first half. Brian had cast his spell and now Shirley took to the stage ready to spread even more magic.

I watched mesmerised, singing along in my head, every number from old favourites, such as 'The Lady Is A Tramp', 'As I Love You' and 'I Who Have Nothing', to more recent successes such as 'Love Story' and 'Till Love Touches Your Life'. I particularly loved the ending of this song, when Shirley would focus her big brown eyes on one member of the audience when singing the words 'Your life', then glancing around to another, she'd repeat, 'Your life'. Tonight, as Shirley sang the number, she ended by looking directly at me as she sang those words. I applauded so furiously that my hands stung and before the evening's performance was over, my watch had stopped. A few days later I sent the watch back to Omega;[3] they reported the watch had been shaken too vigorously and suggested I try to avoid repeating the same action. Well, there wasn't going to be much chance of that!

Shirley's performance was once again electrifying, she could do no

3 My parents bought the watch as a twenty-first-birthday present for me, when we were on holiday in Switzerland. Naturally, it was very special and I only wore it on special occasions. Sadly, many years later it was stolen from our home and although I received some compensation, the watch held priceless memories which could not be replaced.

wrong. Her classics sat happily amongst songs from her recent LP *I Capricorn*, an album dedicated to world-renowned palmist Mir Bashir[4] and which included the track, 'The Greatest Performance of My Life', a number that went on to become one of Shirley's most popular, featuring in concerts for many years to come.

'Tonight I gave the greatest performance of my life' – the words echoed out around the auditorium, delivered with all the passion, strength and feeling we had come to expect. Then Shirley delivered the line that always choked me up, 'If you had been behind the curtain when it fell, you would have seen this actress crying', but I recovered sufficiently to rise to my feet to offer a hearty cheer. I never looked around to see the audience's response – it could be heard and felt – and I knew this was the moment to reach for my bouquet. As I lifted it up and placed it in Shirley's arms, I felt such pride; I was representing the entire audience and I swear the applause grew even louder. After a few words, Shirley walked over to the piano to lay down the bouquet, then after thanking Brian and the orchestra, we were treated to a few extra numbers. When Shirley walked offstage for the final time, the audience slowly started to leave the theatre, each knowing they had witnessed her greatest performance.

That night we made our last journey home to Essex from

---

4 At the time of release of 'I Capricorn', several articles had appeared in the press regarding the high degree of accuracy of Mir Bashir's forecasts. I was fascinated and intrigued by palmistry at the time and made an appointment to see him, for what was termed, a 'general life reading'. I found him to be a very nice, quiet man. My palms of my hands were covered with a black ink, and then I was asked to place them onto a large sheet of white paper. I washed my hands as Mir Bashir retreated to his large armchair, where he began to study my prints. As he handed me pen and paper, he requested I write down everything he would tell me, and during the consultation, he was most specific that I noted every word correctly. I found it quite difficult to write down everything in longhand and attempted to abbreviate one of the facts he had mentioned. This he immediately picked up upon, saying 'No, this is what I actually said, please write that down correctly.' At the time I was unable to recognise or appreciate the slight differences his words conveyed, but he understood and offered me an explanation before I continued to record his predictions, correctly. Was it accurate? Amazingly so. I found Mir Bashir to be a very gifted man and one I was delighted to have met.

Bournemouth. We would be moving to the Isle of Wight within weeks, but prior to leaving Chadwell Heath, I received a surprising letter addressed from The Terrace Suite, The Roof Gardens, The Dorchester Hotel, London W1. 'I would like to thank you very much for the beautiful red roses you presented me with onstage during my last performance in Bournemouth.' I was overjoyed, to say the least.

Moving to 'the island' went smoothly and, as I explained earlier, I made the decision to stay in London during the week and travel to visit my parents at weekends. Something else was also happening in my life, although at this precise moment I hadn't recognised it! I was falling in love, and this was Love with a capital L. We had been friends for some time and knew each other well, but although I was always the dreamer, I never dared to dream he could be in love with me. I had never truly been in love before and I needed to be sure before speaking of such things. One thing was certain, I understood every word of every love song Shirley sang and it made me feel wonderful.

CHAPTER 14

NEVER, NEVER, NEVER

The summer of 1972 was bliss. I discovered I was truly in love as well as something even more magical: he was in love with me. We had been friends for some time before we declared our feelings to each other that summer. Once we did, we realised our love was extremely precious. Our souls united, as if we had been in love before, in another time, another place. We couldn't explain, but the feeling was blissful and we were overwhelmingly happy.

I had been blessed to have been brought up by parents who loved each other so much. When I told my mum that I had received a proposal of marriage, her reply was, 'Do you love him (my parents knew him well)?' When I explained to Mum just how much I loved him, she said, 'Well that's all right, then.' What a reply! That's what true love is all about. On 31 August we became engaged and, at the time, it was the happiest day of my life. We planned for an April wedding and the rest of our lives together.

It would require a book, probably several volumes, to explain the events and characters that lay ahead of us, but by the end of October the man who loved me wrote, 'I think it's best if we do not see each other again.' On reading those words, I felt I would die.

Meanwhile, following the British tour, Shirley had never been more popular. During the summer months, magazines featured news stories of family holidays in Sardinia. Cabaret, television appearances and record releases continued, feeding the public's demand to experience Shirley's remarkable talent. Life for a fan couldn't have been much better, but by the end of the year, for me, life was hard. Somehow I existed from day to day, thanks to my family, members of his family, friends and my passion for anything Shirley Bassey.

I was momentary lifted from my cloudy grey world when watching television one evening. On returning to Britain, it came as a big surprise to Shirley, as she stepped off her plane, to be met by Eamonn Andrews, host of *This Is Your Life*, dressed in a pilot's uniform. With that famous red book in his hand, a shocked Shirley was then driven to the television studio where I watched family and friends taking part in what was one of the most memorable programmes in that popular series.

Then in December, I received tickets from the BBC inviting me to see Shirley record a television performance. A few days later, I travelled alone to the studio, longing to see Shirley. I settled into a seat, and then came an announcement that Shirley would not be appearing. In her place I watched Tony Bennett. He probably sang, 'I Left My Heart In San Francisco', but my heart was somewhere else.

Somehow I got through those dark days, weeks and months, then one morning on my way to work, I turned my head right to look at the traffic before crossing the road. When I reached the other side I had to stop and question myself. I realised I had spent the previous six months simply existing, not even bothering to look when I crossed a road. Mary, I told myself, you must have a wonderful guardian angel, but somehow life has to go on, you owe it to everyone.

I visited my aunt and uncle who lived in Hornchurch fairly often.

My uncle worked at the Ford Motor Company and sometimes, when he was working a night shift, I would stay the night to keep my aunt company, then travel into work the following morning. Auntie was my mum's sister and like my mum was blessed with a wonderful personality and could make you smile. She was fun to be with and a great cook, so I always looked forward to my visits.

One day in the spring of 1973, I arrived at my aunt's to find her listening to the radio whilst preparing dinner in the kitchen. She greeted me warmly as usual and then, rather enthusiastically asked, 'Have you heard Shirley's new record?' I said I hadn't, although I was aware a new single was due for release. Then my aunt said something rather odd, 'Are you sure you didn't ask Shirley to record the number?' 'Ask Shirley, I laughingly replied, 'how could I ask Shirley?' Auntie looked at me somewhat strangely, 'Well wait till you hear it, she replied, 'then you will know what I mean.'

A few days later I heard Shirley's new release and I cried. I understood exactly why my aunt had said what she did. 'Never, Never, Never', could have been written for me and I wasn't the only one saying so!

'Never, Never, Never', had started life as 'Grande, Grande, Grande', an Italian song, written by Tony Renis and Alberto Testa, which became a hit in Italy for Mina in 1972. It only required Norman Newell to write English lyrics and a mega hit for Shirley was in the making, not only in Britain but worldwide. In fact, it became her biggest hit in the United States since 'Goldfinger'. Opening with the line, 'I'd like to run away from you, but if you never found me, I would die', my love, on hearing the song for the first time whilst travelling by car with members of his family, insisted the radio be turned off. He couldn't bear to listen any more. For me, however, the best line comes later, 'although you always laugh at love, nothing else would be good enough for you'. Further into the song, according to the sheet music, come the words, 'I love you, hate you, love you, hate you…' I noted when Shirley performed the song over the years, she always slipped in an extra 'love you' (not finishing with the words, 'hate you'). I liked this addition and felt it had significance, especially as the song was always introduced at concerts with a reference to 'The Italian' (Sergio Novak). Perhaps 'Never, Never, Never' holds a special place in Shirley's heart too, just as it does in mine.

Shirley's growing success in the States led to a second tour which commenced in April 1973 and included two nights, in May, at the legendary Carnegie Hall in New York. How I would have loved to have been at Carnegie Hall, but a trip to the States was out of my league. The concerts were a sell-out and fortunately for all of her fans worldwide, they were recorded. When released by United Artists later in the year as a two-record set with booklet, entitled 'Shirley Bassey, Live at Carnegie Hall', listening to it I was blown away. The recording truly captured the electric atmosphere in the hall, allowing the listener to believe they were part of the standing ovation Shirley received before a note had been sung. Her performance throughout the album is simply breathtaking and the LP rightly became a classic.

Now that my life was getting back on an even keel, my previously established routine of contacting agents, theatre managers, television ticket offices and the record companies, resumed. Whenever I received any relevant information regarding Shirley's engagements, I would contact George and the girls from Birkenhead (Joyce and Reon) and they would reciprocate whenever they heard any news. This way we usually managed to 'keep ahead of the game', a great asset when booking theatre tickets. Still living in an age when not everyone owned a telephone, I in my Wanstead bedsit, shared a phone with all the other residents, so a written application to a theatre for tickets was still very much the norm. Waiting for the reply called for a lot of patience, but the excitement felt when your envelope arrived, and you held your tickets in your hand, is something an email cannot emulate, especially when you discovered the tickets were for the front row.

We had tickets for the front row of the stalls at the Royal Albert Hall that year, and Mum and Dad travelled from the Isle of Wight for the concert. Our excitement grew as we chatted with other fans outside the theatre prior to the doors opening. If my memory serves me well, it was during this tour that we first met Bill, Shirley's chauffeur, but more about that in the next chapter.

Although there are many entrances into the Royal Albert Hall, seat location determines the door through which you enter, but once inside it is easy to get lost along the corridor which encircles the vast auditorium. People travelled along it in both directions and should you have stopped, you would soon have recognised several faces. Tonight, celebrities were out in force to see the artist billed by promotor Robert Paterson as 'The World's Greatest Female Entertainer'. Although we, her fans, had known that for years, I still feared there may have been one or two critics in the hall hoping Shirley might strike a wrong note. Even then, like the present day, some of the press just wanted to report a negative story.

Entering the vast auditorium, we were dazzled by its grandeur of red and gold as we approached our seats. Located near to the stage, our seats offered a lovely viewing opportunity but unfortunately no access to the gangway in front of the stage – a disadvantage for me, but at less I knew Shirley would be able to see (and hear) me clearly from my seat. I guess I always believed it must be nice for her to spot a friendly face when first walking out to face her audience. Tonight there would be no need to worry; Shirley's fans were all around, waiting to present her with a standing ovation, prior to singing a note, just as they had at New York's Carnegie Hall.

Emerging from the rear, centre stage, between an orchestra divided on either side, Shirley looked every bit a superstar in a beautiful pink Douglas Darnell gown. With matching sleeveless coat and a flowing train, the edges of the coat were trimmed with a wide border of pink ostrich feathers. A few of the finer feathers took flight and could be seen drifting in the spotlight's beam, as Shirley stretched her arms out to acknowledge the crowds spontaneous applause. Exposing the coat's silver lining and the gown's five strands of pearls, which lapped diagonally across her dress, pink sequins scattered starbursts around the hall. The lines of pearls gathered at the top of Shirley's right shoulder, held by what seemed to be a cluster of jewels, then dropped down alongside her arm. The dress was simply stunning and immediately became my favourite. The audience loved it too, judging by the cheers and wows that sounded when the silver gown was unfurled.

As the large orchestra, led by Arthur Greenslade, continued to play the opening notes from the arrangements, Shirley graciously accepted a standing ovation from her British fans, and how pleased we were to give it! Singing at her best, songs such as 'Let Me Sing And I'm Happy', 'Day By Day', 'Something', 'I'd Like To Hate Myself In The Morning' and 'Big Spender' echoed around the hall to everyone's delight. Albert would have loved it, that's for sure!

Between numbers a small number of dedicated fans approached the stage to offer small gifts, flowers and a handshake full of love. All were warmly received before the lights dimmed once again and we settled into a stillness which came prior to the introduction to 'Never, Never, Never'. I probably anticipated the number a few fractions of a second quicker than the rest of the audience and jumped to my feet, applauding loudly. My effort was rewarded with a smiling nod from Shirley as she started to gently sing, 'I'd like to run away from you… (maybe she meant it!)'. As I sat back down in my seat, Mum and Dad stared ahead at Shirley, for which I was grateful, because in spite of all my efforts I could not hold back the tears which were starting to slide down my face. My stomach tightened and I wiped a few more tears away. This was the first time I had seen Shirley sing the song live, *my song*, so I had expected the pain. However, Shirley's extra 'love you' at the end, help to dry my tears and I managed to cheer bravely, along with Mum and Dad. They both knew what the song's implications meant to me, so when I turned to Mum, it came as no surprise to see her loving smile.

Shirley was acknowledging the crowd when a well-dressed gentleman walked out onto the stage, carrying what looked like large picture frames. Cheers rang out as people realised it was the television and radio presenter David Frost, there to surprise Shirley by presenting her with ten gold discs. More songs followed as fans flocked to the stage until finally, after several encores, the party really was over. It had been a fabulous evening.

The next day Mum and Dad travelled back to the Isle of Wight and I wrote to Joyce and Reon about the performances we had seen. The girls also attended several concerts during Shirley's British tour, so now I would look forward to hearing there news too!

The year ended with Shirley Bassey being voted the 'Most Exciting Female Singer on TV' by the readers of *TV Times*. Mum, Dad and I had posted separate votes along with thousands of other fans in Britain. Everyone had taken Shirley to their heart after watching TV performances, during one of which she sang 'Never, Never, Never' – *my song!*

CHAPTER 15

BILL

At the start of the mid-seventies, I had begun to settle back into my routine and life was looking more positive. At the start of the new year I had sent Shirley a birthday card, as I always did, together with a letter relating to her previous tour and record release. I never expected to receive a reply, Shirley by that time had hundreds of thousands of fans worldwide and quite honestly no reply was necessary. So imagine my surprise when a letter arrived from Shirley, which read as follows:

> I would like to thank you very much for your Birthday Wishes. Thank you also for letting me know how much you and your parents enjoyed my performance at the Royal Albert Hall.
>
> I must agree with you, 'Live at Carnegie Hall' is a great record. The producer did a great job by capturing that fantastic, electrifying atmosphere of Carnegie Hall.
>
> Best wishes for a happy 1974 to you and your parents,

Yours Sincerely,
Shirley Bassey [hand signed]

Needless to say, my parents and I were absolutely delighted. I couldn't get over my excitement for weeks, but more importantly, we were all delighted that it had been posted from Lugano, Switzerland. We knew this meant Shirley was spending some time at home with her family. Her work schedule each year was incredible, but it was nice to think Sergio was arranging some family time together, in addition to Shirley's professional engagements. A recent *TV Times* article had featured several holiday photos of Shirley, Sergio and their family at their holiday villa in Sardinia. Shirley had looked so relaxed and happy; it was a delight to see.

There was no time to relax for long, though; for soon Shirley would be embarking on more tours: Germany, Belgium and Holland. The Far East beckoned in the summer, where Shirley recorded another live performance at the Kosei Nenkin Kaikan hall in Tokyo, Japan. At the time, the double LP was released exclusively in Japan, and since we were living in a world without the Internet, Shirley's British fans were unaware of its existence.

When August came, it was time to wish Shirley a 'Happy Wedding Anniversary'. The following month I was delighted to receive another letter from her. 'Your congratulations for our 6th wedding anniversary were very welcome.'

But better news was to follow: 'I'll be in England very shortly for my yearly concert tour; here are the dates.' Listed were all the venues and dates throughout the UK. Finally, Shirley wrote, 'Hope you'll be able to find good seats.'

The tour would be opening in Bournemouth, at the Winter Gardens theatre, on 30 September 1974, and I was even more thrilled when I read that Shirley would be appearing for two nights. Shirley's popularity had increased demand, now two nights at each venue around Britain would become the norm. I couldn't write my letters to the theatres quickly enough – after all, Shirley wanted me to have good seats! – and later the same day, my requests for tickets were in the post. I had phoned my parents and we decided there and then to spend the couple of days 'on holiday' in Bournemouth – what a holiday that would be.

Concerts on this tour, along with Shirley's future tours during the seventies, were wonderful experiences for me. I have previously written about the fantastic atmosphere the Winter Gardens produced, but in addition it was also a very exciting place to be a fan, as it offered opportunities not easily accessible at other concert halls. To add to this, during these years, I formed a friendship with Shirley's chauffeur. Bill was a tall good-looking guy, with a great sense of humour and clearly very good at his job. Naturally, he had a great respect for Shirley but he also showed respect to her fans. Always loving a cup of tea, whenever an opportunity arose, Bill would join Mum, Dad and I at a table in the café, even though I often had my ear next to the wooden doors dividing the café and auditorium, trying to listen to Shirley rehearse.

Our 'holidays' always started for me the moment we arrived in Bournemouth. We had booked to stay for a few nights at the Winter Gardens Hotel, located a short walk from the theatre's stage-door entrance. Mum and Dad could actually see the entrance from their bedroom window, that's how close it was. After checking in at the hotel, we made our way to the theatre café where we had a sandwich and a cuppa and chatted to some of the members of the orchestra, who were now beginning to assemble. As this was the first date of the tour, a rehearsal had been arranged; the word 'rehearsal' was magic to my ears since it meant Shirley would probably attend. We didn't have to wait long before news spread among the gathered group, Shirley would be arriving soon.

Only a few fans were waiting by the stage door area when the big black limo (a Rolls-Royce Phantom or Daimler) turned into the grounds, slowly coming to a halt near the stage-door. Sergio and Shirley seemed happy as they emerged from the limo and Shirley posed for me to take a photo. Mum spent a few moments chatting with Shirley, as always asking her how she was and telling Shirley how lovely it was to see her again. Shirley signed a few autographs before finally heading into the theatre. Sergio, as ever, smiled and came and had a chat, once Shirley was settled in her dressing room. With no pushing crowds, it was very relaxed and civil. Thrilled by our encounter, we returned to the café to get a good seat (next to the adjoining doors) from which we could hear the rehearsal for the price of a cup of tea. I was always amazed that so few people gathered in the café during the afternoon, I don't know, perhaps they 'closed' the café but allowed us to stay since we were attending the concert. Whatever, it was fabulous. Even today, I can still recall how I felt when I first heard Shirley sing a few notes, without the full orchestra. I laugh today when I see a vocalist, licking a microphone as though they are about to eat an ice cream. If they were to stand back a few inches from the mic, we probably wouldn't hear them; well, perhaps that would be a good thing! Thankfully, I lived in an amazing time, when I could listen to Shirley perfecting every note, sometimes without any microphone, with only a wooden partition between us.

The first day we were booked for the evening's first performance and had superb front-row seats. We had booked a table at a nearby restaurant to have dinner after the show and then planned to return to the theatre in the hope of seeing Shirley leave after her second concert performance.

During the afternoon Bill surprised me by asking if I would like to keep him company when he went to have dinner after the concert. Obviously, it would be late, but he told my parents he would see me safely back to the hotel. Since Bill and I got on well and shared a similar sense of humour, I wanted to go, so my parents raised no objection. So after Shirley's second concert that evening, we joined the crowds gathered by the stage door. Bill came out and told everyone that Shirley would be leaving shortly but asked us all to stand clear of the car as he drove out of the grounds, since he didn't want anyone to be injured. He told us he would switch on the interior car lights and drive away slowly so that we would all have an opportunity to see Shirley and wave goodnight. A few moments later Shirley came out smiling, entered the car to the sounds of cheering fans, and waved happily as Bill slowly drove away. Mum and Dad stayed with me while I waited for Bill to return. For some reason I thought he would be driving his own car, so you can imagine how my mouth dropped when he collected me in Shirley's limo. The wave I offered my parents as we drove away was rather like the one often see being given by Her Majesty!

At that late hour most places were closing but Bill knew a café which stayed open till late. I will never forget the look on the faces of the customers as we emerged from the limo, me dressed up in my fake fur jacket and Bill in his chauffeur's uniform. All eyes stayed fixed upon us as we chatted away, Bill tucking into what today would be referred to as 'A Big Boy's Breakfast', while I had coffee and cake!

As Bill pulled up outside the hotel where I was staying, I noticed the slight movement of the curtain at my parent's bedroom. Dad was just checking that I had arrived home safely, even though I was in my mid-twenties. Good old Dad!

The next morning, during breakfast, my parents wanted to know about our evening adventure and I tried to explain what it felt like to have been driven in such a beautiful car. Bill had mentioned during the evening that he was going to clean the car the next day, so I'd offered to help. He had laughed and said, 'OK then, I'll see you tomorrow,' but I don't think he expected me to show. After breakfast, Mum, Dad and I strolled around the shops and gardens of Bournemouth, as well as the Royal Bath Hotel, where Shirley and Sergio were staying. Then, after having a little lunch at the theatre café, I was ready to help clean the limo! Actually I have always enjoyed cleaning cars, so to be able to clean Shirley's limo was an exciting experience for me, plus I would have a lesson from Bill on how to 'professionally' clean a limo and the experience might prove useful.

Bill and I had great fun. When we had finished the car was sparkling and I felt rather proud of my handiwork. At the time I carried some business cards which I used for promoting my portrait drawing, so I took out my pen, crossed out the words '*portrait drawings*' and wrote '*car wash services*', then handed the card to Bill. He laughed out loud and said 'I'm keeping this to give to Shirley.'

Later that afternoon, Bill said, 'Would you like to come to the first concert tonight?' (Bill knew we were attending the second concert that evening.) 'I'd love to go', I replied. We then arranged a time to meet and I hurried off to tell Mum and Dad. We had already made an early reservation for dinner, so we would be back at the theatre to see Shirley arrive; now I just needed to get myself ready.

We arrived back at the theatre shortly before Shirley's arrival. It always felt special to be there to welcome Shirley, who offered a cheeky smile as she went into the theatre. Mum and Dad then decided to go for a drink, so I arranged to meet them at the bar after the show. It wasn't long before Bill appeared. 'I gave Shirley your card,' he said. 'What!' I replied. 'What did she say?' Bill replied, 'She asked me why did you do it [wash the car], so I told her.' He said nothing more on the subject, and then beckoned me to follow him. 'If anyone stops you, just say you are with me,' he said as he led me through the corridors backstage. Within seconds we were passing Shirley's dressing room just as Sergio came out.

'Hello,' he said, and walked off in the opposite direction. I naturally thought Bill was leading me towards the rear of the auditorium where I would be offered a seat, but suddenly we turned between some curtains and I was standing in the wings! 'Now stay here until I come back after Shirley's performance and whatever happens don't applaud or cheer, save that for the next performance.' I turned to see the orchestra onstage, almost at my side. As I looked to the right, I could see the first few rows of the audience. I turned to speak to Bill but he had gone and I was alone onstage, but not for long. The musicians started to play the overture and as I looked straight ahead to the opposite side of the stage from where I was standing, I suddenly saw Shirley silhouetted by the stage lights. I thought I must be dreaming and had to pinch myself, and then she stepped out from the wings and took centre stage. The audience went wild; how I managed to control myself, I don't know, for there I was experiencing just what it was like to be Shirley Bassey, the world's greatest female entertainer, that night in Bournemouth.

I couldn't take my eyes off her as I watched and listened to each individual note, trying to record every detail in my brain as she sang, 'Let Me Sing And I'm Happy', 'Something', 'Nobody Does It Like Me', 'Big Spender' and 'Never, Never, Never', to name just a few. The emotion, the precision, the voice reached out to our souls and in return the audience sent back love via their cheering and applause. Towards the end fans came down to the stage, as I had done on many occasions, to shake Shirley's hand. Some offered flowers, some small gifts; all were welcomed with a handshake. I knew just how happy they were feeling and it was lovely to see just how wonderful it looked and felt from Shirley's viewpoint.

I watched as Shirley returned to the wings, and then waited for that precise moment before she returned centre stage. Sometimes she would take a sip from a glass prior to her return and then, towards the finish, another silhouette appeared to help Shirley with the silver-lined coat, trimmed with feathers. This was the signal the end was drawing near. Shirley returned walking slowly along the entire width of the stage as hands rose up out of the darkness. The house lights went up, now the faces of the fans with the outstretched arms, could be seen. Shirley's hand reached out to them all. As hands joined, the cheering continued until finally Shirley took centre stage to end her concert appropriately with the number 'Greatest Performance' ('Tonight I Gave The Greatest Performance Of My Life'). The performance left nobody in any doubt!

Shirley rushed off to the wings and was gone in a matter of seconds. I was left speechless, looking down at the front-row seats where, in another hour or so, I would be sitting. From one dream into another, I thought. Bill brought me back to reality fairly quickly, or maybe it was the chill of the night air as I left the stage-door area. 'Before you go,' said Bill, 'can you just wait by the car as I have to collect a few things which need to go in the boot?' Minutes later Bill placed some packages in the car, and then went back inside again before returning with a massive bouquet of flowers. I was speechless when he handed then to me and said, 'They are for your mum.' 'But they are Shirley's flowers, I can't take them,' I replied. Bill smiled and said, 'I've been told what I have to do with them'! 'Please, please, please thank Shirley', I replied. Bill just laughed, as usual. 'I'll see you after the show,' he said.

I don't know who was happier that evening. I took the flowers back to our hotel before going into the bar to meet Mum and Dad. 'Did you enjoy the show?' was a rather silly question from my dad but I knew what he meant since he followed the comment with, 'Where were you sitting?' I replied, 'I had to stand, Dad,' taking a silent pause before adding, 'but I stood on the stage, in the wings.' They were quite emotional when I told them what Bill had done. Then I turned to Mum and said, 'I have a surprise for you too. Bill handed me a beautiful bouquet of flowers for you, from Shirley.' Mum was speechless as tears started to fill her eyes.

Well, as you can imagine, we were the happiest fans in the theatre at Shirley's second performance. Once again, the atmosphere was magical and she gave her all. At the end all three of us went up to the edge of the stage to shake Shirley's hand and offer a big 'thank you'. We couldn't have been happier or more excited had we had just won the top prize on the pools!

After the show we went round to the stage-door area. Several fans had already started to gather as Bill positioned the limo near to the exit. When he saw us he called me over and said, 'Mary, stand by this door and when Shirley is inside, close the door for me.' Then, having told the crowd what was going to happen, he added, 'And don't make the car dirty, Mary spent all day cleaning this.' Everyone around laughed, not really knowing whether he was joking!

Shirley emerged to tremendous cheers and I successfully closed the door, then Bill slowly pulled away to the sound of applause. We watched until we saw the internal car lights go out as the car headed into the darkness.

Bill drove for Shirley whenever she toured during the winter months, then he would venture off to Spain for the summer to enjoy his passion – fishing. I remember on one occasion, he drove me in Shirley's limo and asked me to 'mind the car' while he went into Woolworths to buy some fishing tackle. What a laugh!

I met up with Bill only on a few other occasions during those years. We would talk about life and rarely spoke about Shirley, but I do remember one day he said, 'I will tell you one thing, there are some fans Shirley likes an awful lot, but just as I will always be a chauffeur to Shirley, you will always be a fan, regardless of what may happen to us in life. That's just the way it is with Shirley.' Those words always remained with me. So Bill, if you ever get to read this book you can take a little credit for its working title,[5] because I am still a fan and very proud to remain one.

The last time I saw Bill, on tour with Shirley, he was looking forward to returning to Spain and left saying, 'I expect I'll see you when I get back next year.' I never did see Bill again. I like to think he may have settled in Spain to enjoy his dream. Whatever, I hope life has been good to him.

---

5 My original title for this book was *I Am What I Am – A Fan.*

CHAPTER 16

SEND IN THE CLOWNS

When Shirley returned to Britain for her 1976 tour, there was a new man in my life. A very good friend had gifted to me a single lens reflex (SLR) camera and as my small bedsit was inadequate for me to continue with my portrait drawing, I decided to pursue my interest in photography, joining the local Wanstead and Leytonstone Camera Club. It was here that I met Bernard.

Bernard was a semi-professional double-bass player with a love for jazz. He greatly admired many musicians and performers, but I had already realised he would never be a fan of anyone, that just wasn't part of his character. However, Bernard was a perfectionist, so I was convinced he would appreciate Shirley's talent and professionalism if he were to see her live in concert, so it was arranged: Bernard would join Mum, Dad and I at the Royal Albert Hall in May. First, however, I would spend a few days in Bournemouth with my parents, attending Shirley's opening concerts and where I dared to dream of capturing some 'action' photographs.

Back in Wanstead I often admired the flowers and arrangements in a small florist's shop located near to my bedsit. I frequently had ideas for presenting Shirley with flowers at Bournemouth, but with my limited knowledge of Bournemouth's florists, I had some reservations as to what could be achieved. Then, one day when I was walking home, I saw a wonderful display of silk flowers in the local florist's window. These artificial flowers were stunning; they looked almost real, were delicate and came in a wide variety of both flowers and colours. For once, a bouquet did not have to be enclosed in cellophane and kept; it could look as beautiful on the day it was given as it had looked on the day of purchase. I stared at the florist's window for some time before deciding to present Shirley with a silk-flower bouquet at the Bournemouth performance.

When I collected the bouquet, which consisted of pink roses, in a variety of shades, and apple blossom, it looked stunning. The florist had done a lovely job and told me she felt very proud that I would be giving the bouquet to Shirley Bassey. With the bouquet boxed up, under my arm, I travelled home to the IOW and I couldn't wait to show my parents. There was great delight when I took the flowers out from the box; my mum and dad hadn't seen silk flowers like these before and thought they were lovely. I was sure Shirley would love them too!

A few days later when Dad drove the car onto the ferry at Yarmouth for our trip across the Solent to Lymington, it marked the start of our short break to Bournemouth. From Lymington, the drive west towards Bournemouth now took on a familiar feel and after an hour or so, we had arrived at the Winter Gardens Hotel. After being shown to our rooms, I safely laid my 'box of treasure' on the bed before rushing across to the theatre where I met up with a few fans and happily discovered that Shirley had not yet arrived – panic over. George Webb arrived and we spent some time chatting about Shirley's latest record and press reports.

It wasn't long we sensed the activity around us increasing, so we headed out to the stage door and didn't have long to wait. Shirley emerged from her limo smiling as we welcomed her, then I asked her if it would be all right to take some photos during her concert, stressing I would not use flash or cause any disturbance. I'm delighted to say Shirley said it would be OK and I happily thanked her. I realised she was putting her trust in me and I was determined not to abuse the situation. Throughout the years that followed, I am delighted to say that whenever I asked Shirley for permission to photograph during a concert, it was never refused. I like to feel she appreciated that I tried to show consideration and respect whenever I clicked that shutter.

Once Shirley was inside the theatre, our small band of fans gathered in the café to listen to the magic! On one occasion following a rehearsal, we were chatting excitedly about Shirley's performance when one of the musician's near us commented, 'She wouldn't be able to sing without a full orchestra.' Well, that was like a red flag to a bull. I told him, in no uncertain terms, that he had no idea what he was talking about. I don't know if Shirley, or someone else overheard our confrontation with the musician but what happened later that evening, towards the end of Shirley's concert, was really uncanny.

Wearing a sparkling black gown covered by a coat of gold brocade, trimmed with ostrich feathers, Shirley walked onstage to a thunderous reception from an audience that had grown to love her more and more every year since her first performance at the Winter Gardens. I had decided to present Shirley with the silk flower arrangement towards the end of that night's performance, then I could concentrate on taking some photographs the following evening when we had ideal seats, front row just left of centre stage. Tonight I would not only listen to every note, I would watch Shirley intensely and mentally record in my head the perfect moments, preparing for tomorrow's concert when I would release the shutter and hopefully capture the shot I wanted.

Over the years I had come to realise that Shirley had an acute sense of hearing, so I wanted to consciously take my photos when Shirley was either singing a loud note or then the audience was applauding. Any noise I made with the camera, when the shutter fired and I wound on the film, as we had to do in those days, would then be reduced to a minimum and not disturb anyone seated nearby. It was fortunate that black-and-white film was available, which allowed me to photograph in low-lighting conditions without using a flash. (The Winter Gardens theatre would announce, before Shirley took to the stage, no flash photography permitted, thereby permitting photography without flash!)

I sat close to the stage with my parents as Shirley sang her way through a tremendous programme. 'Let Me Sing And I'm Happy', 'Yesterday When I Was Young', plus a string of hits including 'Big Spender', 'Never, Never, Never' and 'Something', all featured, receiving loud applause and cheers from the audience. As well as our old favourites, Shirley always included new songs from her most recent LP releases and I particularly enjoyed hearing these, watching gestures which I had imagined whilst playing the tracks at home. On this occasion I hoped Shirley would feature my favourite track from the *Good, Bad But Beautiful* LP, but it never came. I came to the conclusion that the song from the musical *A Little Night Music* was perhaps more suited as an album track than a live number!

After Shirley had performed a few numbers, one or two fans approached the stage to shake her hand. Returning to centre stage, Shirley raised her left hand and exposed her little finger dressed in a splint; she asked the audience to be gentle. She explained her finger had been injured by an overenthusiastic fan at a recent concert (you can just see the injured finger in my photos). As always, we wanted the concert to go on for ever, but realisation strikes that it won't when songs such as 'The Party's Over' or 'This Is My Life' echo around the auditorium. Time for me to jump up from my seat with my flowers and approach the stage, where Shirley was already shaking hands with a few fans. I waited as the audience's applause seemed to hit me in waves, in unison with my fast-beating heart. Shirley turned and smiled and I handed up my bouquet with its large pink ribbon. Thanking me, we 'gently' shook hands before Shirley laid the bouquet across her left arm, to support it, as she progressed along the stage to greet some other fans, who by now had assembled at the far end of the stage. George managed to capture the moment with his camera, and he later sent me a photo, which I still have to this day. In the photo Shirley is holding the flowers whilst I am cheering and applauding as I walk back to my seat.

Although I cannot be positive as to the exact date it started, during the late seventies, Shirley regularly received flowers onstage from the theatre management. I believe this gesture prompted Shirley to hand out flowers to her fans, an expression of love that she maintained throughout her concert tour years.

Back in my seat, Mum and Dad were smiling proudly. I gaze up at Shirley as she started to sing her final number. When it was over the audience erupted and Shirley graciously thanked us before heading offstage. It can't be over; the applause was deafening and shouts for more echoed back from every corner of the theatre. Minutes seemed to pass, yet there was no let-up. 'We want more', the audience yelled. Cheers rose as Shirley returned to the stage. 'One more,' she said to the people standing at her feet, who responded by requesting their own particular favourite. I shouted out, 'Send In The Clowns', but no response. Again I pleaded, 'Send In The Clowns', but my voice was silenced by the roaring of the crowd. A few moments later Shirley chatted with her musical director before returning to the microphone to acknowledge the applause. Finally, Shirley announced, 'I'm going to sing a song *without* the orchestra since they do not have the music with them.' Then looking directly down to me, she added, 'It's called, "Send In The Clowns".' Her musical director, after walking to the piano, began to play the introduction to Stephen Sondheim's haunting melody. Shirley began to sing, interpreting the words and music so beautifully. It was simply magic and I am certain the memory of that performance stayed with everyone lucky enough to be in the audience, for a very long time. It remains one of my most treasured memories.

With the audience cheering and applauding like never before, Shirley left the stage – nothing could have followed that performance. I sat numb in my seat and wondered whether Shirley had heard about our 'conversation' with the musician! I really don't know, but if she had not, it was an incredible coincidence that she had chosen to sing without an orchestra! Eventually I glanced in the direction of the musician with whom we had spoken. He looked very sheepish and lowered his head. Nothing further needed to be said – our case had been proved beyond reasonable doubt!

It took me ages to get to sleep that night. I laid in bed, my head in a spin, songs ringing out and images flowing before my eyes. It had been a wonderful concert and tomorrow we would experience another, which I knew would be just as wonderful. Finally, sleep came.

The following evening Mum, Dad and I settled into our seats in the front row. The SLR camera, with its telephoto lens, sat on my lap. I was experiencing my usual mix of excitement and apprehension, which I had grown to accept – it was part of being a fan. Tonight, however, I had an added challenge, one which I had imposed upon myself. I wanted to capture some perfect images of Shirley in concert. During her performance, as I photographed, I constantly watched Shirley for any signs that might indicate that I was overstepping the mark, but my actions didn't seem to concern her in any way. In fact the smiles and eye contact which came our way helped relieve my apprehension.

I felt I had captured some good shots but nothing would be certain until the film was processed, which I would do, once home. Dad and I discussed how much extra development time we should allow to compensate for the lighting conditions and thankfully we judged correctly. We were delighted when we viewed the roll of negatives; we had some great images of Shirley. Once back at work, I stayed late one evening to produce a few prints. I was so excited by the results and longed to show Mum and Dad.

A few days later I received a letter from The Dorchester Hotel, London, from Shirley, in which she said:

> Thank you very much for the most beautiful silk flowers you presented to me in Bournemouth.
>
> Thank you also for your note. It is a fabulous feeling to know that I have so many loyal Fans like yourself and your parents.
>
> Kind regards, Shirley Bassey.

When I read that letter, it was a fabulous feeling for me!

Only days later we were back at the Royal Albert Hall and on this occasion we were joined by Bernard. Mum and Dad had met Bernard on a few occasions, but Bernard had never previously seen Shirley live in concert. Obviously he had watched several of Shirley's television performances and although he had enjoyed them and admired her professionalism, he would never regard himself as a fan. To put it simply, Bernard wasn't the type to be a fan to anybody even though he enjoyed great music. Actually, he loved music and would name Frank Sinatra, Ella Fitzgerald, Peggy Lee and Tony Bennett amongst his favourite performers, but a fan – no! His music was jazz, so to hear Shirley in concert and watch the reaction of her fans, including myself, was going to be a new experience.

On this occasion we had seats in one of the boxes which encircle the stalls. These were lovely seats from which to indulge in Shirley's concert, not only offering privacy but an opportunity to watch her performance from an entirely different perspective to those we had enjoyed so much at Bournemouth. When Shirley took to the stage, she received a welcome perfectly appropriate for the world-class performer she had become. An hour or so later she left the stage to a chorus of cheers for more and thunderous applause from an adoring audience. Shirley, as ever, had given her all.

I am delighted to say Bernard enjoyed the concert and was also impressed with the photos I had taken. Later I submitted two of the prints to our camera-club monthly competition and impressed the judges – I guess you could say they were a big hit, reaching the top of the hit parade! I hope you like them too.

CHAPTER 17

YOU TAKE MY HEART AWAY

Happy and in love, when it came to work, I felt I needed a new challenge. I had enjoyed working at Queen Mary College but past ghosts lingered and I knew it was time for a change, so in 1976 I applied for the position of medical representative with a pharmaceutical company and, to my surprise, I was offered the job. Initially I had to attend an intense training course and I have to admit there was more than one occasion when I wondered if I had done the right thing. I had to study quite a bit and so my 'fan duties', as I call them, had to take a back seat for a while.

I had, however, sent requests to the BBC for tickets to attend any appearance by Shirley on a television show. Her popularity resulted in the BBC offering Shirley her first six-part TV series later that year, and I was fortunate due to my pre-planning to get tickets to attend some of the shows. In the studio, I loved to watch Shirley give a perfect performance, but I admit I secretly wished she would make a mistake, so I could hear her sing again. Occasionally we would be rewarded with a retake when a technical problem occurred, then Shirley would simply smile and re-record the number.

In October, Shirley featured on the front cover of the *Radio Times* and I remember, every Saturday night for six weeks, the excitement at home as I watched the show with my parents. Shirley also starred at the Royal Variety Performance in November, the show was broadcast live, but sadly on that occasion, I was unable to attend. Life as a fan in 1977 was relatively quiet. When Shirley was abroad, it was always more difficult to get information regarding her engagements. I had heard she would be returning to the States and Japan, but news was limited and I can't remember any further details appearing in the press at that time.

Bernard and I had an important overseas engagement of our own. We had decided we wanted to spend our lives together and chose Rome as our destination to celebrate our engagement and my birthday. It was all very romantic; Bernard had secretly packed an orchid in his hand luggage, as well as the ring which he presented to me on the morning of my birthday. I had taken with me a lovely congratulations card from Mum and Dad together with some money they had given us to celebrate with. Bernard had bought a bottle of champagne, which he had arranged to be placed in the hotel's fridge, but his plan to have a celebration drink at breakfast was postponed when he discovered the fridge had been locked and nobody available had a key! Our morning was spent amongst the stray cats in the majestic Colosseum before having lunch in a delightful restaurant overlooking the Amphitheatre's facade. The restaurant staff certainly knew how to spot a couple in love and asked if we were celebrating a special occasion. After announcing we had become engaged, the waiter appeared with two glasses of brandy and, in broken English said, 'On the house, congratulations.'

It had become a family joke when my mum, on seeing a photo of Bernard for the first time, said he looked like 'Aunt Ada', so when we saw a lovely restaurant in the afternoon called Sergio and Ada's, we had to book a table. We had a fabulous evening and Rome stole our hearts.

In the summer when United Artists released Shirley's latest album, *You Take My Heart Away*, the choice of tracks seemed uncanny. 'Perfect

Strangers', 'This One Is For You', 'I Need To Be In Love', 'Stargazer' and Paul McCartney's 'Silly Love Songs', to name a few. I was not alone in my love for this album; her fans worldwide adored it.

When Robert Paterson announced Shirley's 25th Anniversary Tour, it was rather surprising to see only six venues: the Brighton Centre, Royal Albert Hall, Preston's Guild Hall, Birmingham's Odeon, Manchester's Free Trade Hall and Glasgow's Kelvin Hall. I immediately booked tickets for Brighton and London – it was going to be a great birthday.

When Shirley arrived back in Britain for the start of her tour she announced her intention to semi-retire, news that stirred the press into action. Perhaps this may have been one of the reasons that led to the change of venues. Arranging for Shirley to perform two or three nights at each venue also relieved the pressures of touring. In the official concert programme Peter Clayton, BBC jazz presenter and author of a number of articles and sleeve notes, implied in his article that the process had already begun 'with a cutting down on the touring, an even greater choosiness in the selection of dates and venues, the spending of more time at home'.[6]

However, public demand to see Shirley had increased tremendously during the previous decade and I am sure the choice of venues had been selected to meet ticket-sale expectations. Some of these halls held between four and five thousand people, a vast difference in capacity compared to Bournemouth's Winter Gardens and the like.

The Brighton Centre, a new futuristic building when it opened in 1977, did not hit the right notes with me, but then I guess it wasn't part of the plan to make it easy for fans wanting to see their idol at a stage door! The auditorium was vast and our seats on the night, although central, were ten rows back from the stage, a distance unfamiliar to me

---

6 Peter Clayton's article was again reproduced in the 1979 tour programme and sleeve notes for *Shirley Bassey – 25th Anniversary Album*.

at a Shirley Bassey concert. Selfish I know, but I had grown to love the front row, although I knew the day would come when I would have to relinquish my place. When I turned around to look at the audience sitting behind, I suddenly realised how fortunate we were and felt rather sorry for the fans at the back. How could they possibly see Shirley?

The other aspect relating to the audience which I clearly remember was the number of 'nice young men' sitting near to us. I had never really taken any notice of this before and was reminded of something Bernard and I had heard at a Rod McKuen concert. Rod McKuen had said, 'It does not matter who you love, or what you love, what's important is that you love.' Those words have stayed with me all my life and somehow seemed very appropriate that night in Brighton.

It goes without saying that both of the concerts we attended (Brighton and London) were wonderful, with Shirley singing her heart out through a catalogue of successful hits that stretched across her twenty-five years in show business. She added a few new ones but it was probably 'Goldfinger', 'I Who Have Nothing', 'Something', and 'Big Spender' that drew the loudest cheers and generated a surge from the fans, anxious to stretch out a hand, present a flower or offer a gift. Shirley greeted each and every one with a smile to melt their heart and eventually they returned to their seats no doubt mesmerised by the experience.

I remember at the Royal Albert Hall a young lad, no more than ten years old, who sat in front of us with his father. Shirley had briefly chatted about semi-retirement during her concert, the lad was heartbroken and near to tears as he looked at his father and said, 'We will never see her again.' His father reassured him with these words: 'Don't worry, they all say that, we will come and see her again next year.' That little lad went away very happy and I am sure he still remains a fan today.

There was a wonderful atmosphere as we left the Hall; you could hear voices all around making comments such as, 'I never expected her to be that good', 'wasn't she wonderful', 'such a powerful voice', 'she just gets better and better'. Well, I agreed with everyone as we made our way back to the car. We were all so happy and to top it all, in a month's time I would be marrying Bernard.

We were married on the Isle of Wight at Newport Registry Office, a blessing followed at St Blasius Church in Shanklin, with a reception at the village of Niton. I carried a bouquet of silk pink roses and apple blossoms similar to the flowers I had presented to Shirley in Bournemouth. After our honeymoon Bernard and I each returned to our separate bedsits where we stayed for the next few months until we were able to move into our new home together. Seems unbelievable today, but that's how it happened then.

Whilst we were beginning married life in a house of our own, Shirley had returned to Australia, a country that adored her and was close to Shirley's heart. Later, rumours started to circulate about a breakdown of her marriage and the press started to dig.

The release by United Artists of *Shirley Bassey – 25th Anniversary Album*, a double album which climbed to No. 3 in the British Charts, reached the No. 1 position in Australia and went on to gain Shirley a platinum disc. Having returned to perform at a concert for Prince Charles at Caerphilly, Ron Bell, the court photographer, captured a lovely photograph of Shirley with the Prince clutching a copy of Shirley's album. The photograph was published the next day in several newspapers.

In the spring of 1979, Shirley returned again to Britain to record her second series of *The Shirley Bassey Show* for the BBC. The series was fantastic and featured film clips of Shirley in an assortment of unusual locations such as Cape Canaveral with Captain Charles Conrad, the third man to walk on the moon. (Many of these clips can now be seen on YouTube.) Apart from the location filming, most of the show's content was recorded at the BBC's Television Theatre at

Shepherds Bush Green, London. I luckily attended a number of the recordings since both my parents and I would send in a request for tickets. Fortunately we had both received tickets for the show to be recorded on 14 March. Mum and Dad were going to come and stay with us so we could all attend. I had written a letter to Shirley about her latest album release, also mentioning we would be in the audience for her BBC recording on 14 March and that we were looking forward to seeing her again.

Just prior to my parents leaving home, they received a telegram which immediately filled their hearts with fear. Even in the late seventies, telegrams usually brought bad news of some description, but when they realised it had been sent by the BBC, they offered up a sigh of relief. The telegram read:

> We regret that the Shirley Bassey Show has been cancelled on 14th March owing to industrial dispute stop – Ticket Unit BBC.

Mum and Dad still came to visit and we celebrated my birthday, although we were disappointed about the show being cancelled. I immediately wrote to the ticket unit to request more tickets and shortly after we received tickets for Shirley's final show.

On the morning of 16 March my attention was drawn to an envelope lying on the doormat, addressed to me in red type. It had a London postmark and I looked at it for several seconds, wondering where it had come from, before placing it on the kitchen table where it remained all day until I returned home from work. It was my parents who reminded me about the envelope, so I went and opened it, letting out a scream of delight as I unfolded the page to expose the printed letterhead 'Shirley Bassey'. I excitedly read to my parents:

Dear Mary,

Thank you for your very nice letter and I am glad you like my new LP.

As you will know by now the TV show on the 14th was cancelled, so I do hope you will be able to come to one of the other shows.

Warmest personal regards,

Yours sincerely,
Shirley Bassey [signed]

Today, my set of unused tickets, telegram and Shirley's letter are lasting memories of a show cancelled by strike action, something which fortunately did not happen to Shirley very often.

By the time I had booked tickets for Shirley's British and Scandinavian tour in 1979, the press was reporting on Shirley's marriage breakup and any other gossip about it at that time. We had liked and respected Sergio, having seen him demonstrate his fondness for Shirley on many occasions, so for us it was sad to hear about. It was, however, none of our business. There has always been a crazy element within the press, possibly encouraged by Joe Public, which seemed to think they had a right of ownership to the lives of stars. Generally speaking fans do, at times, face criticism for intruding into the private lives of the people they admire, but personally I have never met a fan of Shirley's that has not shown respect for her privacy. Whenever difficult times have touched Shirley's life, all we have been able to do as fans is to remain loyal and hope the wave of support we offer may, in some way, help see her through.

Following the success of Shirley's TV series, United Artists released an album entitled *What I Did For Love*, which featured Shirley singing fourteen songs from the shows, including 'The Shadow of Your Smile', 'Time After Time' and 'Does Anybody Miss Me'. Shirley also included, at her concerts in November, several of the numbers from the album along with many of the established favourites we all longed to hear again and again. Bernard and I, along with my parents, went to one of the Brighton concerts, where this time we had managed to get fairly good seats, only four rows back from the stage. We had seen George outside and he had chatted to us about the concert, having been on a previous night. Then it was time to take our seats and be entertained by a group called Champagne, but I'm afraid they didn't quite live up to the name.

The interval always seemed to last for ever. I'd be sitting on the edge of my seat, waiting for that moment when Shirley would step out onto the stage. At that instant I would jump to my feet, cheering loudly and franticly applauding until my hands hurt. Wearing one of Douglas Darnell's stunning gowns and a coat trimmed with feathers, Shirley seemed delighted by the welcome offered by her Brighton audience. For over an hour she presented a varied programme which demonstrated her fantastic singing ability as well as her talent to express lyrics like no other. As the show seemed to draw towards its finale, I left my seat and approached the stage, heading towards Shirley. A few other fans joined me close by and when I felt the appropriate moment had arrived, I stretched out my right arm as far as I could. Shirley immediately reached for my hand and I thanked her for the wonderful show. Not expecting a reply, I was taken aback when Shirley said, 'Congratulations on your marriage.' This was the first time I had seen Shirley face to face since mine and Bernard's wedding the previous year. I was so shocked she had remembered, especially after such a long time. I told her, 'Bernard's here', quickly motioning in the direction of our seats. More fans arrived and Shirley continued along the stage as I returned to my seat.

'What did she say?' Bernard asked, having realised I had spent more time than most chatting. When I told him, he looked surprised and I wondered if he thought I had made the whole thing up. The final number sung, Shirley slowly walked crossed the stage holding a bouquet of red carnations. Some of the flowers were handed out to fans standing by the stage; other flowers were thrown by Shirley to some of the fans she had spotted in the audience. Everyone wanted a flower and I was always amazed how accurately Shirley seemed to be able to get the flower into the hands of the person she had selected, especially when so many hands were reaching out to catch the prize. I stood cheering as Shirley approached close to where we were seated; we made eye contact and then Shirley seemed to gesture towards Bernard. Holding a carnation high in the air, Shirley began to swing her arm back and forth, clearly implying this carnation was being aimed for Bernard. Suddenly it was launched and arms shot up everywhere. All I could hear was Bernard saying, 'Get off, get off' as several boys prepared to dive on him. Thanks to Shirley's accuracy, he managed to catch the carnation and offered his thanks to her by waving the flower in the air. Shirley smiled and gave a nod before moving back to the microphone. The enthusiastic audience suddenly became silent as Shirley prepared to offer us an encore.

Although I was still 'in recovery' from all the excitement and enjoyment we had experienced at Brighton, a few days later we attended one of Shirley's concerts at the Wembley Conference Centre. Shirley appeared at the venue for five consecutive nights, the third night being a Royal Gala Performance in the presence of His Royal Highness, The Prince of Wales, in aid of The Prince's Trust. The concert generated lots of press coverage and provided me with reviews and photographs of Shirley with Prince Charles for my scrapbook.

Once again Shirley's performance was sensational and we cheered as heartily as ever, although we were some distance from the stage, but Shirley's singing reached out and filled our souls.

Shirley continued the British leg of her tour in Birmingham before crossing to the continent to close the decade with concerts in Copenhagen, Oslo, Stockholm and Gothenburg.

With 'superstar' status and an ever-growing legion of fans throughout the world, Shirley appeared to have it all!

CHAPTER 18

ALL BY MYSELF

As we entered a new decade, life became extremely busy for Bernard and I, something which had an impact on 'being a fan'. The amount of time now available to me to gather information regarding Shirley's professional commitments had reduced, mainly due to work, but looking after our home also occupied more time than required in my bedsit.

We were both in full employment and although demanding at times, we were beginning to enjoy the rewards earned through hard work. Recently we had returned from an exciting three-week holiday to the United States, where we stayed in New York, Las Vegas, Los Angeles and Hawaii. We had taken a flight on a small plane through the Grand Canyon, strolled on the white sands of Waikiki Beach, toured film sets in Hollywood and booked seats to see Dean Martin in Las Vegas – only Dean failed to show up! It was all very exciting and a dream come true, as we visited the Las Vegas Hotels where Shirley's engagements had broken box-office records, and of course Bernard had to visit the Sands Hotel and Casino!

During our holiday I guess my only slight disappointment came during our stay in New York when I discovered Shirley was *not* due appear at Carnegie Hall – can you believe it! Fortunately, we did get to stand on the steps leading up to this legendary theatre, but how wonderful it would have been if we had discovered 'Shirley was in town' and booked to give a performance at that great theatre.

Unfortunately, much of the news appearing in the British press at that time related to Shirley and Sergio's divorce, which I was extremely sad to read. There was mention that Sergio would continue as Shirley's manager and indeed he was credited for Shirley's management in her 1982 tour programme. The exposure of her personal life to the lens of the press must have added to the pressures of being a star. Shirley has a remarkable talent, a rich gift, but when it was handed out to her, it didn't come with a guarantee to offer immunity from life's emotions.

What I found hard to accept was that for the first time in my life as a fan I did not know where Shirley was living or how I could contact her. Shortly after I had first seen her perform all those years ago, I had known her private address, and that's how it had continued over the years. Even so, I very rarely wrote to her private residence; my letters and notes were usually sent or delivered to stage doors and hotel receptions, because I respected her privacy. I had always felt reassured that in times of sadness (Shirley's, not mine), I knew I could send Shirley a note of support. Now I felt sadness because I was unable to do anything.

So when I heard that she would be performing a concert to mark the reopening of the Apollo Victoria Theatre in London, I had to get tickets, I had to offer support. Originally built as a grand cinema, it closed in the mid-1970s, but after restoration and some conversion, it had now been beautifully restored as a one of London's biggest theatres, with a seating capacity of more than 2,200. Whether I missed the initial announcements or underestimated the demand for Shirley, I'm not sure, for I remember being surprised and a little disappointed when the best seats on offer were row 'O' in the stalls. My only consolation: the seats were by the central aisle, so I would get to the stage.

I met up with George Webb on the day of the concert and we both found it reassuring seeing Shirley as she arrived at the theatre. She had engrossed herself in her work over the previous few months and gave a wonderful performance and, yes, I made it from my seat to the stage, eventually!

Another outstanding performance that year, which George and I attended, was the recording for Thames Television's *Shirley Bassey: A Special Lady.*[7] It featured guests, Richard Clayderman and Robert Goulet and an abundance of lovely songs which Shirley performed beautifully. I felt her new musical director, Michael Alexander, had added a hint of jazz to some of the arrangements, which I enjoyed and which complemented Shirley's style.

The following year, 1981, brought more heartache for Shirley when her mother, Eliza, passed away. Somehow Shirley coped.

Eventually, there was some good news, when M.A.M. and Apollo Leisure announced they would present 'Shirley Bassey's 1982 UK Tour'. Scheduled between September and October, the tour would consist of twenty-five concerts, be held at eleven venues and include four nights at the Royal Albert Hall. Earlier in the year, Shirley who was no longer with United Artists, recorded tracks for a new album entitled *Love Songs*. Issued by K-Tel, the album's sleeve notes were rather minimal but acknowledged Shirley's 'special thanks to Ken Carter for his help and support'. The single, released from the album, 'All By Myself', gave Shirley a sizeable hit but my particular favourite at the time was the 'New York Medley', an arrangement which Shirley had already successfully incorporated into her stage performance, two

7 Fortunately the recording was later released as a DVD and is still available today from various websites.

numbers which share the same title, 'New York, New York', the title theme, and Gerard Kenny's own composition, 'New York, New York, so good they named it twice'.

Thankfully, we managed to get good seats for the concerts at Southampton and the Royal Albert Hall and, if my memory serves me well, Joyce and Reon had booked to see Shirley in concert at Manchester and Blackpool. As always, my parents joined us for the concerts and as always Shirley looked stunning, sang with all her heart and thrilled us beyond belief. Every performance seemed to surpass our expectations, always outdoing all we had previously experienced. During this tour there were times when Shirley and her audience were in unity, overwhelmed by affection which seemed to drift on the air.

Mum and Dad regularly came to stay with us, but as you can imagine, the occasions when we went to see Shirley were extra special. I usually had a few days off work and we would spend most of the time, after a show, chatting about Shirley's performance and reading the press reviews. Joyce would sometimes send me press reviews from the concerts she and Reon had attended, as well as writing lovely descriptive letters about the shows, which I shared with my parents. Mum and Dad loved seeing Shirley and as soon as one tour ended, they, like all fans the world over, began to look forward to the next.

At first the signs were hardly detectable, but prior to Shirley's UK tour in 1984, Dad was beginning to notice slight changes in my mum's 'happy-go-lucky' personality. Visiting friends or relatives were hardly aware of any differences in Mum's behaviour, but the clues were there if you knew where to look. Sadly, my mum was developing Alzheimer's disease, although we didn't know it at the time.

I was delighted when I discovered Shirley was returning to Bournemouth, although now the venue was the newly opened Windsor Hall, which formed part of the Bournemouth International Centre, known as the BIC. Bournemouth always seemed to 'come up trumps' for us and I was naturally delighted when I discovered we had managed to get front-row seats. We immediately booked accommodation at the Winter Gardens Hotel, near to the centre, and planned returning home, with Mum and Dad, in time to attend one of the Royal Albert Hall concerts.

During July and August that year, Shirley spent time recording an album with the London Symphony Orchestra, entitled *I Am What I Am*. I longed for the album's release since it featured fifteen of Shirley's most important songs, with arrangements by Michael Alexander and produced by Norman Newell. Norman was also the lyrist to three of the album's numbers: 'Never, Never, Never', 'Natalie' and 'This Is My Life'. On the sleeve, Shirley had written a note ending with the words, 'I hope my new album gives you many hours of listening pleasure'. Well, it's certainly done that.

It was a damp November day as we mounted the steps leading to the reception area at the BIC, but that really didn't seem to matter. It had taken me some time, earlier that afternoon, to locate the stage-door area where I had deposited a 'good luck' card and letter for Shirley. Later we went for a meal and now we stood near to the bar as Bernard ordered four glasses of Beaujolais Nouveau, which had just been released having found its way across the Channel. Actually, it was a very good year and we had another glass or two before the evening was over. I remember there was a tremendous buzz as the area filled with people, all longing to see and hear Shirley. I noticed a large poster, advertising the concert, across which had been placed a sash with the words, 'SOLD OUT' in red. I managed to speak to one of the staff and asked if I could possibly have the poster after the show; they agreed and I'm delighted to say I was allowed to take it home. The theatre, the largest in the south of England, held over 4,000 people and I admit I to feeling a little proud as we were shown to our seats.

The first half of the show was split between Dave Evans and Wayne King, who were entertaining, but as always they were playing to an audience who were solely there to hear Shirley. We applauded them as though we were rehearsing for Shirley and it helped to calm my nerves. Then, following the interval, we resumed our seats. The lights dimmed, the members of the orchestra took to the stage, and the audience started to clap, whistle and cheer as Michael Alexander, immaculately dressed, walked onto the stage and raised his hands ready to conduct the orchestra. Then it began, that beautiful music every soul in the theatre had come to enjoy. The stage lights flashed in all directions and the audience began to go wild. Yes, we were back in Bournemouth and I loved it.

Suddenly, Shirley was walking out onstage, arms outstretched as if wanting to embrace the entire audience and revealing a sparkling diamanté dress. The audience erupted; the orchestra continued to play the opening score until, eventually, Shirley having taken us under her control, approached the microphone and began to sing. Her first few numbers were expected favourites, such as 'As Long As He Needs Me' and 'As I Love You', and were greeted with wild applause within moments of the audience recognising the opening few notes. Shirley seemed to be singing each number with a greater ease and depth of emotion. Mum always loved the older numbers and if you looked, you would see they still brought a tear or two to her eyes.

It's now impossible to remember every detail, but 'Big Spender' was one number that Shirley never missed out from any show. She only had to say to her audience, 'Here it comes', and we all knew what to expect. Some of the men sitting in the front few rows turned to putty as Shirley began to sing, 'Do you want to have fun, fun, fun…' directly to them. The wives and girlfriends looked on, amused by the idea! The final 'Hey Big Spender…' drew cheers, thunderous applause and shouts for more, which echoed around this vast hall. Momentarily Shirley allowed herself to soak up the atmosphere, and then a few fans seized the opportunity and approach the stage, offering up a gift, flowers or simply their hand. All were accepted with a smile before Shirley changed the tempo and delivered a heart-rending ballad.

The house lights dimmed and the spots panned around the auditorium, offering up the impression that the cops had arrived, as Shirley bounced into her 'New York Medley'. With a fabulous jazzy arrangement, the orchestra let rip during the number as Shirley danced the Charleston, then returned to singing the New York theme, finishing on a prolonged New York, N-e-w Y-o-r-k, which took my breath away. We were so close to her, hearing pure Bassey, no amplification, just vocal power delivering unbelievable notes

We rose from our seats in homage, yet more was still to come. A slower number, which I needed to settle the heart rate. Then Shirley introduces the title track from her latest album, 'I Am What I Am' from the musical *La Cage Aux Folles*. The fans cheered as Shirley slowly began the opening verse, then the orchestra raised the tempo and Shirley roared into the number. When she sings the line, 'Give me the hook or the ovation', the response from the audience is overwhelming.

Whenever I have heard the song over the years, my mind has always taken me back to that fabulous evening. When it ended fans rushed to the stage to reach up and shake Shirley's hand. Flowers were handed up and soon part of the stage resembled a florist's shop. Mum, Dad and I were amongst those lining up along the edge of the stage when Shirley returned onstage with a cluster of red carnations for the fans. Some were thrown out into the audience whilst the others were handed to individual fans standing in front of the stage. Shirley specifically made sure Mum was handed a flower and then gave one to me. We were both over the moon and, once back at the hotel, placed the two carnations into a glass of water. The following morning as we were leaving the hotel clutching our flowers, a lady came up to us and said, 'You must be really great fans to get two carnations'!

A few days later we were at the Royal Albert Hall, experiencing another wonderful concert, but I knew obtaining good seats for this venue, in the years ahead, would become more and more difficult. Mum's health was also likely to get worse, which meant Bournemouth would be a far easier place to visit, so the decision was made: the BIC would become our 'home' venue.

CHAPTER 19

HEY JUDE

By the mid-eighties things were really going well for Bernard and I. Bernard was becoming known in British jazz circles for his photography, after having provided photographs to musicians for publicity purposes and album covers. He was also contributing his photos to *Jazz Journal International*, a monthly jazz magazine for which he eventually became one of the main photographers. His love of jazz led him to photograph several legendary performers in concert over the years and naturally I usually accompanied him. Some of the singers we have been lucky to see in concert include, Frank Sinatra, Ella Fitzgerald, Sammy Davis Jnr., Tony Bennett, Peggy Lee, Sarah Vaughan, Lena Horne, Dean Martin, Liza Minnelli and Billy Eckstine. Who knows, once this book is complete I might write Bernard's biography as a jazz photographer!

The majority of artists mentioned made an impact upon us, some more than others for a variety of reasons, but there were also a few who did not, and I sometimes wondered why I could not recognise the 'star quality' they were said to possess. However, there was nobody amongst these legends who could produce in me the same thrill and excitement I experienced every time I watched Shirley perform.

Having worked hard, we purchased a boat and were learning to sail, and whenever we had any spare time we would head down to the south coast, often incorporating a visit to my parents. It was during one such visit that I arranged to take Mum, along with my dad, to see our doctor. Dad had been very reluctant about the whole thing, but in his heart of hearts he knew, like me, that something was wrong. The problem was I didn't know what, and feared the worst. Mum was such an easygoing person, so the visit didn't worry her unduly.

After spending some time talking to Mum and eliminating various possibilities, the doctor turned to me and said, 'Your mother will not be your mother for much longer.' He must have seen the shock on my face because I thought he meant she was going to die. Then he explained Mum had Alzheimer's disease and what we could expect to happen in the future. My dad found it very hard to accept, convincing himself it might never happen and refusing to let my mum go to hospital for a further assessment. Unfortunately the disease had already begun to take hold.

Later that summer, 1985, Shirley and her family faced a far greater tragedy when her younger daughter Samantha was found dead. We were all deeply saddened when we heard the report on television and I remember my dad telling me that Mum cried. I have no children of my own, yet I cannot think of anything in life more painful than the loss of your child. I wondered how Shirley would cope and indeed if she would sing again, but we felt really bad that we could do nothing to help!

All the newspapers naturally covered the story and the reports were sad to read, but amongst it all seemed to come a glimmer of hope when a reporter, asking after Shirley, spoke to Norman Newell. He told the reporter that Shirley was very resilient and would come through. It was reassuring for me to know that once again Norman Newell was there, a true friend.

Shirley poured herself into her work; it was all she could do. Her fans all over the world were longing to see her. Then came a concert in Australia, a country she loves so much. Shirley walked onstage and was about to sing 'Goldfinger', but nothing came out. Since Samantha's death Shirley had lost her voice on several occasions and eventually went to see voice coach and opera singer, Helena Shenel. She taught Shirley, for the first time in her life, the importance of looking after her voice, teaching her the voice exercises and skills that had served Helena so well.

The following year, after all her hard work, it was announced that Shirley was about to embark on a world tour. Australia, Austria, Canada, England, France, Germany, Holland, Hong Kong, Ireland, Japan, Poland, Scotland, Sri Lanka, Turkey, United Arab Emirates, USA and Wales were all booked into her engagement diary. Fans everywhere longed to see her and I immediately applied to the BIC for tickets. Tony Macarthur was now Shirley's personal manager, and with the Allied Entertainment Group presented the 1986 tour. It's my opinion this was one of the best produced concerts we ever attended, with Shirley offering her audience a new facet of her talent – as an impressionist!

On the day of the concert, once settled at the hotel, we then headed off to the BIC. Now familiar with the venue, I really wanted to see Shirley as she arrived, so we waited outside the backstage area and eventually we were rewarded. We exchanged greetings; it was lovely to see her looking well, and Bernard asked if he could take some photos during the concert. Shirley said it would be fine and Bernard promised to send Shirley copies, which we always did.

When the evening came and we walked down the aisle to the front seats, I was as excited as ever. My eyes were instinctively drawn to the stage microphone, for over the years I had become good at estimating, before even taking my seat, the distance from my seat to the mike. Tonight, we were once again very fortunate in being only feet away from the stage and in a perfect position for Bernard to get some good shots.

Something else was different; as we looked towards the stage we noticed the orchestra would be seated at different levels, ascending to the rear of the stage, allowing the audience to see all the members. At the back of the orchestra a balcony had been erected overhead, which stretched across the length of the stage to a silver staircase; this lead down to the stage area adjacent to the musical director's rostrum. I remember thinking, whatever is going to happen tonight must be special, or that maybe it was a set for some other production currently running at the BIC!

Moments before the members of the orchestra took to the stage, the hall became silent, the atmosphere expectant. Now there was cheering and clapping as the audience began to release the emotion they had been struggling to hold in. Michael Alexander walked onstage and stepped up to the rostrum and within seconds the opening notes from Shirley's overture could be heard. As each and every member of the audience recognised a particular favourite, the applause grew in volume; we knew Shirley would soon appear onstage.

Suddenly our eyes were drawn by the spots lighting up the side of the balcony above the orchestra. Almost immediately, from here Shirley emerged dressed in a voluminous stage coat with graduating tones of pink ostrich feathers, lined in silver silk tissue. She seemed to float above the orchestra in her Douglas Darnell creation. Crossing the balcony with arms reaching out, as if trying to draw in the audience's applause, Shirley descended the silver stairs. Many in the audience rose from their seats to greet her. The orchestra upped the tempo and Shirley began, 'Almost Like Being In Love'. The sound quality was incredible and I thought she was singing better than I had ever heard her sing before. It seemed as though she had discovered a better way to add more control to her voice without forfeiting any emotion, indeed the emotional level seemed to have risen. Shirley's singing had become so natural, seemingly so easy. Of course 'the ease' was the results of years of hard work, practice, sacrifice, talent and the help offered by Helena Shenel, although at the time we were unaware of Helena's influence.

After a ballad or two, there were cheers of delight, from the men in the audience when Shirley removed her coat to expose a glimmering gown with a shirt slit diagonally to the hip. She looked wonderful and as Bernard prepared to take some photographs, Shirley, using the hand mike, moved along the edge of the stage as she sang some of her hits. Each was welcomed with loud applause, and frequently cheers could be heard from various locations throughout the auditorium if Shirley had sung a fan's particular favourite.

True, there was a fairly well-established pattern to Shirley's concert performances, but old favourites would vary, new songs would be introduced and the expected, 'Big Spender' would always be included. Shirley would chat to the audience at certain moments during a concert, but generally what you got was a polished performance of fifteen or more numbers, something few other performers could match. Intermingling amongst the torch songs, you would suddenly be offered a cheeky rendering of 'You've Never Done It Like That'. It was all part of Shirley's remarkable talent; she took us on a rollercoaster of emotion but would always throw in some fun.

Shirley introduced her new single, 'To All The Men I've Loved Before', which I felt at the time deserved greater success. Then it's that number, 'Big Spender', and she has the audience eating out of her hand. It doesn't matter how often you see Shirley perform this number, you still want to see it again and again. Tonight Dad is given a 'personal performance' as Shirley struts along the edge of the stage. Mum is laughing; Alzheimer's hasn't managed to steal her humour just yet.

We stand applauding with all our might. After several handshakes, the atmosphere changes again as we are offered an emotional ballad, the ending of which leaves Shirley and the audience drained. Shirley rushes offstage and is gone for what seems like several minutes. For the first time, I look at my watch. It can't be over. Calls for Shirley ring out as the orchestra continues with the overture, then the hall erupts as she once again walks out onstage.

This time Shirley is wearing a stunning dress which glitters like diamonds and is edged at the hem with pink ostrich feathers. She chats with her musical director and then, as the lights dim, she puts on a wig! The music starts up, but it isn't the Bassey that we recognise: it's one of Tina Turner's hits and Shirley is strutting her stuff, offering us an incredible impression of the Queen of rock 'n' roll. Bernard snaps away with his camera. There is tremendous laughter and applause from the audience to which Shirley responds, 'We've had enough of that', then jokingly throws the wig in the direction of Michael Alexander. It was lovely to see Shirley having such fun, yet I never saw her 'do impressions' again. Who knows, perhaps business managers advised her to stick with the proven formula!

The 'New York Medley' once again brought wild applause, along with 'I Am What I Am'. The audience having now learned to cheer and offer the standing ovation at the appropriate moment, when the lyrics demanded it!

The concert had been fabulous and then, when you thought it couldn't possibly get any better, came 'Hey Jude'. I found Shirley's version of this Lennon and McCartney number simply unbelievable and the rest of the audience seemed to agree. There applause almost raised the roof off the BIC. When Shirley repeated the final 'na, na, na, . . H-e-y J-u-d-e', I swear I thought my ears would burst. From that very moment I adored the number and was over the moon when Shirley re-recorded the song for her *Hello Like Before* CD, nearly thirty years later. If you haven't bought this CD, buy it, put your headphones on and close your eyes. Let your imagination take over, then you will begin to feel what it was like to be there that night.

As the show reached its climax, Shirley stood before a crowd of fans packed together along the edge of her stage. These were not young teenagers but mainly middle-aged members of the public. They could have been doctors, bank managers, whoever, yet each was drawn towards Shirley, such was her magic. During the last few minutes the strength of the applause had not eased for one moment as Shirley continued to shake hands with as many people as possible. Finally, one more number was called for, 'This Is My Life'. Shirley, now clad in her silver coat, delivered the song beautifully. Mum stood up and cheered her approval along with the audience, which clearly touched Shirley. Then, suddenly Shirley was climbing the silver stairs. As she danced across the balcony, her glittering coat trailing behind her, the audience gave a thunderous roar. Then Shirley turned and gave a final wave, before finally exiting the stage.

After a while the fans standing near to us started to make their way back to their seats. We sat in ours for a while, almost spellbound, trying to relive every moment. We had enjoyed the concert so much, it was Shirley at her very best and I wanted it to remain clear in my mind for ever. Yet my heart went out to my mum because I knew her memory of the evening, would be short-lived.

During the weeks ahead Bernard set about producing the photographs he had taken during the concert. We sent copies of the best photos to Shirley together with a letter congratulating her on a wonderful concert. We didn't include any photos taken of her 'doing her Tina Turner' impression, although we referred to them in our letter. It came as quite a surprise when, several months later, we received a thank you note together with a request for photos of Shirley doing her impression. Naturally, we were delighted and sent copies to her manager.

Shirley pressed on with her world tour, thrilling hundreds and thousands of fans. I continued to scan the music press for reviews, news of television appearances and recording schedules. Any opportunity to see Shirley had to be followed, although with my own heavy work schedule, it wasn't always possible. One example was the Royal Command Performance in 1987, which I was unable to attend. Fortunately we were able to see Shirley's fabulous performance when the show was screened on television shortly after. My dad managed to take some photos from the television and the image I remember so well was one taken from behind Shirley, as she looked out to the audience. That shot really gave the viewer the opportunity to experience the thrill Shirley must have felt, performing for Her Majesty the Queen, Prince Philip and the entire London Palladium audience. Shirley looked stunning, with a new hair style, in a black net gown by London fashion designer, Murray Arbeid, decorated all over with silver glittery stars of varying sizes. It therefore seemed appropriate that Shirley should sing the song she had recently recorded for the London Tourist Board, 'There's No Place Like London'. Shirley gave the Gerard W. Kenny and Lynsey De Paul number her all, but it would soon become clear that the song was unlikely to pose a threat to 'New York, New York'!

When Shirley embarked on her British tour the following spring, 1985, she was represented by friend and antiques expert, Yves Mills. We booked for Shirley's concerts at the BIC, Bournemouth and one of the Royal Albert Hall dates.

At every concert Shirley sang her heart out with such power that you could only wonder from where the energy came. The 'New York Medley' again proved to be one of the highlights of every concert, although Michael Alexander was no longer there to conduct the orchestra; this was now in the hands of Peter Tomasso. From the moment Shirley launched into 'Diamonds Are Forever', the emotion flowed back and forth between 'star' and audience. 'The Magic Is You' received a tremendous applause, along with a few tears. More tears flowed with 'And I Love Him So' as we remembered Shirley's own heartache. A change of tempo and she soon had us swinging along with, 'I Am What I Am' and 'Hey Jude', both of which received thunderous applause and cheers which generated a siege of fans towards the stage. A couple of beefy attendants tried to keep the fans back, but I knew just how the fans were feeling and we would not be moved. Instead we knelt or sat down in the aisles as Shirley sang her final two numbers, 'My Way' and 'The Greatest Love of All'.

Flowers, gifts and handshakes were now an established part of the

Bassey experience. Then she gave a final wave, calling out, 'Goodnight' before adding, 'I'll be back'. That too, was music to our ears.

Before returning to the BIC in 1989, Bernard and I saw Shirley in cabaret at the Circus Tavern in Purfleet, Essex. I seem to recall the engagement had been booked at short notice and indeed I wondered why Shirley was performing at the venue. It had attracted big names in the past; we had attended a wonderful concert by Ella Fitzgerald in 1975. Who could forget Ella asking her audience to light their cigarette lighters or strike a match, as she sang 'Everytime We Say Goodbye'. It was magic, but sadly now, in 1989, the venue was lacking!

On the day of Shirley's concert, I had just only returned home a few days after being in hospital following routine surgery, so our neighbour kindly offered to drive us to the venue. I wasn't supposed to stand for long on my bandaged leg, yet I remember giving Shirley a 'standing' ovation when she took to the stage. It was a good concert but not one of Shirley's best, or perhaps I wasn't feeling at my best. I remember I couldn't make it to the stage. Immediately after the concert Bernard tried to find out if I could see Shirley but he was told she had already left the theatre and I can't say I blamed her!

The year went on to bring other joys; the first was news of a Spanish album entitled *La Mujer*. At the time I had a lot of difficulty in obtaining the album and when I eventually received my copy, I immediately visited our brother-in-law, who spoke a little Spanish, in an attempt to understand the lyrics to the new songs on the album. I loved Shirley's singing at the time but the album wasn't very successful here in the UK, mainly because it didn't get any publicity. The album had been the idea of Grammy Award-winning producer Leonardo Schultz and Shirley had taken Spanish lessons to complete the project. It certainly gained her new fans following the album's debut with her performance at the Viña Del Mar International Song Festival in Chile in February 1989.

However, it was Shirley's concert tour towards the end of the year that produced the most excitement. Back again at the BIC, which always had a special feel to it I think partly because the audience always seemed to consist mainly of fans. That may seem a strange comment requiring an explanation, but I say it because a London audience would occasionally seem to contain too many people who were there 'to be seen', rather than being there to see the performer. In later years it wasn't always the fans that occupied the front seats. I felt the make-up of an audience often influenced the atmosphere and I'm sure Shirley could sense that too! However, let's return to the BIC.

I could hardly control my excitement as Shirley walked out onstage wearing a stunning creation by Zandra Rhodes. Stage smoke filled the air and Bernard managed to capture a little of the effect in his photo, which shows Shirley in her lavishly embroidered cape featuring an abstract design of silver thread, beads and sequins, edged with large white feathers. As you would expect, the atmosphere was electric as Shirley delivered her first few numbers. Then the cape was removed, revealing what appeared to be a full-length white silk gown, but later we discovered the outfit actually consisted of a skirt slit to the waist and a matching sleeveless tunic, both beautifully embellished with silver pearls and sequins.

Shirley was singing beautifully; whether a ballad from the soul or an upbeat medley, each was delivered perfectly. Then came a surprise – Shirley 'tugged' at the bottom section of her gown, revealing her legs. Now she was simply dressed in the one remaining piece of her three-piece creation – the glamorous tunic with its deep cowl back. The audience cheered approvingly and the orchestra began 'Big Spender'. It's a wonder that first aid did not have to be administered to the gentlemen sitting in the front row!

Like so many of the concerts we had experienced before, Shirley gave her all and in return fans flocked to the stage. It was nice to see young fans approach the stage, possibly the sons and daughters of some of Shirley's original fan base, plus others who had 'discovered' Shirley through recordings such as 'The Rhythm Divine', which she recorded with Swiss group Yello. My parents represented the other end of the age spectrum; my dad would be eighty later that year, yet when we all gathered to hear Shirley sing, age seemed irrelevant. 'Hey Jude' rang out and the audience, with arms held high in the air, waved from side to side in time with Shirley's singing. Mum loved the number as much as I did and I wondered if she would ever be able to see Shirley perform live again.

Had you glanced at my mum as we walked back to the hotel that evening, you would have been forgiven for thinking nothing was wrong, but Alzheimer's had taken it's hold over the last few years and once we arrived at the hotel her anxiety levels rose. Dad and I had learned with practice how to help relieve Mum's fears momentarily, but as we knew only too well, they could return within minutes. Our tried-and-tested methods of reassurance would then be repeated over and over again finally her anxiety eased. Dad loved my mum to bits and he had vowed to care for her for ever, but watching the disease change the woman he loved was a nightmare for him.

The next concert at the BIC was our last as a family and I wanted it to be special. I managed to get front-row seats, although they were towards the end of the row, a little too near the loudspeakers for my liking, but I was pleased we were close to the stage. Some weeks prior to the concert I had made a request to Shirley's management, asking if I could take my parents backstage after the performance so they could say thank you to Shirley for all the years of pleasure she had given them. I explained the circumstances and the management were aware they had been fans from the beginning. Following several phone calls I was given some assurance that it might be possible. It would depend on what was happening on the day and obviously it would be up to Shirley, but I was given a backstage 'contact' and told to speak with him prior to the show.

On the day of the concert I found it difficult to control my nerves, but as I walked, with Bernard, through the maze of corridors backstage to Shirley's dressing room, I felt optimistic. I believed it would happen if only Shirley was asked! When my 'contact' appeared from Shirley's dressing room, I offered my request and explained the circumstances, doubting whether this young man could really understand! Perhaps I was expecting too much when I tried to explain that although my mum wouldn't remember anything the next day, my father and I would have the memory of Mum 'saying her thank you to Shirley'. 'I don't know if it's possible, where are you sitting and I'll let you know,' was his reply.

We arrived at our seats early; the anxiety of waiting for a reply was almost too much to bear as we watched the auditorium begin to fill. Suddenly a figure appeared from behind the stage curtain and it was my contact, but he didn't appear to be looking for me. I waited while he adjusted the curtain but I couldn't bear it any longer, I had to know, so I called over to him. He came over and I asked, 'Can we see Miss Bassey after the show?' 'She has an engagement and must leave immediately after the show,' was the response. I was speechless, I wanted to say, 'Did you actually ask Miss Bassey?' but I didn't. I think I was so disappointed, I could not have faced the rejection if he had said 'Yes', so I said nothing. When I turned and looked at my dad, disappointment was etched across his face.

Shirley's performance that evening and the audience's enthusiasm was as thrilling and exciting as it had ever been. I adored her interpretation of the Jeff Silbar/Larry Henley song, 'Wind Beneath My Wings', and as Shirley sang the final lines, I admit the tears were rolling down my cheeks.

Next morning, at a cottage we had rented near Bournemouth, I took a cup of tea into the bedroom where my mum and dad were sleeping. They both sat up in bed and I handed Mum a cup of tea, She looked up at me then turned to my dad and said, 'Who's that?' I looked at Dad and the tears began to form.

CHAPTER 20

I'LL GET BY

As we entered the nineties, Bernard and I were enjoying life to the full. We had good jobs, worked hard and were looking forward to the rewards our hard work offered. We had a thirty-foot motor sailer moored on the Hamble and planned to go on a short cruise around Britain on a somewhat larger vessel, the *Queen Elizabeth 2*, or *QE2*. It was particularly special because the shipping line, Cunard, was celebrating its 150th anniversary. The cruise would form part of the celebrations, climaxing with a visit on board by Her Majesty the Queen and Prince Philip, as the ship returned to its berth in Southampton.

A week before our departure, Dad phoned to tell me he had read in the *Radio Times* that Ken Bruce would be presenting a special show during our cruise, featuring passengers' requests from the ship. Dad said, 'Do you know Ken Bruce?' to which I replied that I did not know him but I thought I would recognise him. So I told Dad, 'If I see him I'll try and get a request played for your wedding anniversary.'

Immediately following the cruise, my parents would be celebrating their fiftieth wedding anniversary and we had a small party planned for family and friends on the IOW. I didn't really hold out much hope of seeing Ken Bruce, let alone getting a request, but I decided to write my request to him on a greetings card and carry it with me, so if a sudden opportunity presented itself, I could hand him the card. The request I wrote, was for a song by Shirley Bassey.

The first few days of the cruise were thrilling; we were met by fantastic receptions in Liverpool, Cobh, Ireland and Greenock, Scotland, but Ken was nowhere to be seen; in fact, when I asked the ship's staff about the radio show, they had no knowledge of what I was talking about and looked at me rather strangely.

Bernard too, had almost given up hope with me, especially when I spotted a young man wearing a cardigan on board, wearing a BBC logo, and I approached him. As it happened, he told me Ken Bruce was not yet on board but he would pass on my 'request', which I quickly handed to him.

With so much happening during the cruise, I soon forgot about the request until the following evening when we received a phone call in our cabin. I was startled to discover it was the producer of Ken's radio show and he started to ask several questions about the cruise. Then I thought, what's all this about and asked, 'Well, will Ken Bruce do my request?' I was so shocked when he replied, 'I'll tell you what, you can come and do it yourself!'

Bernard came out of the bathroom and said, 'Who have you been talking to for so long?' When I told him I was going to be on Ken Bruce's show, which would be taking place from the bridge of the ship, Bernard looked a little disappointed, knowing that passengers could not go to the bridge. Then I said, 'It's OK, they said you can come too.'

The next evening we were in Cherbourg, France and had already received instructions regarding where we should meet our bridge 'escort'. The radio show was due to be broadcast live at midnight and I was excited, although from Dad's information I expected other passengers to also be taking part, so that eased my nerves. We arrived at our rendezvous and were escorted to the bridge where we were introduced to Captain Woodall, Paul Daniels and the producer, to whom I had spoken on the phone. 'Where are the other passengers?' I asked and nearly died when he replied, 'Oh, there is only you.'

Everything happened so quickly. I heard someone say, 'By the way, we can't play Shirley Bassey, it will be Ella Fitzgerald since the records have been pre-selected.' Suddenly I was sitting in front of a microphone at a small table, opposite Ken Bruce, and we were chatting like long-lost friends about the cruise and my parents' anniversary request. Then Ken said, 'Now what record would you like us to play?' and I replied, 'Well, I wanted you to play Shirley Bassey, but I've been told it's got to be Ella Fitzgerald.' There were roars of laughter from Ken and everyone all around, and then he said, 'Now you have given the game away.' I whispered, 'This is a rehearsal, isn't it?' He gave a big grin and shook his head from side to side. We were 'live' on air.

I felt terrible having made such a blunder, yet the producer and Ken Bruce thought it had been so natural; in fact Ken later featured the interview request again on his programme the following weekend, actually on the day of my parents' anniversary. I hadn't been able to contact Dad about the broadcast from the ship but he had decided to listen to the live show and said he felt so happy and very proud when he heard the interview. So that was my claim to fame in the nineties, but at least I managed to utter the words, 'Shirley Bassey'.

Mum and Dad's fiftieth-anniversary celebration was a lovely occasion held in a restaurant, which they frequented often, so Mum felt quite at home. Mum was always a laugh at any party and she did not disappoint us on this occasion, joking with a nephew who resembled my dad at the same age. The only thing was, she thought he was her husband! Mum didn't recognise my niece, or my niece's children, whom she loved very much and I had now become my mum's best friend from her teens. Somehow, it didn't matter, we all laughed, sang and enjoyed the celebrations.

In Manchester, Mickey Martin had been presenting 'International Cabaret' in the Peacock Suite, at the Hotel Piccadilly. Bernard and I had stayed at the hotel to see Vic Damone and *Dynasty* star, Diahann Carroll, in cabaret and after an enjoyable evening we had spoken with Mickey and were delighted when he told us he had booked Sammy Davis Jnr for the cabaret at the hotel. The following morning we became one of the first to book for Sammy's engagement and as we left Mickey's office I noticed a photo of Shirley on display. 'Are you going to book Shirley Bassey?' I cried. I hadn't expected the reply that came, 'Actually, Sammy Davis Jnr isn't very well, so Shirley is going to step in if he can't make it.' Naturally, we did not want Sammy to be ill, but knowing we were booked to see either Sammy or Shirley was a bonus.

Sadly, Sammy was unable to fulfil the engagement and the press was informed that Shirley Bassey had been booked. With our reservation already secured, we knew we had the very best seats at a table located immediately in front of centre stage for Shirley's performance on the second evening of her engagement, so we were looking forward to our visit immensely.

We arrived at the hotel on the day of Shirley's first show and to Bernard's delight, checked into the hotel as the members of the Count Basie Orchestra and jazz legend Nancy Wilson, arrived. Apparently, they also had a 'gig' in Manchester.

That evening we dined in the hotel's restaurant and then later decided to go to the Peacock Suite when Shirley was due onstage. The Peacock Suite was a long rectangular room with a modest stage at one end. From the entrance, at the rear of the suite, it would take 'a lifetime' to walk to the stage, dodging between the numerous circular tables, each of which could seat approximately twelve people. We noticed a guy standing near the rear door and started to chat. It turned out he was one of the musicians in the Count Basie Orchestra and having played for Shirley, when she performed with the orchestra in the States, he wanted to catch her performance. Bernard explained this to the doorman sitting by the rear exit and after the offer of a drink, he said we could stand and watch from the back. Nobody noticed as we slipped in under the cover of darkness, as the house lights dimmed.

When Shirley came out onstage, she seemed miles away, but I felt so lucky to be watching her perform, knowing that the next day it would be even better. The sound was not at its best from where we stood, but Shirley gave a great performance and the Manchester audience gave her a tremendous reception. The musician beside me swung from side to side, clearly enjoying the show, and towards the end we both managed to sing along to 'Hey Jude', with our arms waving in the air. It was a wonderful evening, even though I had to restrain my enthusiasm.

The following evening promised to be a whole different experience. Dressed in our evening attire, we walked through the Peacock Suite to our table at the very front. Bernard and I had previously decided to choose the seats (our tickets simply stated a table number) which backed onto the edge of the stage. It meant we would not be facing the entertainment during dinner, but when Shirley was due to perform, we would turn our chairs around and face the stage. We arrived at the table and selected our seats. The room was packed to capacity with little space between the tables once everyone was seated. Dinner consisted of a ten-course set menu, with the main course 'Blanc de Volaille au Xeres Shirley Bassey', named after the star. Once we had wined and dined, there was the usual buzz as the audience began to settle into their seats. When we stood and turned our seats around to face the stage, one or two of our table companions realised why we had chosen our seats; honestly, my knees were touching the edge of the stage. The microphone stand had been place within inches of me, never had I ever been so close. Fans couldn't rush to the stage here, you had to be there from the start, and we were the lucky ones.

Everyone rose when Shirley emerged in a beautiful sleeveless coat with a flowing train in orange silk chiffon, the gown encrusted with two-tone tangerine and pink sequins, edges and collar trimmed with a deep border of tangerine ostrich feathers. The coat was lined in gold silk tissue. Appropriately Shirley immersed herself in 'Goldfinger', followed by 'Diamonds Are Forever', before standing centre stage to greet the audience. As Shirley stood before us, I almost wanted to laugh because I realised we were so close, I could have tickled her toes! Perhaps she read my thoughts, because at that moment Shirley looked down and said, 'Good evening'. I watched in admiration as the orchestra began to play the opening notes from the 1954 movie, *There's No Business Like Show Business*. Originally the song was belted out by Ethel Merman, but Shirley's wonderful rendering showed no signs of strain. I looked up to see her using all the skills she had acquired throughout her life onstage and I was in awe of the control she now had over her voice. Then came the 'New York Medley' and the room became alive with roaming spotlights and stars, all highly appropriate for the occasion. We applauded loudly along with the other diners, all of whom had taken Shirley to their hearts. Of course a cabaret audience can be quite different to a theatre audience, but Shirley knew only too well how to win them over.

With her coat now removed, Shirley looked even more stunning in the sparkling, orange gown, embroidered with beads and crystals, another of Douglas Darnell's striking creations. The straps of the gown crossed above the low-cut back, from which hung two strands of beads, crystals and pearls. There were cheers of approval from the audience. Lifting the microphone from the stand, Shirley then walked along the edge of the stage as she sang 'When You Smile', addressing her lyrics to selected individuals along her path. As she did so, the microphone cable constantly slipped over the edge of the stage, dropping onto my knees. I found myself having to frequently put the cable back on the stage. Shirley must have been aware something was happening but she didn't seem to worry. Perhaps she realised I, more than anyone, would know when she needed more cable!

Once the applause and cheering subsided, the lights dimmed as Shirley stood centre stage and began, 'The Wind Beneath My Wings'. I had never heard it sung better, I was close to tears. With so little distance between us, we were listening to pure Shirley, no amplification, just that incredible voice with which she made every song her own. It seemed unbelievable; it was magic!

A few words to the audience followed and then it was time for 'Kiss Me, Honey, Honey, Kiss Me' and more fun with those lucky enough to be near to the stage. Again wild applause followed before Shirley returned, once again, to centre stage to perform 'Don't Cry Out Loud', followed by 'I Am What I Am', which had the audience on its feet. Shirley returned to another ballad, my own special favourite, 'Never, Never, Never', and naturally, the Italian was mentioned! Stevie Wonder's, 'For Once In My Life', a song which Frank Sinatra often performed in concert, was now given the Bassey treatment and how the audience loved it. I was mesmerised by the whole experience.

The introduction to 'Big Spender' roused the audience to fever pitch as Shirley started singing the number to a gentleman at the far end of the stage. Then she was standing in front of Bernard singing, 'I don't pop my cork for every man I see…' Now, as I have previously tried to explain, Bernard never became excited by any performer, so when Shirley had finished her number and turned to Bernard to say, 'Was that OK?' I began to worry! Bernard, rather coolly replied, 'It was alright,' at the very moment when every other man in the establishment was turning green with envy. 'Well, I had better do it again,' Shirley says to Bernard, as the orchestra strikes up the opening notes. As Shirley crouched immediately in front of him, I learned over to whisper in Bernard's ear, to which Shirley jokingly reacted by saying, 'Leave him alone'! Everyone around us laughed and we were all delighted to be treated to a second performance of 'Big Spender'.

Finally came 'Hey Jude' – it was unbelievable. Everyone rose to their feet, cheering, shouting and applauding. A crescendo of sound was being directed towards the stage, offered to Shirley Bassey in appreciation from her audience.

Mickey Martin had written, in the programme, that we would experience a truly memorable night and indeed we did. Only one more song was necessary, the song that told the whole story: 'This Is My Life'.

CHAPTER 21

DON'T CRY OUT LOUD

In the summer of 1991, the words from the Peter W. Allen and Carole Bayer Sager song, 'Don't Cry Out Loud', which Shirley had sung in Manchester, surfaced in my mind on numerous occasions.

We'd certainly 'had it all' when we returned from our holiday that summer, and we were looking forward to seeing my parents, who were coming to stay with us for a couple of weeks. I knew how much Dad, in particular, was looking forward to a rest since he was now doing everything at home. Although friends and relatives assisted when they could, Dad was a very independent person and frequently refused offers of help. This was a situation that was beginning to cause concern.

We met Mum and Dad at Waterloo Station and we had to laugh when Dad introduced us to Mum's new 'friends' whom they had met on the train. They were football fans travelling back from a match and looked a rather formidable group, but Mum had started to chat with them and once she discovered they were from West Ham, then they were 'the salt of the earth'. (Mum was born in West Ham). The fans carried my parents' bags along the station platform and seemed genuinely sad as they waved goodbye to my mum. As we drove home all seemed well. I was still Mum's 'best friend', not her daughter, but that didn't matter.

During the week that followed Dad managed to catch-up on his sleep and life became as settled as it could under the circumstances. Then, on Saturday, Mum suddenly became very restless, far worse than any of us had seen previously. Although my parents were due to spend a further week with us, I suggested to my dad that perhaps it would be best if we took them back home to the island the following day. Dad didn't want to do that and dismissed the idea.

The following day Mum seemed more relaxed and after breakfast I suggested washing her hair. This always went down well, since Mum loved having her hair done. I would act the hairdresser and treat her as my favourite customer. Bernard went off into the garden and Dad decided to walk to the local shop to get a Sunday paper, as I began to pour warm water over Mum's head, followed by shampoo. Mum and I were well into the routine, laughing and gossiping as I began to dry her hair, when the door dell rang. I opened the door expecting to see my dad; instead there was a stranger asking if I was Mr Pilgrim's daughter. A little surprised, I replied I was and then... 'I'm afraid your father has had an accident'. My first thought was, it can't be too bad, Dad has told this man where we live. I rushed out to Bernard, told him to look after Mum, and said I was going to see Dad.

The man took me in his car to the scene. A crowd of people had gathered around on the pavement, a few hundred yards from the newsagents. I quickly made my way through the crowd to reach Dad, who was conscious but only just. His first words were, 'Who's with Mum?' and I reassured him Bernard was taking good care of her. Fortunately two people who lived nearby administered first aid and undoubtedly helped save my father's life. He had been hit by a car, which had mounted the pavement, throwing him up into the air before landing on the bonnet of the car, from where he was then thrown back onto the pavement, several hundred yards further along. The car driver had stepped out of the car, glanced at this dying eighty-year-old, my dad, and then driven off at high speed.

Eventually an ambulance arrived and Dad was taken to the nearest A&E department where ironically I had called, in my role as a medical representative, a few days before. When I arrived at the hospital, the waiting became horrendous, before I was told Dad was being transferred to a ward. If all goes well, we will operate tomorrow. When I told the doctor, 'my mum has Alzheimer's and was being looked after by my husband,' he coldly replied, 'I could have her sectioned if you like.' Those words cut into my heart, I was horrified.

Dad miraculously surprised everyone, surviving through the night, and the next day he went into theatre. His injuries included two broken legs, one of which was a compound fracture, a smashed knee cap, a broken arm, smashed shoulder joint and collar bone, six broken ribs, a severe cut to his head, plus multiple bruising all over his body. When I saw him in ITU after surgery, he did not make a pretty picture and he insisted that I should *not* let Mum see him looking like he did. We managed like this for a few days but then Dad's doctor said it would be good for them both to see each other and as Dad was being transferred back to the ward the next day, we agreed to take Mum to the hospital. I had told Mum, Frank (my dad) was in hospital and asked if she would like to go and see him. It didn't appear to worry her at all and she simply relied, 'Oh yes.'

I could hear my heart pounding as I walked into the ward with Mum. I looked around for Dad – you couldn't really miss him. He was lying in a bed close to the sister's office, each leg in plaster, one fully and one from the knee down. There were bandages around his chest, bandages around his head, a plaster cast engulfing his left arm and shoulder. Only a small area of his body was visible and that was black, through bruising. Then I looked at Mum as she casually walked up to the bed, looked straight at Dad and said, 'Hello, Frank. Have you fallen over, you silly fool?' For once, I was grateful Mum had Alzheimer's and therefore couldn't comprehend the severity of the situation. Dad looked up and seeing Mum laughing burst into tears.

Three days after the accident, my boss telephoned me to ask when I would be returning to work. I never did. As the days, then weeks, passed, Bernard and I came to accept our life had changed. I knew I had no option but to look after Mum and Dad and thankfully Bernard supported my decision. I thanked God that he did; had he not, I don't know what would have happened!

Three months later, Dad was transferred to the hospital on the Isle of Wight. There he remained for a further two and a half months, during which time he underwent further surgery to his shoulder, arm and right leg. I had given up my job and returned, with Mum, to my parents' home, from where we routinely departed every afternoon and evening to visit my dad. I was fortunate that Mum's sister lived nearby with her husband and they were available to entertain Mum, whenever it became necessary.

During this period Bernard remained at home in Essex, although he visited us on the island as often as possible, given our resources. We also placed our house on the market, for sale, intending to permanently move to the island as soon as possible. In fact Bernard and I 'lived apart' so to speak, for ten months, finally moving to Newport in August 1992.

I goes without saying, Dad had many hurdles to cross, and he often suffered from anxiety and depression, but his willpower to get back home was incredible and it was driven by his love for Doris (Mum). Shirley's music also played a part; he listened to it constantly in hospital and frequently had requests played for him on the hospital radio. On one of our visits, Dad was delighted to hear that I had booked tickets to a show at the Ryde Theatre. Aunt, Uncle, Mum and I were going to see Maxine Barrie, the winner of the 1990 *Stars In Your Eyes* for her performance as Shirley Bassey. Normally we would never go to see what is now referred to as a 'tribute act', but then times were not normal.

On the evening of the concert, we arrived at the theatre early. Mum went with my aunt and her husband for a walk while I was going to try and speak to Maxine Barrie. I had a plan, although I didn't really know if it would work! Once inside the theatre, someone directed me to the stage where Maxine was rehearsing. I remember thinking it would never be this easy with the real Shirley. I waited at the side of the stage until Maxine finished her number, but I had been spotted and Maxine came over to me. I introduced myself and apologised for interrupting her rehearsal and then said, 'I'm a great Shirley Bassey fan.' She smiled and said, 'Oh no, that's my worst fear.' I explained as quickly as possible, Mum and Dad's circumstances and said I was bringing my mum to the show that evening. She appeared genuinely upset. Then I said, 'I would like to ask a big favour but I will fully understand if you say no. Maxine replied, 'What is it?' I asked if I could bring my mum backstage to meet her, after the show. 'Of course you can, but come during the interval since I have to catch the ferry immediately after the show.' I was delighted and thanked her, adding, 'There is only one problem, Mum will think you are Shirley Bassey and I'm not sure what she will do.' 'Don't worry, that will be fine,' came Maxine's reply.

When I joined my aunt and uncle, I let them in on my secret, and then we made our way to our seats in the stalls, a few rows back, centre stage. Some things never change, I thought, as we took to our seats. When the music started, Shirley's overture, Mum was delighted and started to applaud with great enthusiasm. Maxine walked out onstage in a glittering diamanté coat and gown and my mum rose to give her a standing ovation. I was rather surprised, and also rose to my feet, but the person most shocked was Maxine. However, she played her part well, acknowledging our applause before going into her opening number.

I genuinely enjoyed Maxine's performance. She had been a performer for many years before her 'overnight' success on the TV talent show, and gave a very good performance as Shirley. Obviously her voice did not have the power of Shirley's, and that special magic, which is Shirley Bassey, was missing, but her act was accurate and enjoyable. Taking into account that Maxine only had a small group of musicians to accompany her, the effect was terrific and I gained respect for the lady.

Mum was also enjoying the performance and was quite excited by the end of the first half. When she sat down at the start of the interval I asked if she would like to go backstage to see Shirley. Mum replied, 'Oh, we can't do that.' Then I told Mum it was OK because I had already asked and she had said we could go and see her. Mum couldn't get up from her seat quick enough. We went through the door leading to the backstage area and started to climb the stairs towards the dressing room. At that moment Maxine came out from her dressing room and started to head down the stairs, from where she would go to the wings. When she spotted us, Maxine called out, 'Hello, are you enjoying the show?' Suddenly, Mum stretched out her arms and cuddled Maxine as though she was greeting a long-lost friend. 'Shirley, you were wonderful,' she said. 'It's so lovely to see you again… and thank you so much.' Maxine was clearly taken aback. We saw Maxine after the show and I thanked her most sincerely, she told us she would love to return to the island to perform a show as herself. Before leaving, Maxine gave me with a signed photograph for my dad, wishing him a speedy recovery. When Maxine left that night, she *truly* knew what it was like to be Shirley Bassey.

When we visited Dad the next day, he was delighted to hear of Mum's experience and placed his personally signed photo on his bedside table for all to see. I'm sure the entire ward had heard the story by the end of the day.

Sadly, Dad spent Christmas in hospital, which he found very

difficult, but a few weeks later, he came home for a weekend visit. This was mainly to see how he would cope. Both legs were still in plaster and social services arranged for some sort of 'monkey lift' to be fitted, above his bed, to enable him to pull himself up. A few weeks later, Dad came home for good. Mum was clearly delighted to have him back in the bungalow and would wander into his bedroom, often having dressed up, using whatever items took her fancy. Dad and I were in stitches one morning when Mum suddenly appeared in her corsets, with her shirt pulled up to her chest, balancing an egg box on top of her head, performing on tip toes like a ballet dancer. How we laughed, often through our tears.

In the summer of 1992, one year after Dad's accident, Bernard and I moved permanently to the island. Bernard worked hard decorating our home while I spent most of my time at my parents' home. Although Dad accepted some help initially for himself and Mum, it soon diminished over time. He eventually managed to walk and regained some use in his arm. Prior to the accident, they had frequently gone out, by car or bus, and Dad still hungered for this life. We took them out as often as we could but the time came when I needed to get a job and eventually I became employed, part time, as a practice manager at a GP surgery. Bernard also found himself a part time job as a quality inspector, which at nearly sixty years of age was some achievement.

Joyce, from Birkenhead, would regularly send me wonderful, descriptive letters whenever Reon and herself went to see Shirley in concert. Through these letters, newspaper reports, reviews and television appearances, I managed to continue to follow Shirley's career.

At the beginning of 1993, it had been wonderful to watch the TV programme *This Is Your Life*. Shirley had been surprised by yet again, in Part 2 of her life, by 'the big red book', in front of five and a half thousand fans, whilst receiving a standing ovation at the Royal Albert Hall in December. It made me long to see her again.

Everyone had been telling Bernard and myself we should get away for a short break, so when we read Shirley would be appearing with the 10,000 voices of the World Choir in Cardiff, we wondered if it might just be possible. Happy in the knowledge that care would be provided for my parents, we booked seats for the concert being held at Cardiff Arms Park on 29 May and two nights' hotel accommodation. We were a little apprehensive when we left the island to travel to Cardiff but we understood as much as anyone that we needed to recharge our batteries. To see Shirley perform in her home town would certainly do that for me.

After checking into our hotel in the centre of Cardiff, we went in search of a nice restaurant nearby for dinner. I distinctly remember everywhere we went you could sense the buzz. It seemed everyone in Wales was gathering here for tomorrow's concert and each overheard conversion always contained one word, 'Shirley'. The place had a magical atmosphere and we were very glad to be part of it.

The following day I was delighted when I discovered in the Virgin Record Store, a new CD by Shirley. I purchased the CD which had been released by Icon Records in 1992 as *The Bond Collection*, unaware at the time that the recording was made in 1987 and the CD released against Shirley wishes. Now it has become something of a rarity, since Shirley later obtained a permanent injunction against Icon Entertainment, preventing further manufacture or sales of the record and all unsold copies were withdrawn from sale.

As we joined the crowds of people walking towards Cardiff's Arms Park, my own excitement grew. I knew our seats were some distance from the stage but somehow, at this venue, it seemed irrelevant. Tonight it was about atmosphere, generated by an audience of 30,000 who had come to see Shirley Bassey sing with the combined voices from 182 choirs. When we eventually found our seats, we felt very privileged to be experiencing the event.

Although we enjoyed the evening's programme, it seemed we had been waiting for ever for Shirley to appear. The weather had not been kind and we welcomed the bright orange rainwear which S4C, the Welsh-language television channel, distributed freely amongst the audience. It certainly offered us added protection from the rainfall, which had begun prior to the orchestral introduction of 'Goldfinger'.

As Shirley walked out onstage, Cardiff Arms Park erupted; the whole city must have heard the cheers. She looked wonderful in the lovely Zandra Rhodes gown we had seen her in at Bournemouth. With a backdrop consisting of hundreds of men in white shirts and black bow ties, the effect was stunning. Her performance, although limited to only a few numbers, confirmed what the people of Cardiff already knew: the world's best singers are Welsh. Shirley delivered 'Something' beautifully. An image of Shirley was forged on my mind during that number. At one point the lights beamed from above, highlighting the rain drops and seemingly converting them into diamonds. Suddenly a bird flew into the beam of light as Shirley looked up towards the heavens. The crowd fell silent as the bird flew back and forth across the beam of light, while Shirley continued to sing. The moment was inspirational. Like me, perhaps the bird thought he was in heaven.

'Big Spender' was performed a little more slowly for this concert but wasn't lacking in appeal because the choir joined in with Shirley for the number. The audience loved the fun and Shirley clearly approved of her 'backing group', turning to blow kisses of thanks. Then came the final number, 'Hey Jude', with the choir joining the audience for the 'na-na-na-na'. It was unbelievable. Nothing more can be said except, thank you Shirley, thank you Cardiff, thanks you Wales.

When we arrived back home the following day, all seemed well. I loved telling my parents about Cardiff, our weekend trip and Shirley's performance and although Mum never fully comprehended the tales I told, she certainly recognised and enjoyed Shirley's voice when we played the CD. Of course, Shirley's recordings were always being played at home. That year EMI issued, on the Music for Pleasure Premier label, a new recording entitled *Shirley Bassey Sings The Songs of Andrew*

Lloyd Webber. I remember playing the CD for the first time, it blew me away and I thought it was sensational. Shirley had interpreted every number brilliantly and her voice had never been better. Even today, it remains one of my favourite CDs.

Later that summer Bernard and I looked forward to another short break, which we had seen advertised earlier in the year. A travel company had advertised a tour package to Jersey, which included flights, a couple of nights hotel accommodation and most importantly, good tickets to see Shirley Bassey in concert at Fort Regent. Naturally we had booked the package immediately, hoping that, when the time came, we could arrange for care for Mum and Dad for the few days we would be away.

We were sad to leave Mum and Dad and it would seem strange without them, but good care had been arranged and Dad understood. After settling into our hotel in St Helier, Bernard and I decided to look for a nice restaurant where we could book for dinner later. Good food was always high on our priority list, so we were pleased to discover a charming place near our hotel. We also discovered, to our delight, a theatre near the restaurant where Danny La Rue was starring in the musical, *La Cage aux Folles.* As we had a free evening the following night, we decided to try and book, and managed to get tickets for seats in the front stalls. As we left the booking office I jokingly said to Bernard, 'I wonder if Shirley will come to see Danny, they are good friends.' Bernard just grinned but I knew what he was thinking, There she goes again, dreaming!

That evening we had a lovely meal and sat at a table next to a couple of guys who started chatting to us. After some general chat they asked if we had come to Jersey to see Shirley Bassey. At the mention of her name, I could talk for hours, so I told the guys about our trip and how we had just booked to see Danny La Rue the following evening, adding that he was a friend of Shirley's. One of the guys replied, 'We know, we are working with the show and Shirley's coming tomorrow evening, but keep that to yourselves.' I couldn't believe what I was hearing but they assured me it was true.

The next day I strolled around with Bernard, in a dream. Could it be true? I tried not to get too excited. As we took to our seats, I looked around the theatre but there were no empty seats nearby, then I turned and looked up to the royal circle and there, in the centre, was a line of empty seats. The house lights dimmed and I quitely said to Bernard, Shirley's going to be in the royal circle, then in the darkness I looked up and saw her walk in with her companions. Nobody seemed to be aware of what was happening and we sat back to enjoy the musical. Just before the interval, I turned and looked up. Shirley was leaving her seat and I guessed she was heading backstage.

When the lights went up I told Bernard what I had seen and we decided to wait on the staircase to the royal circle when the bell sounded for the audience to return to their seats. I was terribly nervous as after all, Shirley was having a night out with friends and the last thing she probably wanted was to see a fan. Anyway, would she remember me? – after all, I hadn't seen her face to face for five years. I decided I would stand back and be discreet, something that's hard for a fan. We stood on the landing halfway up the staircase, which by now was empty, wondering if anyone would appear. Suddenly a person was coming up the stairs and I heard, 'Hello, it's lovely to see you.' It was Shirley. I shook her hand, muttering we were sitting in the stalls and that we would be coming to see her tomorrow evening. 'Oh good,' she replied.

Bernard and I finally made our way back to the stalls; fortunately we didn't need to disturb too many people. We sat watching the rest of the show in a daze. The show was very well received by the audience and when Danny La Rue came back onstage to acknowledge the applause, he announced Shirley Bassey was in the audience. Cheers rang out, and then Shirley stood up and took a bow. Danny and Shirley then called out to each other, about their 'frocks'. What a fabulous night it had been.

The next morning I phoned Dad and relived the experience of the previous evening. When I told him Shirley had said it was lovely to see me, I could tell he was close to tears. Obviously he would have loved to have been with us but now trips like that were no longer possible. I knew he would tell Mum all about our night out and for a short while she would be as happy as he would then play one of Shirley's albums and Mum would start to sing!

That evening we headed for the Gloucester Hall, located within the vast leisure, conference and entertainment complex known as Fort Regent, once a ninteenth-century hilltop fortification above St Helier. We were happy to discover our seats were only a few rows back from the stage and more importantly, near to the aisle, which meant I could get to the stage. As we sat waiting for the interval to end, I thought how I missed sharing the excitement with my parents, but I knew Dad, at least, would be thinking of us. The orchestra started to play and the hall echoed to the sound of 'Goldfinger' as people rose to give Shirley a standing ovation. As Shirley acknowledged the audience, it seemed clear that she was glad to be back in Jersey as she threw herself into 'Goldfinder', followed by 'Diamonds Are Forever'.

The concert followed Shirley's now established pattern, old songs like 'Kiss Me Honey, Honey', new songs such as 'Wind Beneath My Wings', blue songs like 'Don't Cry Out Loud' and, of course, the not-to-be-excluded fun number 'Big Spender'. With the town staging *La Cage aux Folles*, Shirley could do no wrong when she stood centre stage and slowly began, 'I Am What I Am'. I half expected Danny La Rue to jump out in his glamorous 'frock', but of course he had his own performance to give that night. When Shirley sang the words, 'give me a hook or the ovation', a mighty cheer rose from the audience and the orchestra stepped up the tempo.

I didn't want it to end, but then I never did. It was time to head for the stage, so at the end of the next number I made my apologies to a couple of people next to us and quickly walked to the stage. As soon as Shirley spotted me, she came over and with hand outstretched, gave a lovely smile, just like the night before. I felt wonderful. To the delight of the audience, a few more numbers followed and then, finally, it was over.

CHAPTER 22

WISHING YOU WERE SOMEHOW HERE AGAIN

Late in 1993 my greatest joy, as a fan, came when I heard the news that Shirley had been honoured in the Queen's Birthday Honours list. Then on 18 February 1994, Shirley was invited, by the Queen, to Buckingham Palace where she received her CBE, making her a Commander of the Order of the British Empire. The photographs which appeared in the press the following day featured a delighted Shirley, accompanied by her daughter Sharon and friends Beaudoin and Yves Mills, displaying her medal with pride. However, the press cuttings would have to lie and wait, along with the accumulation of other cuttings and reviews collected throughout the past several months. Alzheimer's had begun to engulf our family and we were losing the battle.

Bernard and I knew it would happen eventually, but even so you are never really prepared. The time had come when we were unable to provide the full care and support Mum now required and although we had some help from others, it was not enough. Dad, too, had his problems. Our dreams were rapidly fading, only to be replaced by fears, self-doubt, guilt and anxiety. Those dark times are not for the pages of this book!

During the summer of 1994, the sad day finally arrived when our GP told my father, 'Your wife *must* go into a residential care home.' Bernard and I realised it would be so much better for Mum, which it was, but knowing that did not make the situation any easier. Thankfully, Mum settled in well, which offered some comfort.

After a matter of weeks our GP insisted my father should join my mother at the care home, initially for a few weeks 'respite'. Very reluctantly, Dad agreed but in our hearts we knew he had lost the will to live.

The GP had also made the suggestion, as he was concerned about my health, that Bernard and I should take a break. Therefore, when we discovered Shirley would be performing at Plymouth during her forthcoming tour, we applied for tickets. We managed to get front-row seats and I permitted myself to dream once more.

We booked a hotel, for three nights, located by the edge of the Cornish coast, yet within easy distance of Plymouth. I had not seen Shirley 'up close and personal', as they say, since Jersey three years earlier, so I was looking forward to saying 'hello and thank you' once again, at the end of her concert. There was a concern, however – Dad wasn't eating. Then prior to our trip, he developed a chest infection and was admitted to hospital. We proposed cancelling our trip but after a few days Dad showed signs of improvement and the hospital staff assured us he was doing fine, so we decided to continue with our plans. The day before our departure we visited both Mum and Dad; everything was in place regarding care at both the care home and the hospital. We were also reassured by my aunt and uncle that they would visit Mum and Dad and, if necessary, inform us should any unforeseen problem occur.

When we drove onto the ferry at Yarmouth to cross to Lymington on the mainland, it seemed as though a weight had been lifted from our shoulders. Suddenly the day seemed bright and the journey, although fairly long, was delightful. Finally, I was dreaming of seeing Shirley again. I found it hard to believe it was going to happen. We stopped on route for lunch, before travelling on to Plymouth then crossing the River Tamar via the Saltash Toll Bridge. Finally, early evening, we arrived at the hotel, looking forward to a glass of wine, dinner and an early night.

As we approached the hotel reception, I had a strange feeling something was wrong. When we introduced ourselves, the receptionist immediately said, 'We have had several phone calls for you.' Passing us notes upon which phone numbers had been hastily written, she said, 'Can you please phone the hospital and your aunt.' We were quickly shown to our room, from where we returned the phone calls, expecting to hear Dad had taken a turn for the worse. The news we received was far worse: Mum had fallen and was in hospital with a broken hip. The surgeons planned to operate the following morning.

After breakfast, the following morning, we checked out of the hotel. We were heading home, but first we had to make a detour into Plymouth to return our front-row tickets for Shirley's concert.[8]

We finally arrived back on the island early evening and headed immediately to the hospital. As we entered the surgical ward, I had no idea what to expect. Suddenly we spotted Mum; she had a great big smile on her face and was waving to us from her bed. I couldn't believe it. We gave her a big hug and kissed and then I explained to her that she had a fall and was now in hospital.' Casually Mum replied, 'Am I, that was silly.' Shortly after my aunt and uncle arrived, so we used the opportunity to go and see my dad, who was also in the same hospital. I must admit I was not looking forward to seeing him. I had a vision of my father saying, referring to Mum's accident, 'I told you this would

8 A few weeks later the theatre refunded the price of the tickets to us; obviously they had resold the tickets. How lucky those two people were, obtaining 'our' front-row seats on the day of the concert. I hope they enjoyed the performance!

happen.' Thankfully, it wasn't as bad as I feared. In fact he spoke very little, yet I sensed he was pleased to hear Mum had recovered so well from the operation.

I will never know if it was the effects of the anaesthetic or medication, but Mum's memory seemed to improve for a few days after the operation. When we visited one evening we were delighted to see Dad at her bedside. He had not seen her for several weeks and it was wonderful to see him holding her hand whilst they happily chatted together. It was clear for all to see how much they loved each other. Later a nurse came to take Dad back to his ward. I distinctly remember, as he left the ward, he turned back to wave to Mum and there were tears in his eyes. They never saw each other again; Dad died a few days later.

I didn't want Mum to be told of Dad's passing, yet when we arrived at her bedside it was clear to see, she knew. The ever-present smile had been wiped away, replaced by one or two tears which slowly trickled down her cheek. The smile was rarely seen again.

I was not told by the hospital that Mum had suffered a stroke, only that she should be discharged to a residential nursing home. The staff at the home were very caring and kind and I visited every day, but the person I went to visit had already 'gone'. Mum's shell lay in front of me but 'my mum' was no longer there. It was a terrible experience.

Within a few weeks of my father's death, Mum suffered another stroke and died peacefully soon after.

The previous three years had been horrendous and anyone who has experienced something similar will understand when I say, Mum's death was a welcome relief.

CHAPTER 23

AS IF WE NEVER SAID GOODBYE

Grief is something we all have to face in our lives and we learn, in our own way, how to live with it. Initially I engrossed my-self in my work, but in time Bernard and I began to think about our lives, something we had not allowed ourselves to consider for some time.

Our circumstances meant we had not been able to attend any of Shirley's concerts during her recent tour, which celebrated her fortieth anniversary year since her show business debut. Thankfully, Joyce's letters were a delight to read, always arriving promptly after Joyce and Reon had attended one of Shirley's concerts. I finally started pasting my collection of press reviews and articles into the scrapbook and eventually life, as a fan, began to get back on course. The most recent reviews were acknowledging Shirley's 'almost operatic power and purity blessed with a deeper, richer timbre than before'; these were words written by theatre critic Jack Tinker after attending Shirley's concert at the Royal Festival Hall. Of course, many of her fans had already noticed some of the gradual changes occurring in

Shirley's voice; however, it was always nice to see her getting proper recognition of her talent and hard work, especially when it came from the national press.

In November that year, 1994, the Variety Club of Great Britain held a 'Tribute Luncheon to Shirley Bassey, CBE' at the Savoy Hotel in London. The following Monday, 28 November, Shirley closed the first half of the Royal Variety Performance, in the presence of His Royal Highness the Prince of Wales. Appearing in a striking dress decorated with layers of white silk tassels, which danced in time to Shirley's every movement, the performance was regarded as the evening's showstopper. Later, when I watched the television broadcast of Shirley's performance, I felt the thrill and excitement pouring back into me.

I hungered to see Shirley in concert again, so we decided we would go to a concert as soon as possible, although we knew there would be a wait; Shirley had only just completed her recent tour. A few months later we heard the news we had been waiting for: Shirley would be returning to Jersey in the summer, to make a reappearance at Fort Regent. We were delighted when we discovered a short-break package was available again, similar to the one we had experienced during Shirley's last concerts at the venue, so we booked immediately.

After arriving in Jersey we went to meet the tour representative at the hotel for her introductory welcome and the distribution of tickets for Shirley's concert, which we were attending the following evening. Pleasingly, the tour group consisted mainly of Shirley Bassey fans, so it wasn't long before everyone started to chat. As each surname was called, the tour representative handed out a white envelope to a recipient, which they clutched in their hand as if they were receiving a large cheque from Ernie. Then our name was called and I quickly took hold of the envelope, opening it almost immediately. To my surprise there were four tickets inside. Bernard and I had obviously booked two tickets, but we both looked at each other and immediately knew for whom the 'other tickets' were meant. Feeling rather sad, I handed back the two spare tickets, expecting nothing more would be said, but the representative insisted the booking had been made for four people. We explained the hotel and flights were booked for Bernard and I only; however, no explanation could be found! Eventually, having checked that everybody had received their correct tickets, the representative reluctantly took back our spare tickets.

Since we had missed seeing Shirley during her 40th Anniversary Tour concerts, I wanted to present her with something at Jersey, as a thank you, as well as to mark the occasion of her forty years in show business. Prior to coming to Jersey, I had looked for weeks for something suitable. It's difficult enough to choose a present for a friend or relative, but what do you buy a 'star'. Eventually I spotted a curved crystal photo frame which would hold three photographs. Each individual frame was edged in gold and although this type of frame is now readily available, at the time it was stylish and unusual. Bernard and I selected three coloured photographs, from ones he had taken, which we felt captured the atmosphere of Shirley in concert. When we placed the prints in the individual frames, we were delighted by the result. I packed the completed frame carefully on a pad of pastel-coloured tissue set within a gold gift box, since this would allow Shirley to see the framed photos as I presented the frame to her. The gift wrapping would also protect the frame from any accidental damage.

As Bernard and I made our way to Fort Regent for Shirley's final concert, I was understandably filled with many emotions. I had been so lucky to have had such wonderful parents with whom I had shared so much. Once inside the auditorium, I felt they were with me as we made our way to our seats. Bernard and I were not surprised to find two empty seats near ours; often Shirley fans would miss the first half of a show, only to take up their seats after the interval. However, tonight, when the lights dimmed for the second half of the concert, the two seats remained empty. I found it rather consoling to imagine my parents were sitting there!

From the moment Shirley walked onstage, I was once again captivated. She was wearing one of her favourite black gowns, a Douglas Darnell creation. In fact Shirley liked this dress so much, she requested another to be made in white and this she'd worn during her recent 40th Anniversary Tour.

We had good seats, approximately six rows back from the stage. A few years ago I would have hungered to be in the front row but now I found I was content to sit and watch Shirley from a reasonable distance, enjoying every note, movement and gesture performed to perfection. Now it was young men who mostly occupied the front-row seats, but what did that matter, whether fans from forty years ago or 'new recruits', we were all here to enjoy Shirley's performance. Her opening number generated a tremendous response from the Jersey audience, loud applause, cheering and ovations from various sections of the audience. Everybody around us were enthusiastic fans and I knew we were going to have a wonderful evening, although I thought Shirley's new musical director, Colin Green, seemed a little apprehensive.

The concert followed what had now become an expected pattern of 'hits', such as 'Kiss Me, Honey, Honey, Kiss Me', 'As I Love You', 'I, Who Have Nothing', all of which received tremendous applause. Intermingled were the saucy numbers, such as 'Big Spender', then the emotion of Shirley's own life were featured through songs like 'Never, Never, Never' and the newly recorded 'With One Look'. This number showed off Shirley's talents as a performer and left the audience thinking the song could have been written for her. Andrew Lloyd Webber may have written the number for the musical, *Sunset Boulevard*, but now Shirley had taken ownership, along with another song from the same show, 'As If We Never Said Goodbye'. The audience's applause was deafening. Individuals approached the stage, arms outstretched in search of Shirley's hand, as she waltzed along its edge. Many were lucky, some gripped tightly to their prize, but all eventually returned to their seats, waiting for the next number.

The performance continued with Shirley offering other stunning renderings, amongst which the 'New York Medley', 'I Am What I Am' and 'Hey Jude' were the most popular. Whilst the audience poured out its appreciation, I decided it was time to approach the stage and present my gift. I had not seen Shirley up close since our last visit to Jersey and I wondered if she would still remember me. My concerns quickly evaporated as I drew near. Shirley was heading towards me wearing that lovely smile that said all I needed to know. I removed the lid from my gift box, exposing the crystal frame for her to see, then handed the package up to her. As she took full hold of the box, Shirley crouched down as if to indicate to the audience the gift was heavy, before looking at the photographs within the frame. I was delighted by Shirley's comments before she eventually placed the box on the piano for safe keeping and I returned to my seat. The final number brought cheers, thunderous applause and the now customary standing ovation.

Within the hour, we were heading back to our hotel, memories of the evening spinning through my mind. Everything had seemed like it had always been. The magic had remained and I felt my parents' presence, somehow, had been with us. Tomorrow we would fly home but the memories of the evening would last for some time.

Next morning fog lingered over Jersey and we wondered if our flight back to London would be delayed. We had experienced delays due to fog on previous visits to Jersey. The island's airport is tiny when compared to Gatwick or Heathrow; you could even call it minute. Members of the party staying at our hotel were booked on various flights to different destinations, so we were departing the hotel at intervals throughout the morning. When Bernard and I travelled to the airport, the fog had mostly cleared, but we found the airport heaving with passengers due to delayed departures. We spoke with some of the fans we had met during our visit, before proceeding to check-in for our flight.

A few minutes later, as we were walking away from the check-in desk, absorbed in examining our seat numbers, something suddenly caught my eye. A group of people were about to cross our path and one person in particular caught my attention. Smartly dressed in a navy blue denim trouser suit and sporting a panama hat and large sunglasses, it was Shirley Bassey. I quickly responded with a hello and thanked her for the fabulous concert. Nobody else seemed take any notice and soon she was heading off towards departures. Several private jets were preparing to take-off between commercial flights, so as we waited for news of our departure, we chatted with some other fans who had seen Shirley enter the airport. They were booked on an afternoon flight, departing an hour or so after ours. I suggested to them that we would probably see Shirley boarding a private jet shortly. I couldn't believe it when one of the fans said, 'No, Shirley is on the flight before ours.' When they told me the flight number, I nearly died. 'We're booked on Shirley's flight,' I said.

Bernard and I decided to be ready to go to the departure gate immediately the flight was announced. I was so excited and could not believe we would be flying home on the same flight as Shirley. We were first to arrive at the departure gate and took up our position by the exit door. Within minutes an airport courtesy bus arrived and parked almost in front of us, a short distance from the steps leading to the plane, and out stepped Shirley. An air stewardess carried a large bouquet of pink flowers and stood by her as she waited to board the aircraft. Bernard asked the security guy on the gate if he could step outside to take a photograph of the aircraft (we didn't want anyone to know we had recognised Shirley) but his request was rightly refused. However, he suggested Bernard take a couple of photos through the glass door – I hope you will agree, the results were not bad, considering the circumstances.

One or two people boarded the plane prior to Shirley climbing the steps. My heart was pounding, the minutes seemed like hours as we waited patiently for the announcement. Bernard and I were the first to board the aircraft and my fear was we would be directed to board at the rear of the aircraft, but thankfully we were shown to the steps near to the cockpit area. I cannot express how exciting that was for me. Minutes before I had watched Shirley mount the steps and now I was going to be flying with her. As we were directed through the first-class area the compère from Shirley's concert said hello to me. I can only imagine he had recognised me from the moment I'd presented Shirley with my gift. As we passed, we spotted Shirley sitting at the rear of the first-class section, occupying the window seat. I nudged Bernard, who was walking ahead of me, and he quickly leaned across the seats and started to sing the first line of Frank Sinatra's classic, 'Come Fly With Me'. It certainly brought a smile to Shirley's face but neither of us wanted to draw attention to her, so we continued to our seats. We were sitting three or four rows behind Shirley, divided only by the first-class-economy curtain. I actually had, like Shirley, the window seat. I always adored flying, so knowing I was looking out onto the same clouds as her seemed surreal. I felt I was in heaven.

When the plane landed I suggested to Bernard that perhaps we should not 'press our luck', so we decided to make our way to baggage reclaim and leave Shirley in peace. However, as we left the aircraft Shirley was still close by and once we had collected our trolley we found we were, almost by accident, standing by Shirley as if drawn like a moth to a flame. We all waited to collect our luggage. Shirley had placed her lovely bouquet of flowers in the handbag rack of the trolley, an appealing image which Bernard had noted. Not many people had yet arrived at the baggage claim, so Bernard said, 'I think I will ask Shirley if I could take one quick photograph.' I warned him Shirley might well say no, but I could see why he wanted to try and capture the image.

He politely asked Shirley if he could take a photo of her with the flowers. She replied, 'I'd rather you didn't', which Bernard accepted without any fuss, but Shirley followed this by saying, 'I'm quite happy for you to photograph me while I'm working, but I'm not working now.' Like Bernard, I knew he was asking a lot and hadn't really expected Shirley to agree, but to hear Shirley refer to her talent as a performer as working really took me by surprise. Had it really become work as I thought of work? I hoped not!

We remained where we were, waiting for our luggage, as more and more people arrived. Some were now beginning to recognise Shirley and those who had not, soon realised she was 'somebody', the flowers being a bit of a giveaway. Shirley was passing the time talking to Colin Green whilst, annoyingly, people approached and took photographs. Nobody appeared to even consider Shirley. I told Bernard, 'At least you had manners!'

The conveyer belt began to roll and people's luggage started to arrive. Both Shirley and I had picked up cases and most people were already making their way through the arrivals exit. We stood side by side watching two small cases emerge onto the belt; somehow they had become entwined. Oh no, I thought, as I recognised the Louis Vuitton piece of luggage hooked onto my fake designer suitcase. As the pieces approached we both reached out and took hold of our individual handle, then gave a tug. Thankfully, the cases parted and we each placed our item on its appropriate trolley.

Whilst in Jersey, Shirley had given an interview to the press in which she said she would be returning to London following her concerts, to see her daughter, Sharon, and the grandchildren. As Shirley and I approached the exit, I wished her an enjoyable time with her family before saying goodbye. Bernard and I then stopped to watch as Shirley continued through to the arrivals hall. No longer the performer, nobody seemed to recognise the mum who was longing to see her daughter.

It had been a wonderful weekend but very emotional too. Returning home this time was sad because I could no longer share with my parents the thrills and excitement of seeing Shirley. In the past we had shared and enjoyed every moment together; now they had both gone.

The following month I received a letter which warmed my heart.

> '...Miss Bassey has asked me to thank you so much for the lovely photo display she received in Jersey. She thought the photographs were lovely and I know she is going to find it a home in a prominent position in her apartment. Thank you for your kindness'

Bernard and I were delighted and I know Mum and Dad would have been very proud.

CHAPTER 24

DO YOU KNOW WHERE YOU'RE GOING TO

In July 1995, Shirley returned to her home town in Wales to perform at Cardiff Castle. Recalling her days as a twelve-year-old schoolgirl, when she wanted to sing before Her Majesty the Queen, Shirley was now living her dream before the audience of 10,000 fans, many of whom had travelled from around the UK to see her perform at this unique venue.

The year also saw Shirley touring Northern Europe, the Middle East and America, as well as recording and releasing the first of two CDs for PolyGram. The first, entitled *Shirley Bassey Sings The Movies*, featured a selection of her favourite compositions from the movies and included 'Try A Little Tenderness', Makin' Whoopee', 'Crazy', 'Love on the Rocks' and 'Arthur's Them (Best That You Can Do)'. I confess, on first hearing the CD I felt the musical accompaniment sounded rather synthetic. However, it was the style of the nineties and went on to become very successful both in the UK and overseas.

In September, Shirley recorded *An Audience With Shirley Bassey* for

LWT at the London Television Centre before a celebrity audience that included Max Bygraves, Lionel Bart, Britt Ekland, John Mills, and many more. Like so many of Shirley's fans, we were thrilled when we watched the televised show. It was, I believe, and still is, one of the best shows to feature Shirley ever produced for television.

I know I have said this before, but in the past I have been so very lucky. I attended so many of Shirley's television recordings and, yes, it helped that at the time I was living on the outskirts of London, a young woman with few commitments. Now our lives impose greater restrictions, so what had been possible as a fan in my teens, today presented greater obstacles. Shirley's popularity was at an all-time high. The constant demands from fans throughout the world must have made Shirley wonder, 'Do You Know Where You're Going To', whenever she sang the song from the film *Mahogany*.

Nineteen ninety-six was a mammoth year for Shirley. Following on from visits at the beginning of the year to the Far East, New Zealand and Norway, she headed back to the UK for a nationwide tour. Commencing in April at the Brighton Centre, she played fourteen cities before ending with a record-breaking nine nights at London's Royal Festival Hall, in June. Today we take very much for granted the information we can access on the web. Nowadays we can access details of Shirley's New Zealand concert, but back in the nineties the main source of information was the concert programme. I have collected many over the years, from a single sheet to the large-format glossy twenty-eight page souvenir programme that accompanied the 1996 tour.

My excitement moved up a level when I entered the concert hall (the Bournemouth International Centre) to find the programme seller waving the golden souvenir, which had glamorous photos on the front and back covers, across which was written 'Shirley'. Inside were more delightful photographs, several of which had been taken during the recording of *An Audience With Shirley Bassey*, as well as 'Royal Command' photos and stills from the film *La Passione*. Once we had settled in our seats, glancing through the programme was compulsory for me. That year I had particularly enjoyed reading Shirley's welcome message and the two-page feature about her latest challenge, her film debut in *La Passione*, written and produced by Chris Rea.

La Passione tells the story of a ten-year -old son of an Italian immigrant with an obsession for Ferrari and motor racing, and especially real-life racing driver Wolfgang Von Trips, who died following a crash at the Monza Gran Prix in 1961. It is the story of a passionate fan, so you can understand why it appealed to me. In the film Shirley plays herself in a stunning dream sequence. Unfortunately, at the time, the film was not widely distributed, so I remember only a few televised extracts.[9]

Now, almost twenty years later,[10] Chris Rea has re-released *La Passione* but to my dismay when I received the order Dame Shirley was missing – her part in the film had been cut. The CD/DVDs were quickly returned.

Needless to say, every concert we attend during that tour was fabulous. On every occasion my excitement grew, just as it had always grown throughout the years. I admit there were times when we had endured a poor first half of a show, when I wondered, Will I be as thrilled as before by Shirley's performance? But any momentary doubt always vanished the moment she walked onstage. There I'd be jumping up from my seat, cheering and applauding as hard as I possibly could.

I can't offer a precise explanation for this emotion, but I know it is a form of love. Every true fan will understand, and many will have experienced what I always feel. From the opening number to the finale encore, Shirley entertains. It's a combination of many ingredients, each chosen and mixed with experience, passion and love, to deliver the perfect feast. The recipe is now tried and tested and the fans love it. We

---

9 When I wrote a few lines about *La Passione*, I thought I should check to see if my recollections were correct, so I did the usual Google search. To my astonishment I discovered Chris Rea's *La Passione* CD/DVD was due to be reissued the following day, so I placed an order.

10 November 2015.

cheer in recognition each time we hear the opening notes to several 'Bassey' classics. We meditate throughout the love songs and join in the fun during 'Kiss Me, Honey, Honey' and 'Big Spender'. Then we analyse a new number from Shirley's latest recording, 'Crazy', sung so smoothly and softly. (Yes, Shirley can sing softly.) The audience, now represented by all age groups, cheers its approval and Shirley leads us into her next number. 'I Am What I Am' blows us away, as does 'Hey Jude' and 'This Is My Life'. Fans rush to the stage and Shirley shakes hands with the faithful. Another number leads us to believe we have experience the best performance Shirley Bassey has ever given. Well the truth is, it probably is, but wait until the next one!

Shirley ended her tour with nine sell-out concerts at London's, Royal Festival Hall and in doing so established, at the time, a record for the longest run by a solo artist at the venue.

The year also saw the release of Shirley's second CD for PolyGram, entitled *The Show Must Go On*. The CD featured 'Slave To The Rhythm', 'Where Is The Love', 'Every Breath You Take' and 'One Day I'll Fly Away'. Along with her TV appearances, Shirley certainly gave her UK fans plenty to enjoy during the year.

Shirley acquired more fans the following year when she returned to the charts, courtesy of Will White and Alex Gifford, members of the duo the Propellerheads, with the single 'History Repeating'. The duo reportedly wrote the number with only one singer in mind and tempted Shirley into the studio. At the time it seemed an unusual combination, but it worked and the song entered the charts and became a 'dance floor' hit in the clubs both in the UK and overseas. The making of a video for 'History Repeating' later featured on Shirley's DVD *Divas Are Forever*.

Sadly I was unable to attend, in 1997, neither the Castle Howard nor the Althorp Park outdoor concerts. Held in the summer, they were billed as 'Shirley Bassey's 60th Birthday Concerts' and were extremely successful. A relative (the daughter of the aunt who gave me my first

78 rpm recordings of Shirley) attended the Althorp Park concert and telephoned me the following day with a full report. She was so excited by Shirley's performance that we spent ages on the phone discussing the concert. In fact, when I replaced the receiver, I realised we had probably spent as much time chatting as Shirley had spent onstage. Fortunately for fans, the two concerts were recorded and later released on CD as *Shirley Bassey, The Birthday Concert*, confirming once again, that Bassey 'live' is fabulous.

The following May, 1998, we returned to Bournemouth's BIC for the second night of Shirley's Diamond Tour. Although we no longer had front row seats, I still experienced the same butterflies of excitement as I had from the very beginning. The feelings never receded and the thrill of seeing Shirley in concert never diminished. She could always whip up her audience to fever pitch, creating an atmosphere so charged you felt her magnetism all around. We listened, applauded and cheered our way through fifteen or so songs and nearly one and a half hours later, Shirley finally left the stage.

A few days after a concert, I would write to Joyce who always reciprocated with descriptive letters detailing the performances she and Reon had attended. During Shirley's tour they normally travelled to Manchester, Blackpool or Cardiff to see her perform and on some occasions, even travelled down to London. They, like me, had witnessed and enjoyed Shirley's exceptional talent for several decades

The Diamond Tour ended in Britain with ten nights at the Royal Festival Hall, breaking the record previously set by Shirley in 1996, and then it was home to Monte Carlo for a well-earned rest.

Later in 1998 Shirley returned to London to record a 'special' for the BBC entitled *Viva Diva*, then, four days later, gave a very special concert in front of the Pyramids in Cairo. At the time I had no knowledge of these engagements but thankfully, due mainly to the rapid development in technology through the decade, these performances were recorded and we can now enjoy these in our homes.

Viva Diva was screened by the BBC on New Year's Eve 1998, and was, at the time, one of the best television specials ever produced. Featuring the cast from the musical *Chicago*, Shirley gave two great performances, featuring the show's hit tunes 'Razzle Dazzle' and 'All That Jazz'.

The following February, Shirley returned to Australia for concerts in the cities of Perth, Canberra, Melbourne, Brisbane and Sydney. In addition, an outdoor concert was given at Wyndham Estate Winery, Hunter Valley. These winery concerts were extremely popular and were attracting the world's top entertainers. Other performers that year included Tony Bennett.

During the summer of 1999, Shirley returned to the UK to record tracks for the Official Rugby World Cup (RWC) album, *Land Of My Fathers*, and a video shoot for theme song 'World in Union' at Cardiff's Millennium Stadium. Shirley also recorded an appearance, along with Welsh opera singer Bryn Terfel, for the *Des O'Connor Show*. At the RWC Opening Ceremony in October, Shirley took to the stage in a Sarah Perceval creation which resembled a Welsh Flag. The kaftan, in green, white and red cotton, featured a red dragon motif, embedded with Swarovski crystals, gold beads and braid with a large rhinestone for the eye. The matching chiffon coat featured a similar dragon motif on the back. Shirley looked wonderful and sung beautifully and photos appeared in almost every newspaper of her wearing her 'Welsh flag'. A few days later she returned to the stadium for the closing ceremony, wearing the same 'flag', to sing 'We'll Keep A Welcome In The Hillside' along with Bryn Terfel and Michael Ball. What an occasion!

As the century was drawing to an end, Bernard and I decided to celebrate the start of the new Millennium with a stay at a wonderful hotel. On the morning of 31 December, engrossed in our luxury surroundings, I unfolded the morning newspaper and was ecstatic to see a photograph of Shirley along with the announcement that she was to be made a Dame in the New Year's Honours list. Shirley's family, friends and fans certainly rejoiced that night; in fact, Shirley is reported to have said that when she had first learned of the news, several weeks earlier, she thought she was going to have a heart attack. Apparently she hardly went out after learning of her inclusion in the list, for fear of letting the secret out before the official announcement on 31 December.

It goes without saying that I sent a congratulations card, although I had now come to accept the likelihood of Shirley actually receiving my good wishes was extremely unlikely. The fan base had grown considerably compared to the early years of being a fan. Joyce, Reon and I were, nevertheless, determined to let Shirley know we were still loyal fans and proud of her achievements, so we discussed the possibility of attending one of Shirley's coming performances at the Cardiff International Arena. Fortunately, Joyce knew someone who worked in the box office, so there was a good chance we would be able to obtain tickets for seats near to the front, even though it was Shirley's home town. It was a lovely idea and once Shirley's Millennium Tour dates were announced, Joyce went into action.

Bernard and I would also be booking to see Shirley at what had become our 'home venue', the BIC, yet we were delighted to be going back to Cardiff. It seemed impossible to believe that Joyce, Reon and I had not seen each other for probably three decades, yet our shared love of Shirley's artistry had bonded us throughout our lives. Bernard had never met Joyce or Reon, although he naturally knew about them through our letters, so he was looking forward to the occasion.

Whilst we made plans for our visit and booked a hotel, Shirley was performing in the United States at MGM's Grand Hollywood Theatre in Las Vegas. This was followed by an extremely successful tour throughout the States before returning home to prepare for the UK tour.

Shirley's Millennium Tour opened in May in Bournemouth, and what a reception Shirley received. I think everyone wanted to congratulate her on becoming a Dame. Between songs, fans approached the stage with flowers and gifts and once again it was a magical performance. We came away totally captivated and, as ever, I remained in a dreamlike state. I probably wrote to Joyce immediately after the concert, since the Cardiff dates were two weeks away and I wanted her to know we were going to experience something truly exciting. Joyce had managed to get seats in the third row, so we would all make it to the stage, somehow!

We arranged with Joyce and Reon to meet at our hotel for our reunion. As soon as they walked into the foyer, we recognised each other instantly! After introducing Bernard, the chatting quickly gathered momentum and soon it was like old times again. I had brought with me a copy of the photo of the three of us which we had taken with Shirley outside the London Palladium and as we looked at it, recalling the day so long ago, we wondered where those years had gone. Bernard took some new photographs of us holding our original photo, with Cardiff's International Arena as our backdrop. We were all so excited about that night's concert; the years had not changed how we felt when it came to seeing Shirley. Finally, we arranged to meet later, prior to the show.

The atmosphere in the auditorium was fantastic and my butterflies had taken off on their usual flight, but I had now become accustomed to this reaction and knew the butterflies would 'land' as soon as the music began to play. As we settled into our seats, I was a little surprised to see a couple of 'bouncers' emerge from the wings to take up positions between the first row of seats and the stage. Unfortunately, one of the guys, built like a retired rugby player, choose to stand in line with Bernard and I, which I found a little worrying since he seemed to be looking directly at us. I told myself this was a sign of the times and it would not dampen tonight's experience.

Soon we were listening to a cocktail of musical notes from the orchestra, which were drowned in a sea of cheers rising from the adoring audience. Shirley had walked onstage. Flashlights fired from every corner of the auditorium; it seemed everyone wanted to capture the moment and Bernard too raised his camera to his eye, although he would not be using flash. Shirley, clearly happy, roared into her first number, then suddenly the bouncer leaned over the people sitting in front of us and shouts to Bernard, 'No photography.'

Bernard immediately replied, 'I'm not using flash', and I asked him to put the camera on his lap until the end of Shirley's number, believing nothing further would be said. As Shirley ended her number to thunderous applause, more flashes followed, but these did not appear to concern her, although I do appreciate that flash photography can be disturbing to both artist and audience. The fans continued to give Shirley a wonderful reception and Bernard again raised his camera in preparation for a shot. Abruptly, a dark shadow descended upon us, the bouncer was back but this time he was threatening.

'No photography,' he said as Shirley was about to begin her second number. Bernard quickly replied, 'Shirley has given me permission and I'm not using flash'. 'They all say that,' came his reply, followed by words we couldn't believe we were hearing. 'Give me your camera, or I'll have you removed from the theatre.' REMOVED FROM THE THEATRE, I nearly died. The thought of being removed from Shirley's concert was unthinkable. She was now singing her second number and the people sitting nearby were clearly looking concerned for us, so I quickly persuaded Bernard to hand over his camera, something I secretly feared he would not do. Thankfully, he knew what this concert meant to me, so he reluctantly agreed.

Shirley looked stunning in a glittering silver dress as she announced to her audience, 'Hello Cardiff, it's lovely to be back home again.' Her audience, largely consisting of people in our age group, had almost certainly followed Shirley's career since her early days, so it was a wonderful experience to be amongst like-minded fans. It didn't take long before they started to approach the stage, some bearing gifts and flowers. Shirley seemed delighted by it all and continued her programme with an array of numbers we all wanted to hear. 'Big Spender', 'I, Who Have Nothing' and 'Hey Jude' received rapturous applause and had the audience standing on its feet. However, some of the loudest applause came when Shirley told her audience just how the little girl from Tiger Bay was terribly proud and greatly honoured to be a Dame. Everybody seemed to cheer with delight, and then Shirley began another number. The 'New York Medley' and 'I Am What I Am' almost had the audience dancing in the aisles. The applause seemed to increase after every number, with Shirley singing at her very best.

I couldn't wait any longer; I had to get to the stage. 'Come on,' I said to Joyce and Reon and we quickly rushed for the stage, along with several other fans. Then out of the corner of my eye I caught a glimpse of 'that dark shadow' and for one moment a terrible thought crossed my mind: If he stops me now, I think I will hit him. I put the idea out of my mind, I was standing in front of Shirley now, and as I reached out to shake hands I was conscious the bouncer was stepping back. I knew Joyce and Reon were nearby but wasn't quite sure where, since several fans had now made their way to the edge of the stage. Then I unfolded my sheet of photographic paper, lifting it up to show Shirley the image of herself, Joyce, Reon and I, taken outside the London Palladium all those years ago. Shirley smiled affectionately as I informed her, 'We are all here again tonight.' To my astonishment, Shirley pointed to me and relayed, 'one', then looking around at the fans gathered at her feet and spotting Joyce and Reon, Shirley pointed to each in turn, saying, 'two and three'. A few more words were spoken before we all managed to get a handshake. It was wonderful to know Shirley remembered.

Shirley's arms must have ached after all the handshaking that evening. The auditorium became silent once again and then she threw herself into another song. We became absorbed in the emotion, laughed at the fun, and then all too soon, after several encores, it was time for the final number. On the final note the audience erupted, clapping and cheering before rising to its feet to enthusiastically reward Shirley with a well-deserved standing ovation.

It had been a wonderful evening; we even collected Bernard's camera without so much as a word from our 'dark shadow'. We left the theatre in a dream and I continued to wonder how Shirley's performances always seemed to get better and better. That, I guess, is Shirley's magic! I continued dreaming when we returned home, although I knew it would bring sadness because it was a time when I missed my parents very much. I had always loved talking to them about Shirley's performances; it had given us all so much pleasure. I miss that sharing!

Shirley continued with her Millennium Tour, attended by fans old and new, throughout May, before concluding with ten nights at the Royal Festival Hall in June. The engagement received rave reviews and broke Shirley's own previously held attendance record at the venue. The new century had begun well.

CHAPTER 25

THANK YOU FOR THE YEARS

As we headed towards the summer of 2000, life couldn't have been better. We continued to work hard; Bernard had officially reached retirement age, yet continued to work, on a part-time basis, in a job he enjoyed. I had planned to work at the surgery for several more years before thinking of retirement. We loved to travel and had compiled our travel 'bucket list' some time ago, so now we planned to add some 'ticks' to the list.

Actually, we had already begun the previous year, when we enjoyed a Mediterranean cruise, the highlight of which was the return flight home from Pisa, Italy, on Concorde. Before moving to the IOW, Bernard was connected with Concorde through his work in the aerospace industry, so for him it was an extremely special event. We had managed to arrange a visit to the flight deck and were overjoyed when it actually took place while the aircraft was in flight. It was a magical experience and I was permitted to capture the occasion on camera for the album.

We planned our next adventure for early 2002, when we would

visit South America and Antarctica. We were looking forward to the experience immensely, but secretly, whenever we booked any holiday arrangements, I dreaded the thought that our holiday dates would clash with Shirley's return to Britain to tour. Thankfully, it never happened.

By the late summer of 2000, I was contemplating the words Mir Bashir had told me many years before, 'Life will have its ups and downs…', after my employer informed me, she would be taking early retirement. My employment at the surgery would terminate at the end of January 2001. It marked the beginning of a 'down' period in my life, which lingered for two years. The support from Bernard and friends, along with *the music,* helped to see me through. We had thought we would need to cancel our holiday to South America and Antarctica, but thank God we did not. The scenery alone was breathtaking, beyond belief. Antarctica, untouched by man, majestic, pristine, magnificent, is a place which touches your soul. We returned home, our batteries recharged, to face a year which can only be described as disastrous. Somehow we found the strength to battle through, and eventually I took on a new role at a graphic design company.

The sun began to shine, in 2003, when I heard news of Shirley's forthcoming tour, although when I read its title, 'Thank You For The Years', I knew the words conveyed a message no fan wanted to hear. This tour would probably be her last. It was difficult to believe this tour would mark fifty years in show business for the star and that, earlier in the year, Shirley had celebrated her sixty-sixth birthday. Large venues that would accommodate up to 12,000 fans were chosen in the cities of Glasgow, Manchester, Birmingham, Cardiff and London, at all of which Shirley would undoubtedly give the performance of her life.

Shortly after the announcement of the tour our local newspaper ran an advertisement from an island coach company: they were arranging a trip, with accommodation, to Shirley's Wembley concert on 14 June. Needless to say, we immediately booked.

On the day of the concert we boarded the coach, along with other fans, for a journey which would first take us across to the mainland, by ferry, before continuing by coach, to the Marriott Hotel near Heathrow Airport, where our overnight accommodation had been booked. Along the journey the conversation centred on Shirley, whilst our driver played her CDs through the PA system. Neither had really been a necessary ingredient, since we did not require any motivation to get us to our destination, but it was an enjoyable addition. As I gazed out of the coach window, whilst travelling along the motorway, I thought of all the thousands of fans heading from the far corners of South England, and beyond, to be at tonight's concert. Many of us had probably shared the experience of sitting in the same audience at various concerts in the past, but we would probably never meet. Tonight we would be joined together again, united in showing our appreciation to Shirley, before again returning home, charged by our memories. My dreaming continued and soon I realised the coach was pulling onto the forecourt of hotel. We quickly checked into our room, hung up our best clothes ready for the evening, and then arranged an early table booking in the restaurant. I was never able to eat very much before a concert, but we needed to eat something substantial before our departure to Wembley Arena.

A few hours later, having dealt with all the necessities and wearing our 'Sunday best', we again boarded our coach. The journey, which started well, soon slowed to what seemed like a walking pace, until finally we saw the iconic shape of Wembley Stadium looming ahead, triggering our excitement to a higher level. I had never liked Wembley Arena. It seemed to take ages before our driver was able to park, and then it took forever to get into the building and then what seemed like a lifetime to find our seats. Considering the size of the arena we had fairly good seats, although it would not be possible for me to 'escape' to the stage. Although I was disappointed by that aspect, I knew my cheering would reach Shirley and so I was grateful to be sitting as near as we were to the stage. The interior of the arena was grey and dull,

Shirley deserved gold, glitz and red velvet. However, the audience was star quality and generated an atmosphere that was second to none.

I remember nothing of the first act, then after the interval the audience began to buzz and then those four thumping notes with which John Barry introduces 'Goldfinger' thundered around the arena. The audience went wild, applauding, cheering and whistling as they rose to their feet the moment Dame Shirley walked onstage. She looked stunning in her jewel-encrusted dress, which featured a slit designed to expose her left leg when required! Every artist dreams of a standing ovation but few receive one before even a note has been sung. The ovation continued for five minutes before Shirley was able to continue with Mr Bond's most recognisable theme and understandably received a wonderful response again from the audience, the word 'Gold' still echoing around the arena. Then the classic Nat King Cole number, 'What A Day It Has Been', which took me back to my day with Valerie and the Mayfair Hotel. Another oldie, Albon Timothy and Michael Julien's 'Kiss Me, Honey, Honey, Kiss Me', granted Shirley the opportunity to expose that left leg to fans sitting in the front row.

This was Shirley at her very best, performing to a live audience and obviously beginning to enjoy the occasion. Already some of her fans had approached the stage, bearing gifts, allowing the rest of us a short phase to catch our breaths. A few words of welcome from Shirley, and the promise of a wonderful evening received more enthusiastic applause, before the lights began to flash across the arena. It was time for Shirley's 'New York Medley'. I loved her jazzy interpretation of the classic 'New York, New York' and the sensitivity Shirley brought to 'Arthur's Theme'. Then came some of the Bassey classics, 'Diamonds Are Forever', 'Something' and 'I, Who Have Nothing' (not necessarily in that order). It only took a few moments for the audience to identify a song, and then wild applause would fill the air. Shirley would offer a bow of her head in gratitude as she sang each song with all the passion and perception her audience had come to know. Following on with another song from the *Something* album, Shirley brought new meaning to the Doors' 'Light My Fire'.

More loud applause followed while fans at the stage reached for Shirley's hand. A smile, before Shirley introduced Willie Nelson's melancholy 'Crazy'. Then we really began to wonder if this roof would hold when Shirley went into 'Big Spender' and 'I Am What I Am', two numbers that could never be left out. The audience was on its feet for another ovation.

A new battalion of fans rose up from their seats as Shirley weaved her arms and swayed her hips to the disco dance hit 'History Repeating'. Tonight Shirley, and the audience, clearly enjoyed the performance.

Shirley had now been onstage for at least an hour, although I haven't taken my eyes off her for one moment to look at my watch. Although we were sitting several rows back from the stage, it felt as though Shirley was singing just for me. This is one of the reasons, I believe, why her popularity has continued to grow over the years. I realise Shirley is singing to us all, but she makes each and every one of us feel unique and special.

As the cheering subsided, Shirley spoke to the audience and introduced a new song written by Andrew and Elizabeth Neve, entitled 'Thank You For The Years'. Shirley added, 'So many of you out there have been with me almost from the beginning, but it's also good to see young faces in the audience. This song says it all.' The audience fell silent and Shirley began to sing, 'I thank you for the years…'

The atmosphere was charged with emotion as she delivered the lyrics with such genuineness. When it came to the final verse I am sure I shared the same feelings as every fan in the audience: we wished we could sing these words to Shirley. As the music ended it was clear for all to see that Shirley was fighting to hold back the emotion. The audience had gone wild and I thought this is going to be the end, but Shirley had other plans. After a brief departure, she was back onstage, shaking even more hands and accepting gifts.

The performance continued with earlier classics, 'As I Love You', the fast and furious 'Johnny One Note', and the song which had always pulled at my mum's heart strings, 'As Long As He Needs Me'. Another classic, 'The Lady Is A Tramp', again showed off Shirley's singing capabilities, as well as her sense of fun.

Nobody wanted this to end, but how long could it continue! My own personal favourite, 'Never, Never, Never', brought back the emotions. Then came 'What Now My Love' and 'Where Do I Begin (Love Story)', which fittingly suggested the end was near. The applause which followed every number just seemed to intensify, with fans including myself rising from their seats to offer a standing ovation on each occasion. Then, after more than one hundred minutes, Shirley launched into 'Hey Jude'. The power with which she delivered this number was unbelievable. She gave it her all and then, on the final chorus, coaxed the audience into joining in. United we sang along, our arms raised high, swinging from side to side in unison. Then silence fell as Shirley paused momentarily, drawing in all the power she could muster before the final 'H-e-y J-u-d-e' resounded around the arena. It couldn't have ended on a better note.

Back at the hotel that night, I wrote down on two sheets of Marriott notepaper, the title of every song Shirley had sung that evening – I wanted to remember every one. The notepaper remains inside my souvenir programme today and although the order of performance may not be entirely correct, be assured the song list is complete. It was an outstanding performance of twenty-two songs that expressed Shirley's fifty years in show business.

As we travelled home the next morning, I relived the performance in my mind. Sadly, although I did not know it at the time, it was to be the last time I saw Shirley perform live.

When we arrived I longed to play the CD, *Thank You For The Years* (Sony Music Entertainment (UK) Ltd), which had been released to coincide with the tour. Ironically, the CD also offered twenty-two tracks, six of which were new recordings. The beautiful Burt Bacharach/ Hal David 'I Just Have To Breathe' took me back to that other occasion when I heard Shirley sing, 'Send In The Clowns', with just a piano. I loved the track and was delighted that Shirley had chosen to record it, solely with piano. The CD became very popular, entering the album charts and providing Shirley with a silver disc.

There was another reason too, for all my excitement, an announcement from Christie's, the world-famous auction house, appeared in Shirley's concert programme. In September they would be holding a Gala Charity Auction, entitled 'Dame Shirley Bassey, 50 Years of Glittering Gowns'. I knew I could neither attend the auction nor bid for a dress but that did not stop me from wanting to obtain as much information as I could.

I received further details and ordered the hardback catalogue. I remember thinking it was a rather expensive catalogue, but the proceeds were going to good causes. However, when the catalogue arrived, I was thrilled, it was worth every penny. It contains a lovely interview between Shirley and Douglas Darnell, as well as illustrations and full descriptions of every gown. Along with Shirley's autograph, embossed in silver, there is also a Swarovski gem, which hangs from the satin bookmark. The catalogue is a treasure any fan would love to own.

The auction was a tremendous success and widely reported in the press. Shirley's glamorous gowns had raised £250,000 for her chosen charities.

The same year Dame Shirley received the Légion d'Honneur from the Ambassador of France, His Excellency Gérard Errera. In his tribute to Dame Shirley, he spoke of the pleasure she had brought, over the years, to millions of French fans.[11]

---

11 The ceremony can be seen on YouTube, uploaded by Wedding Videos Northampton.

CHAPTER 26

THE LIVING TREE

During the latter part of 2003, I gave up working as a practice manager and decided to reduce my working hours for the remaining few years before my retirement. There were still many places Bernard and I wanted to visit, so we took the decision to try and experience as much as possible, for as long as we could.

We had grown to love cruising and so, when the opportunity came to book for Cunard's newest liner, the *Queen Mary 2*, for its first transatlantic crossing to New York in April 2004, we, along with some friends, jumped at the opportunity. The holiday would include staying for a few nights at the Waldorf Astoria, New York, home to the Empire Room where Shirley had performed in the late sixties and early seventies, before flying home. You could say that once our booking was confirmed, I found myself in a 'New York state of mind' for some time.

At that time, I had been thinking of producing a limited-edition postcard from a beautiful blackand-white photograph which my father had taken of the original RMS *Queen Mary* in the Solent. I wanted the funnels to be painted Cunard red and my father's signature to appear on the postcard, so a friend helped me to create the necessary computer files, which we then sent off to the printers. When I discussed the idea, some people just laughed, but I saw the project through and by February 2004 I had a launch of my own planned.

On 8 January 2004, Dame Shirley celebrated her 67th birthday. It was also a very important day for everyone in Southampton as Cunard would be celebrating the naming of the *Queen Mary 2*, by Her Majesty the Queen, before an invited audience of two thousand people. Four days later, the ship was due to depart from the port on the ship's maiden voyage and on board would be Dame Shirley Bassey. The announcement, made shortly before the departure date, stated Shirley would be performing on the stage of the onboard Royal Court Theatre, the two-storey state-of-the-art theatre which offered tiered seating for over 1,000 passengers. I would have loved to have been there, but it wasn't to be. However, we booked a ferry from the island on the evening of the departure to watch the liner leave its berth, as fireworks filled the night sky. Then as the *QM2* slowly made its way along Southampton Water, rounded Calshot and sailed through the Solent, we enthusiastically waved 'bon voyage'. I dreamed every silhouette I spotted waving back from the upper decks was Dame Shirley and my excitement helped to kept me warm. So Shirley, if you did wave to what seemed like a little ferry, now you know who it was waving back!

Sadly for the passengers, the Bay of Biscay did not provide calm seas through the first day and night . Manysuffered from sea sickness, including Shirley. To make matters worse, her suite was located on an upper deck, not the best place to be when a ship is sailing through a storm. Regretfully, that night the performance had to be cancelled, but the following evening passengers were treated to a performance the like of which only Shirley knows how to give. Her audience rewarded her with eight standing ovations.

On St Valentine's Day, my own launch of 'Hey No 1… the Queen Mary' postcard gave me a tremendous thrill. The *Isle of Wight County Press* had featured an article and I offered to do a signing session at the County Press shop. This had never been tried before (launching a postcard), so the shop's staff and I were not expecting a great uptake. As I approached the shop, I couldn't believe my eyes – a queue lined the street. Two hours later I had sold over three hundred postcards. I was so delighted and prayed somehow Dad would know.

In April we boarded the *Queen Mary 2* for the liner's first transatlantic crossing to New York. We too experienced rough seas and strong winds, which shattered a glass windshield and terrified our friends in a suite below.

We 'lived the dream' aboard the ship. One evening, in the Royal Court Theatre, as I looked down onto the stage from our balcony seats, I imagined I was watching Shirley. The applause I gave the actual performer that evening, was probably more than they deserved!

The arrival of the liner at New York Harbour was unbelievable. It was the first passenger ship to enter the harbour since the horrendous catastrophe of 9/11 and hence security was at maximum level. Yet it seemed every New Yorker' wanted to welcome the ship and its passengers. Ashore, banners welcoming the *QM2* flew from every lamp-post. During our stay we were treated like celebrities wherever we went. On our final evening in this 'never sleep' city, we joined a dinner cruise to watch the *QM2* and *QE2* depart, in unison, from the harbour. As the fireworks lit up the night sky we joined in with the singing. Naturally, it was 'New York, New York', but I sang Shirley's version (sorry Frank)!

On our return home, as I was contemplating our wonderful experience, my thoughts strayed, as they often did, to Dame Shirley. I hoped life would now offer her the opportunity to see and enjoy the world like any other person rather than always having to play the 'star'. Like any fan I wanted to see and hear more of Dame Shirley, but that said, my main wish was for her to enjoy her life.

In 2005 Dame Shirley Bassey returned to the town of her birth to star in the Royal Variety Performance, held at Cardiff's Millennium Centre. Performing before Her Majesty the Queen and His Royal Highness Prince Philip, Shirley almost raised the roof with 'Goldfinger' before introducing a new number entitled 'The Living Tree'. The song had been written by Never The Bride duo Nicky Lamborn and Catherine Feeney, who reportedly left the song for Dame Shirley at her gym in Monte Carlo. The accuracy of the story is unimportant, but thankfully Shirley received the number and the rest is history, as they say. Once again, that night in Cardiff Shirley demonstrated how she could weave the lyrics of a song, 'Let me dance until my shoes cry…', into an emotional performance, as soft and smooth as silk with gold threads running through. It was quite simply, beautiful.

Her performance ended with a standing ovation, not only from her audience, but also from the entire cast of performers. It was thrilling to watch and richly deserved.

Two thousand and six was a very exciting year for Shirley and her fans. In June, a short tour, consisting of five venues, took place. Regrettably we were unable to attend, for various reasons, but the news I received confirmed Shirley's performances were as great as ever. Fortunately, for the fans like myself who were unable to attend a live concert, there was television, which provided us with *Another Audience With Dame Shirley Bassey*. We heard news of Shirley's appearances at charity events and read various news stories, but for me the most significant event occurred near Christmas.

One evening we had been casting a casual eye over the television adverts when suddenly a figure appeared, in a red M&S dress, and launched into 'Get The Party Started'. One note and I instantly recognised Dame Shirley's voice, although I had never heard her sing the Linda Perry number before. I was so thrilled by the performance, the very next morning I rushed into our local Marks and Spencer store. I remember a rather surprised sales assistant looking at me in a slightly strange manner when I said I wanted to purchase the CD of 'Get The Party Started' by Dame Shirley. Another assistant was consulted but nobody, except me, seemed to know anything about the advert.

It didn't take long for the song to become a big hit, not only with Shirley's loyal brigade of fans but also with the British public. I am probably correct in assuming its success had not been anticipated since no CD had been produced at that time. Had it been, Shirley may have found herself celebrating her first Christmas No. 1.

The following summer, we were rewarded with the CD *Get The Party Started*. It seemed apparent that Catherine Feeney and Nikki Lamborn had worked closely with Dame Shirley on the CD's production and I was delighted to see 'The Living Tree', the number which Shirley had performed so well at the Royal Variety Performance, featured. Most of the album, however, consisted of remixed tracks of some of Shirley's hits, yet I am sure it helped to introduce her to a whole new generation of fans. For me, one or two of the remixes just didn't work – perhaps I was growing old! I was, however, so delighted to see the CD enter the Top Ten, at No. 6 in the album charts, especially since Dame Shirley had dedicated the album to her daughter, Samantha.

One other factor also contributed to the album's success – Glastonbury.

When I first heard Shirley would be performing at Glastonbury 2007 on the famous Phoenix Stage, I thought if only it could be the Isle of Wight Festival. Perhaps Shirley, you could add that one to the 'bucket list'. However, I did give it a lot of consideration, but knowing the concert would be televised, we reluctantly decided to abandon the idea of the mud fest!

Dame Shirley went suitably prepared for the wet weather, which had turned the Glastonbury fields to mud. Her diamanté Wellingtons probably received as much press attention as her stunning pink Julien Macdonald gown, but they were a necessary requirement for her to get to the stage. Somehow it seemed appropriate that our 'Diva Shirley' should be booked for the 5pm slot on the stage, which takes its design from the Pyramids in Giza.

Dame Shirley admitted to being nervous, but once onstage the vocals chords fired up and, accompanied by musical director, Mike Dixon and an impressive twenty-three piece orchestra, Shirley roared into, 'Get The Party Started'. The audience loved it and the party had begun. 'Light My Fire' followed, and then the Bond medley, before a double serving of 'Big Spender' was demanded by the adoring crowd. Glastonbury may not have resembled any of her typical venues, but it was clear Shirley could weave her magic here, just as easily as if she had been singing to an audience at the Royal Albert Hall. This particular evening, however, her audience was younger than usual; they waved flags and banners, joined in the chorus and stood in mud, yet they showed their appreciation for Dame Shirley in just the same way as other fans throughout the world. Applause, cheering and shouts for 'more', rang out after every number. Then came 'The Living Tree' and Shirley's new infantry rallied at her feet along with the faithful from the past.

Watching, as I did, on television, it seemed unbelievable that Shirley was now in her seventies, singing to a new generation, which tonight included her own daughter Sharon and Sharon's children. Then Shirley remembered some of the 'oldies' in a medley which included, 'Never, Never, Never' and 'As I Love You', before ending with an immortal performance of 'I Am What I Am'. The response was stupendous. Dame Shirley had won a glorious victory on the muddy fields of Glastonbury.

The following day, I went to the newsagents to gather reports for the scrapbook and was horrified to read an incident which had occurred during Dame Shirley's helicopter return flight to London. It became necessary for the pilot to make an unscheduled landing, in playing fields. Thankfully, all turned out well.

Later the same year, Dame Shirley attended Sir Elton John's 'White

Tie and Tiara Ball', in support of the Elton John Aids Foundation, and performed at the Swarovski Fashion Rocks concert, in aid of the Prince's Trust, at the Royal Albert Hall. Both events received wide press coverage to the delight of fans.

At the time of the Royal Albert Hall event, Bernard and I were thousands of miles away, in Uzbekistan, enjoying a wonderful holiday. We were fortunate to have reached a stage in our lives where we now had fewer commitments, so in September we embarked on a twenty-eight-day journey that would take us six thousand miles across Asia, travelling the famous Silk Route by private train.

We had boarded Russia's *Golden Eagle* Trans-Siberian train in Moscow and were some way into our adventure by the time we arrived at Samarkand, Uzbekistan's second largest town, regarded as the 'Crossroad of World Cultures'. Known for the mosques and mausoleums, the town is as old as Rome and was undoubtedly one of highlights of our journey.

It was here that we experienced a very special fashion show of our own. Held in a grand family home, once belonging to a nineteenth-century Jewish silk merchant, we were treated to a wonderful dinner. Later, students from Samarkand's Fashion College modelled, along an impromptus catwalk, gowns, coats and scarfs of their own designs. The garments were stunning, a melting pot of colour, culture and tradition, unlike anything we had seen at home. Several members in our group made purchases and I have to say it was the one occasion in my life when I wished I had been a size ten or less!

A few days later, as we travelled overnight through the desert, I looked out from our train compartment and was astounded by the unbelievable beauty of the night sky. The sky was filled with sparkling diamonds, or so it seemed. As the train rattled its way through the darkness, I sat captivated by the spectacle. I continued dreaming for some time and wondered if Shirley had also had the opportunity to experience treasures like this… I hope she did.

A few days later we were crossing 'no man's land' between Kazakhstan and China by coach, having left our faithful *Golden Eagle* at the Kazakhstan border. The crossing into China was like something out of a Michael Caine movie and we all breathed a sigh of relief when we boarded our new train, described as China's Orient Express. Let's just say the Venice Simplon-Orient-Express, it was not! However, it probably was China's best train, judging by some of the others we saw during our adventure, so we couldn't complain.

We rarely spent a night on board the train, staying usually in five-star luxury, but on the occasions when it was necessary for our journey, we had some wonderful parties with our fellow travellers, the majority of which hailed from Australia. It was on one such night, whilst travelling on the train from Jiayuguan to Xian, during a conversation at dinner that I happened to mention Dame Shirley Bassey (remember, I could talk forever about Shirley, given an opportunity). At that very moment the Chinese agent aboard the train passed by and said to me, 'She was on this train last year.'

'What!' I replied. 'Are you sure it was Dame Shirley Bassey?'

'Yes, I'm sure it was her, she sings the songs in the Bond films.' Then he added, 'She had an entire carriage on this train', before continuing along the corridor.

Could it be true? I would never know but I was so excited by the revelation. To think, here we were following the route of Marco Polo and now it was possible I was following in Shirley's footsteps.

It was a fabulous party that night. *'I danced until my shoes cried'* – what a wonderful, descriptive lyric from 'The Living Tree'.

CHAPTER 27

AFTER THE RAIN

It rained heavily in 2008. In May, Dame Shirley was rushed to hospital in Monaco, suffering from abdominal pains. Following emergency surgery her doctors later advised against travelling to London, where she was due to perform at Nelson Mandela's 90th birthday concert. Shirley's illness was of great concern to her legions of fans. Unfortunately, like most news stories, once the initial story had been released, no further news followed, so it was an anxious time upon which we placed our faith in those words of wisdom, 'no news is good news'. Dark clouds also lingered over Bernard and I that year, but as always we managed to pull through by recalling our special memories, playing the music we loved and dreaming of experiences still to be enjoyed.

Summer, for us all, arrived in 2009. Bernard and I had booked for a touring holiday in Ireland, a country I had always wanted to visit. It is a beautiful country and we found the people warm and friendly. I have always been good at spotting faces in a crowd and one day, whilst we were visiting a small town, my attention was momentarily drawn to a particular lady as she passed by. Ironically, she too glanced at me but we each continued, in opposite directions, without speaking. When I caught up with Bernard, already several yards ahead, I said to him, 'I have just seen someone the image of Shirley.' Well, you can guess his reply. At the time, of course, we had no idea that Dame Shirley was in Ireland, so I had no reason to even imagine it could be her!

A few months later, to my surprise, I discovered that Dame Shirley Bassey had spent most of the summer recording a brand new CD at Grouse Lodge, near Ballymore in central Ireland. So, did I see Dame Shirley during our visit to Ireland? I will never know. Nevertheless, I believe we are all offered experiences in life which may seem, at the time, to have little rhythm or reason, yet they register in our soul.

Towards the later part of the year, Dame Shirley released the newly recorded CD, *The Performance*. Her lifelong fans were always delighted when news came of a new CD release, but this one was different, mainly because the songs were *new*. The concept had been to invite contemporary songwriters to submit new material specifically for Dame Shirley Bassey. It became quite a challenge for all concerned and although Dame Shirley, now in her seventies, had little to prove, I am sure there must have been one or two people lingering in the wings, hoping to spot a flaw. They should have known better – the title of the CD is the clue. Dame Shirley worked on each set of lyrics, interpreting all in a manner and style unique to her. She would feel the song and know exactly how she wanted it performed. On hand, helping her to achieve her goal were musical director Mike Dixon, and conductor David Arnold.

During the production of *The Performance* CD, interviewing and filming were undertaken for an episode of the BBC's *Imagine* series, to be entitled 'Dame Shirley Bassey: The Girl From Tiger Bay'. The programme, screened to coincide with the CD's release, offered a wonderful insight into Shirley's approach to her professional life. I thoroughly enjoyed watching her sing and adapt each new composition, accompanied solely by her musical director on piano. I admired the professional manner in which Mike Dixon worked with Shirley. Both embraced a mutual respect for each other, something which had obviously developed through years of working together.

Dame Shirley does not read music, which somehow makes the outcome even more amazing. Maybe it's intuition or some other inner sense, I just don't know, but whatever it is, it tells her exactly how to deliver a song, and on that count Dame Shirley had never failed to achieve the desired effect.

The programme, produced and directed by Dione Newton, also featured interviews with several of the songwriters chosen to write for CD. Several of the composers featured needed little introduction. The Bond master, John Barry, with Don Black, submitted, 'Our Time Is Now', and sadly it was to become John Barry's last composition. David Arnold, Gary Barlow, Neil Tennant of the Pet Shop Boys, and the Manic Street Preachers, had also written especially for Dame Shirley, so I longed to hear the result.

I immediately purchased the CD on the day of release and played and played the disc, until each new number was fixed in my mind. This had been the first new recording for several years, so I needed a little longer to 'study', if that's the right word, the composition and performance I was hearing. Listening to Dame Shirley's vocals was sensational. However, if I am being honest, I found some of the recording a little too electronic at times. Don't misunderstand me, I loved the CD, but I am more at home with strings than electric guitars.

They say there is always an exception to every rule and it came, for me, with Richard Hawley's, 'After The Rain'. It is a breath of air on the CD, magical, soft and one of the finest examples of what Dame Shirley Bassey can do with a song.

I also loved the Manic Street Preachers/David Arnold, 'Girl from Tiger Bay', with that clever opening lyric: *'There's a crack in every pavement. Underneath there is a beach'*.

Another personal favourite of mine was undoubtedly the Neil Tennant/Chris Lowe,'The Performance of My Life', although I confess it did remind me of the Roberto Sandro/Oscar Anderle/Robert Allen song with a similar title,'The Greatest Performance of My Life', which featured on the 1972 LP, *I Capricorn*.

I read Tennant reportedly wrote 'The Performance of My Life' initially for 'a diva'. Like all things in life, thankfully fate played a part and the song finally reached Dame Shirley. Is there anyone other than her qualified to perform this number? I don't think so. She sings the lyrics, telling us that to live, Dame Shirley has to give the performance of her life –and then she does just that!

There is no doubt David Arnold had successfully produced a contemporary sound which appealed not only to Shirley's lifelong fans but also brought a new generation to Dame Shirley, her music and the art of The Performance.

There was one other song from the CD that would become significant to Bernard and I and that was Rufus Wainwright's,'Apartment'. Earlier in the year we had celebrated Bernard's seventy-fifth birthday at a lovely hotel near Newbury and due to an error over our booking, we were offered the owner's suite. It was beautiful, consisting of a large lounge, bedroom and bathroom, and I fell in love with it. I remember saying to Bernard,'If there was a kitchen, I could live here.'

We were still living in the house that we'd bought when moving to the island in the early nineties. We loved the property, which dated back to the 1830s and had Grade II listing, but as we were getting older we began to find it was becoming more difficult to maintain. On a couple of occasions we had looked at 'downsizing' were unable to find anything we liked within our budget, so the idea became filed at the back of our minds. As time went by, Bernard frequently heard me singing the chorus from 'Apartment' until eventually, in 2013, it happened, but more about that later.

Back to October 2009 and we are sitting in the comfort of our home, yet even here the butterflies are beginning to flutter as I anxiously wait for the BBC's Electric Proms concert from London's Roundhouse, to commence. Finally it begins and we watch members of the audience, filled with anticipation, entering the theatre along with commentators attempting to describe the atmosphere, but I have little need for this; I just want the magic to begin. Relief comes as the orchestra begins to play and then, almost instantly as if sensing the need of her fans, Dame Shirley Bassey walks out, lighting up the stage in a sparkling silver gown perfectly appropriate for her first number, 'Diamond Are Forever'. The audience roars its approval and the magic begins.

We are treated to a further sixteen numbers, five of which come from *The Performance* and accompanied by the song's writer, in some cases. I was delighted that Dame Shirley had chosen the numbers which had become my favourites. Old numbers or new, all were wonderful, with Dame Shirley singing at her very best, giving the performance of her life. Since the concert is available for all to see on the Internet, I will not go into further detail. Watch and enjoy it yourself; it is possibly the best Dame Shirley concert ever recorded.

The 'revival' of Dame Shirley, as some newspaper reporters referred to it, was like a celebration for fans everywhere. Now in my sixties, I discovered I was just as thrilled as I had been when I was sixteen to read or hear news about Shirley and I was delighted she seemed to be living a more content and happy life. Her charity work continued and today we can thankfully view performances, of which I had little knowledge at the time, on the Internet.

In 2010, Dame Shirley performed at Sting's Save The Rain Forest concert, along with a host of stars, at New York's Carnegie Hall. Then, later in the year, she returned to Cardiff to appear before thousands of fans, including Prince Charles, in the Welcome to Wales opening concert to the Ryder Cup, at the Millennium Stadium.

In the meantime, when the music wasn't playing, Bernard and I planned more travels since there was still so much we wanted to see. We decided to book a long cruise, which would take us to Asia and South Africa, but it almost didn't happen due to a health scare. Fortunately, near the departure date, I was granted consent to travel and on 4 January 2011 we embarked on our 'Grand Asian Voyage' aboard P&O's *Artemis*. It was a holiday of a lifetime, visiting so many wonderful places and cultures – Japan, Thailand, China, Philippines, and South Africa, to name a few. *Artemis* was a very friendly ship and became our 'home' for nearly four months and we were sorry to hear the news that the ship would be leaving the P&O fleet shortly after our return to Southampton. A new ship would be joining the fleet, *Adonia*, and she was the talk of officers and crew on board *Artemis*. During our cruise we even attended a presentation about the new ship, yet nobody ever discussed or spoke about who would launch the ship, in May. When we disembarked in April, we had no idea Dame Shirley Bassey would become '*Adonia*'s godmother'.

On 21 May, in a glitzy ceremony, Dame Shirley looked pure class. Naming *Adonia* in the traditional manner, she pressed a diamond-shaped button to release a bottle of British fizz, which smashed against the ship. Sparkling silver ornaments drifted through the air. Later guests attended a gala dinner and Dame Shirley treated them to a fabulous impromptu performance of 'Diamonds Are Forever' before fireworks lit up the skies above Southampton in celebration. I, along with every fan, would have loved to have been on board to see Dame Shirley become the ship's 'godmother'.

Early in the year, Dame Shirley appeared at the Royal Albert Hall, in a star-studded 80th birthday gala for Mikhail Gorbachev, performing 'Diamonds Are Forever' and 'The Lady Is A Tramp'. Returning to the same stage in May, to honour the late John Barry, Dame Shirley stole the show at the Classic Brits Awards. A posthumous award to John Barry, for 'outstanding contribution to music' was a first and accepted by Don Black. In the tribute which followed, Dame Shirley's performance of 'Goldfinger' brought the audience to its feet.

It rained again in January 2012, when I entered hospital on the mainland for surgery. I thought of Dame Shirley frequently during my recovery; my vocal chords had been damaged during the operation. Over the next three months I sounded more like Mickey Mouse than Mary Long and although it was a time of concern, it made Bernard laugh when 'Mickey' tried to sing the line: 'All I need is an apartment'.

That summer brought great excitement to millions of people throughout Britain and the world as we all united to celebrate Her Majesty the Queen's 60th Jubilee. As part of the celebrations, on the evening of 4 June, a Diamond Jubilee Concert was held at Buckingham Palace, in which a host of stars performed. The classy Dame Shirley Bassey sang only one number, 'Diamonds Are Forever', and what a performance she gave.

As the year progressed Bernard and I turned our thoughts, once again, to the idea of downsizing. Then one morning, whilst glancing through a magazine, an advertisement for a new housing development caught my eye. The very same day we spotted a hoarding which carried a similar advert and since I knew the site location very well, we decided to visit the following day.

Next morning, upon visiting the development, we viewed a 'show apartment'. We were both impressed and Bernard was warming to the idea, so we took up the offer to view an apartment which offered a separate kitchen (as opposed to a kitchen/ diner), since this was an important requirement for Bernard, who for much of the time is my 'chef'. When we walked in to view what is now our apartment, I knew we had found our new home, although it took Bernard a little longer to come to the same conclusion. The rest, as they say, is history, but it did not happen without a few problems along the way.

In May we were due to exchange contracts when Bernard suffered a heart attack. It was a nightmare, the lyrics, 'this girl just can't take it anymore', from Richard Howley's 'After The Rain', readily came to mind. Thankfully, Bernard made a remarkable recovery and we owe our gratitude to the wonderful team who cared for him.

In August, we moved into our apartment, which truly is 'all I need'. We love living here and I thank my God, fate led us here!

News of Dame Shirley, in 2013, seemed lacking or perhaps I had become preoccupied with all that was happening in our own lives. However, one prominent event earlier in the year had dominated the headlines. Dame Shirley had been invited to perform 'Goldfinger' at the 2013 Academy Awards, in Hollywood, to celebrate the fifty-year milestone of the James Bond film franchise. Other performers that night included Adele and Barbra Streisand but it was Dame Shirley who stole the show. Appearing onstage in a stunning gold gown, shegave an amazing performance of what has probably become the most famous of all the Bond themes. Befittingly, the star-studded audience rose to give Dame Shirley a standing ovation, claiming her the real winner!

The idea of writing a book had been going through my mind for a while, although at first I had no clear idea regarding the direction I would take. When we made to decision to downsize, I knew I would have to make some tough decisions as a fan. My scrapbooks of press cuttings from the early days, which to be fair had faded over the years, would probably have to go, but not before reading them through yet again and retaining any necessary information. Naturally, all other memorabilia was sacred and would remain, but I needed to recover some space.

We settled into our apartment quickly and with winter approaching I discovered I now had time to write. Suddenly, whilst I thought about my life as a fan, I realised this was what I wanted to write about. Ideas seemed to fall easily into place and so in the autumn of 2013, I began. In December, I looked forward to receiving a Christmas card from Joyce, since it would always include updates and chat about Shirley, as did mine to her. As yet, I had not told Joyce of my plans to write a book about life as a fan. A week later Joyce's card arrived and I eagerly opened the envelope to read the news normally contained within. On this occasion it simply said, 'I haven't read anything about Shirley, isn't it sad.' Well, those words brought it all into focus.

I was going to write a book for Dame Shirley and her fans, many of whom were just like Joyce, Reon and I.

It may have been winter but the rain had gone!

CHAPTER 28

HELLO, LIKE BEFORE

The new year, 2014, had brought a new challenge, one which offered me immense pleasure as I rummaged through box files containing old diaries, programmes, press cuttings, photographs and negatives. Finding the prized mementoes was never a problem since they had always been neatly retained in albums and for once I was grateful that I had been so methodical throughout my life. As I looked through the pages, it was a delight to revive my deepest, happiest memories and attempt to transfer them into words.

Finding and selecting the photographs for this book presented another challenge since it required transferring the original format, film, into an acceptable digital file suitable for today's technology. It was all good fun and I was amazed at how quickly the time seemed to fly. As I became more engrossed in my project, I had not really noticed the lack of news relating to Dame Shirley, as Joyce had. When I had started to look at the Internet more frequently, mainly to confirm my own details and dates, like any fan I looked at websites such as the 'Shirley Bassey Blog' – the Unofficial Dame Shirley Bassey News website. Actually, I was amazed one day when I recognised myself in an early photograph the site had displayed from the George Webb Collection. However, if I am honest, I'm not totally comfortable with the net since I find so much of what appears seems to originate from rumours and conjecture.

After several months of more rumours that appeared whenever I did the occasional Google search – 'new album', 'concert tours', 'concert tickets', 'world tours' – to my surprise and huge delight, finally I was looking at a photograph which showed Dame Shirley standing in the centre of the renowned Abbey Road Studios, surrounded by musicians. Under the photograph, copyright of Sony Music Entertainment (UK) Ltd., were words which brought music to my ears, 'NEWS COMING SOON'.

Somehow I knew the news would be special, and indeed it was. Dame Shirley Bassey had spent most of the year working on a new album with producer/musical director Stuart Barr and the Royal Philharmonic Orchestra. Wow! As if I needed to be tempted, the press releases announced *Hello Like Before* would be released in three versions: CD, deluxe CD and vinyl, and would feature songs Dame Shirley loved, admired and that came from the heart.

Surprisingly, you may think, until that moment I had never bought any CDs or albums through the Internet, but times were changing fast, so I plucked up courage, tapped at the keyboard and ordered the deluxe CD. I had not heard a single track; I didn't need to because I knew Dame Shirley and the Royal Philharmonic Orchestra would produce magic.

While waiting for the release date I continued with the book, but something kept nagging in the background. I had been so excited by the news of Dame Shirley's new recording, I was hungry to write and thank her. When I suggested this to Bernard he simply said, it will never get to her and rejected the whole idea as if it were some childish fantasy. Bernard and I have always shared everything, so I felt a little sheepish when I wrote my letter to Dame Shirley, in October, without telling him. Something compelled me to do it, although I also prepared myself for the highly likely possibility that I would not receive a reply. I repeatedly told myself too many years have passed since you last saw Dame Shirley, yet here you are hoping she will remember you as a fan – crazy!

I recognised the expression, from so many years before, when the post-office assistant glanced at the envelope addressed to 'Dame Shirley Bassey'. Then I attached the appropriate postage and blue 'By Air Mail – Par Avion' sticker and handed it back to the assistant for posting. I could do no more, so once home I returned to working on the book and placed the contents of 'the letter' to the back of my mind.

The November release date finally came and as promised the CD arrived in the post. I quickly removed the protective covering and gazed at the cover. Dame Shirley looked stunning and it seemed unbelievable that she was now in her seventies. Then I had that moment of fear, just like the feeling before a concert when I would ask myself, 'Will Dame Shirley still be as good?' The fear increased as I pressed the 'play' button on the music system, then the sounds of musicians playing the rhythmic beats to 'This Is What You Are', by Alessandro Magnanini and Mario Ranno, hit my ears. Moments later, Dame Shirley's began singing, 'take me out and knock me down'. Well that nearly happened as I continued listening to the track. I had never previously heard the song but instantly fell in love with the song and orchestration.

Naturally, I was more familiar with Sting's 'Englishman In New York', and probably would never have thought of it as Dame Shirley material. I had, however, always loved her singing numbers that took on a jazzy feel, such as 'New York, New York'. I had to chuckle, as Shirley's Welsh accent seemed highly appropriate when singing an elongated 't-a-l-k' and 'Y-o-r-k.', proving there had been no need for her to be an Englishwoman to master this number.

Like Dame Shirley, Bernard and I have seen Peggy Lee perform

'Fever' on a number of occasions; in fact one of Bernard's photographs of Peggy Lee is one of several published in Bruce Crowther and Mike Pinfold's book, *The Jazz Singers*. It's fair to say 'Fever' is Peggy Lee, just as 'Goldfinger' is Dame Shirley Bassey, both are all time classics. Dame Shirley offers up a tremendous interpretation of the John Davenport and Eddie J. Cooley number. With respect, I'm not sure Peggy could ever have managed 'Goldfinger'!

I sat mesmerised as I listened to every note, every syllable, and every word. This was the Shirley I adored, singing to perfection with a fabulous array of musicians around her. Interestingly, the album was produced by Dame Shirley and Stuart Barr and I offer my congratulations to them for producing an album which has almost captured the atmosphere of a live performance. For a studio recording this is some achievement, in spite of it being Abbey Road!

Fun is on hand when Dame Shirley is joined by Paloma Faith in 'Diamonds Are A Girl's Best Friend' by Jule Styne and Leo Robin. It somehow befittingly follows Shirley's re-recording of 'Goldfinger', written by John Barry, Leslie Bricusse and Anthony Newley. It seems a couple of notes were wrong on the original version, which Dame Shirley has finally been able to correct. I wonder how many of her fans can 'spot the difference'. The style then changes, returning to reflect on the lovely Arthur Butler and Phyllis Jean Molinary 'Here's To Life'. It's simply beautiful and brings tears to my eyes every time I play the album, as does Jimmy L. Webb's, 'MacArthur Park'. I loved the song when it was a hit all those years ago for Richard Harris, but I never understood it then. Now I do, thanks to Dame Shirley's interpretation and the feeling she pours into the song.

Just to show I am not totally biased in my opinion, I do have one reservation regarding the *Hello Like Before*, and that is the Paul Geoffrey Spencer (Dario G) track 'We Got Music'. I personally do not feel it quite sits along with the rest of the material on the CD. Perhaps I am not alone in my opinion since the vinyl album does not include the track and I prefer to play that set. It is without doubt a masterclass: it's perfection, it's pure quality and it's magic, just as I knew it would be.

During the weeks that followed I played the tracks at every opportunity until the words and music became fixed in my mind. I read the odd negative review, some seemingly preferring *Performance*, but my preference is definitely *Hello Like Before*. It's the album I would choose to take to my Desert Island.

On 13 November 2014, Dame Shirley Bassey performed before the Duke and Duchess of Cambridge at the Royal Variety Performance, held at the London Palladium. The show was televised on 8 December, with Dame Shirley performing two numbers, 'The Lady Is A Tramp' and 'I'm Still Here', the latter from the *Hello Like Before* album. She looked and sounded fabulous and well deserved the standing ovation awarded to her.

A few days later Bernard walked into our apartment with the day's post in hand. Holding a larger than usual envelope he jokingly called out, 'Shirley's sent you a Christmas card.' The envelope had come from Monaco, but he thought it was from a neighbour's daughter, who works out there, so he was trying to tease me. I dived for the envelope, taking it quickly from his hand, and then carefully opened it to reveal the contents. 'Yes,' I cried, 'you didn't think I'd get an answer if I wrote to Dame Shirley, did you?' Bernard looked at me astounded, then delight beamed across his face as I had pulled out a beautiful photograph of Dame Shirley Bassey, personally signed to me. I was so excited; I danced around the apartment, a teenager again. When I finally calmed down sufficiently to show Bernard, he was truly delighted for me. I could not have been happier had I won Ernie's jackpot. Oh, the joy of being a fan. Later that day I went into town and purchased a frame encrusted with sparkling diamantés, perfectly appropriate for housing my treasure. Displayed in our lounge, I look at it every day. This seems, perhaps an appropriate point at which to press the pause button on my life story.

A year further down the road and I have completed this book. It has been a marvellous experience and as life's journey continues, I will continue to dream for sure. How wonderful it would be to see Dame Shirley Bassey again, to simply say hello, thank you, and perhaps sip a glass of champagne!

One thing is certain: I will continue to be a very proud fan.